U.S. AGING POLICY
INTEREST GROUPS

**Greenwood Reference Volumes on
American Public Policy Formation**

These reference books deal with the development of U.S. policy in various "single-issue" areas. Most policy areas are to be represented by three types of sourcebooks: (1) Institutional Profiles of Leading Organizations, (2) Collection of Documents and Policy Proposals, and (3) Bibliography.

Public Interest Law Groups: Institutional Profiles
Karen O'Connor and Lee Epstein

U.S. National Security Policy and Strategy: Documents and Policy Proposals
Sam C. Sarkesian with Robert A. Vitas

U.S. National Security Policy Groups: Institutional Profiles
Cynthia Watson

U.S. Agricultural Groups: Institutional Profiles
William P. Browne and Allan J. Cigler, editors

Military and Strategic Policy: An Annotated Bibliography
Benjamin R. Beede, compiler

U.S. Energy and Environmental Interest Groups: Institutional Profiles
Lettie McSpadden Wenner

Contemporary U.S. Foreign Policy: Documents and Commentary
Elmer Plischke

U.S. AGING POLICY INTEREST GROUPS

/// *Institutional Profiles*

EDITED BY

David D. Van Tassel

AND

Jimmy Elaine Wilkinson Meyer

GREENWOOD PRESS

NEW YORK • WESTPORT, CONNECTICUT • LONDON

Library of Congress Cataloging-in-Publication Data

U.S. aging policy interest groups : institutional profiles / edited by
David D. Van Tassel and Jimmy Elaine Wilkinson Meyer.
    p. cm.
   Includes bibliographical references and index.
   ISBN 0-313-26543-7 (alk. paper)
   1. Aged—Government policy—United States. 2. Pressure groups—
United States—Directories. I. Van Tassel, David D.
II. Meyer, Jimmy Elaine Wilkinson.
HQ1064.U5U22 1992
305.26—dc20   91–29198

British Library Cataloguing in Publication Data is available.

Library of Congress Catalog Card Number: 91–29198
ISBN: 0-313-26543-7

First published in 1992

Greenwood Press, 88 Post Road West, Westport, CT 06881
An imprint of Greenwood Publishing Group, Inc.

Printed in the United States of America

The paper used in this book complies with the
Permanent Paper Standard issued by the National
Information Standards Organization (Z39.48–1984).

10 9 8 7 6 5 4 3 2 1

CONTENTS

———————— / ————————

CONTRIBUTORS

/

Susan Abraham

Andrew Achenbaum

Susan Alexander

Robert Altman

James Banks

David Bernatowicz

Janice A. Cafaro

Emily Cherniack

Maris J. Deneke

Nancy C. Erdey

T. Dean Handy

Gretchen J. Hill

Gabriela Hohn

Beth DiNatale Johnson

Kimberly S. Lenahan

Phoebe S. Liebig

Jean R. Linderman

Qiusha Ma

Jimmy E. W. Meyer

Elizabeth Midlarsky

Glen Milstein

Joan Organ

Julieanne Phillips

Donna Polisar

Cleve Redmond

Renee Romano

Donald Shafer

Mary B. Stavish

Tamara Zurakowski

Annette Zygmunt

PREFACE

/

This book is intended as a reference guide to organizations that influence U.S. public policy regarding aging and the aged. The eighty-three organizations profiled here include the most visible players—such as the American Association of Retired Persons (AARP), the National Council on the Aging (NCOA), the Gray Panthers, and the National Council of Senior Citizens (NCSC)—as well as less obvious choices whose unique focus or future potential as a policy force warranted their inclusion—such as P.R.I.D.E., Zonta International, and Children of Aging Parents (CAPS). Not included are official government groups—such as the National Institute on Aging (NIA) or the U.S. Administration on Aging (AoA)—or groups focused more on recreation, research, or service than on advocacy—such as the Over the Hill Gang, the Ethel Percy Andrus Gerontology Center, and Elderhostel. Associations whose advocacy for the aging is part of a broader focus, such as the American Psychological Association (APA) or the American Public Health Association (APHA), are generally not included unless they target more than 50 percent of their resources toward issues related to aging. Organizations with a local focus appear only if their work is—or was historically—of import to national policy. Appendix A lists names and addresses of some of the groups that are excluded, as well as pertinent groups on which there was little information and/or that did not respond to our queries.

An introductory essay contains background on advocacy for older persons in America and provides context for thinking about public policy and aging. Following this essay is a chronological list of enacted federal legislation mentioned in the text, and following that is the alphabetical arrangement of interest group profiles. Former names of organizations are listed, followed by a *see* reference to the current name. Separate profiles were written for divisions of larger associations if the groups enjoyed some degree of autonomy, such as the constituent

units of NCOA. These groups are profiled under the name of the larger association; a *see* reference follows the division's name. A cross-reference from an
organization mentioned within an article to its profile elsewhere in the book is
indicated by an asterisk the first time the organization is mentioned. A variety
of contributors prepared entries; the author's name—or co-authors' names—
appear at the end of each entry.

Each profile follows the same format:

1. A statement of the organization's type and purpose.

2. Origin and Development: Provides historical information on the organization.

3. Organization and Funding: Includes details about the group's structure, membership,
   governance, and funding.

4. Policy Concerns and Tactics: Describes the organization's policy activity—specific
   issues, methods of advocacy, participation in coalitions, cooperation with other
   organizations.

5. Electoral Activity: Presents the organization's attempts to influence the electoral process, by political action committees or other means. This section is not included if
   the group does not engage in such activity.

6. Publications: Describes the communications of the organization—journals, newsletters, important books, other media, and, in a few cases, computer databases.

7. Further Information: Presents selected citations of material published about the organization in magazines, journals, or monographs.

The book contains two appendixes, Appendix A, described earlier and Appendix B, listing the 1991 members of the major political coalitions of aging
organizations: the A.S.A.P. (Advocates Senior Alert Process), Generations
United, the Leadership Council on Aging Organizations (LCAO), the Long-
Term Care Campaign, and Save our Security (SOS). Additional selected monographs and reference sources on aging and policy are included in a selected
bibliography at the end of the book.

Information presented in the profiles is of a summary nature rather than ex-
haustive. Sources included a questionnaire that was sent out by the editors and
returned by about half the groups, congressional testimony, political action committee data from the Federal Election Commission, material published by the
organizations themselves, and telephone interviews with organizational leadership. The source of quoted material within the articles is unpublished material
from the groups unless otherwise stated. General reference sources, such as the
Encyclopedia of Associations (Gale Research, 1991), the *Handbook of Aging
and the Social Sciences* (Binstock, Academic Press, 1990), the *U.S. Directory
and Sourcebook on Aging* (American Association for International Aging, 1989),
the *Resource Directory for Older People* (NIA, 1989), and the *Encyclopedia of
Aging* (Maddox, Springer, 1987), were helpful for some associations. Not all
of these sources were inclusive of or useful for all of the groups, which led to
a variety in the amount of detail presented in each entry. Interpretation of the

organization's impact on the policy sector, compared to other groups, is generally left to the reader. Each organization had an opportunity to read its profile and make factual corrections and/or suggest changes, and over 90 percent of the groups took advantage of this opportunity. Since we determined the final content of the profiles, however, they can in no way be considered official.

We made every attempt to present up-to-date information, but the state of flux within the aging network may negate our efforts to some extent. For example, in the three months before and after this book was written, at least five of the major organizations—Gray Panthers, American Association of Retired Persons, National Council on the Aging, Alzheimer's Association, and National Council of Senior Citizens—moved their national headquarters. One group, the Gray Panthers, shifted its whole base of operations from Philadelphia to Washington, D.C. These changes have been incorporated into the book; inevitably, there will be other recent changes that we could not include.

We must thank a variety of people who contributed to the book in its varying stages. Renee Romano, Qiusha Ma, and Sherry Goldstein, research assistants early in the project's history, laid much of the groundwork. Julieanne Phillips and Mary K. Porter researched many organizations, often to no avail, before the much larger list of possible inclusions was honed to the present number. Joan E. Organ helped bring the project to completion. The librarians at Freiberger Library of Case Western Reserve University (CWRU) were of great assistance in tracking down materials. The CWRU Center for Aging and Health also proved a useful resource.

Sarah J. Snock deserves a special thanks for all her patient word processing, her endurance of many stylistic changes, and her quiet encouragement. High kudos go to our authors and, especially, to the organizations that provided the information for the heart of the book.

REFERENCES

Binstock, Robert. *Handbook of Aging and the Social Sciences*. 3d ed. New York: Academic Press, 1990.

Encyclopedia of Associations. 25th ed. Detroit: Gale Research, 1991.

Maddox, George, ed. *The Encyclopedia of Aging*. New York: Springer, 1987.

National Institute on Aging (NIA). *Resource Directory for Older People*. Washington, D.C.: NIA, 1989.

U.S. Directory and Sourcebook on Aging, 1989–90. Washington, D.C.: American Association for International Aging, 1989.

INTRODUCTION: U.S. AGING POLICY INTEREST GROUPS

————————— / —————————

Serving and advocating the needs of the elderly has become "an aging enterprise," according to Carroll Estes (1979). It has certainly become big business, involving millions of people and thousands of agencies. The eighty-three organizations profiled in this book represent a portion of the private national organizations that deal with some aspects of old-age policy in the United States. The U.S. population of people aged 65 and older, close to 30 million in 1991, represents 12 percent of the total population. Although many would argue that there is no national policy on aging, certainly a wide variety of major programs exists to benefit the elderly, from Social Security, Medicare, housing, research, and employment to a host of other specialized programs and agencies. Over 200 congressional committees and subcommittees bear responsibility for some aspect of federal old-age programs and/or services, representing 29 percent of the national budget—more than the defense budget. Most of these programs, with the exception of Social Security, originated in the 1960s and 1970s, as did more than half of the organizations profiled in this book. In fact, serious concern for the needs of the elderly in the United States has emerged only recently.

In the past few decades, we have heard such phrases as the "graying of America," "senior movement," and "senior activism," which refer to the development of a plethora of organizations serving and advocating the needs of the elderly. There are hundreds of government programs and agencies serving a variety of needs of the most dependent elderly citizens. All of this gives rise to a number of questions: Why did this happen so recently? What about the role of interest groups? What is their nature, and what are their prospects for influencing national policy in the future?

Why did this concern for the elderly hit the national scene so late and with such sudden impact? Although the nation has cared for its older citizens almost

since its founding—through family care, private facilities, and government programs—the breadth of public concern and activism revolving around the needs
of the elderly is primarily a phenomenon of the post–World War II years. Policy
toward dependent elderly in the nineteenth century was similar to family policy;
that is, the state had no business in family matters. A family was expected to
take care of its own dependent elderly, children, and those members disabled
physically or mentally. If a family neglected its duty, the community or the state
stepped in with laws requiring family support of its dependent members. If that
support was not forthcoming, the municipality-, county-, and state-sponsored
institutions for the indigent poor—almshouses—took charge. In the decades
after 1850, states established institutions for the blind, the deaf, the mentally
retarded, and the insane, as well as orphans. As each of these special groups
was filtered out of the almshouses into specialized institutions or asylums, by
the end of the nineteenth century the almshouse became largely the refuge of
the indigent elderly. In the 1870s, church-related old-age homes began to appear
in large, urban communities trying to serve the morally fit indigent or "deserv-
ing" poor.

The federal government entered the arena in connection with aging Union
veterans. During and immediately after the Civil War, Congress passed legislation awarding pensions to Union veterans and to the widows and families of
Union soldiers who had been killed. Federally supported hospitals were built to
care for veterans with war-related injuries and diseases. In 1884, Congress
declared in an appropriations bill that old age was a war-related condition that
qualified Union veterans for government support. This action laid the groundwork
for what were essentially old-age homes for Union veterans. By 1913, support
of these hospitals, homes, and pensions constituted nearly 18 percent of the
federal budget (Achenbaum, 1988). Confederate veterans were not eligible for
such federal support, but the southern states and private charities supported
veterans' homes throughout the South.

Even if the values of individualism and laissez-faire had not dominated the
nineteenth century, there would have been little additional concern for the needs
of the elderly, since they constituted such a small portion of society: less than
2 percent of the population was over 60 years old at any time before 1900. That
percentage grew only gradually during the first third of the twentieth century.
Nevertheless, a variety of groups in the late nineteenth and early twentieth
centuries launched old-age pension movements that, by 1935, had resulted in
the establishment, in thirty-five of the forty-eight states, of noncontributory,
means-tested pensions for the indigent old at 65 or 70 years. All but South
Carolina had legislated mothers' pensions by 1935. In addition, twenty-four
states had pension programs for the needy blind, and a few states had adopted
unemployment insurance. In 1935, Congress passed the Social Security Act,
encompassing all of these programs in its eleven titles, including old-age survivors and disability insurance, commonly referred to as Social Security.

The Social Security Act aimed at nothing less than providing for the general welfare of Americans "by establishing a system of federal old-age benefits, and by enabling the several states to make more adequate provision for aged persons, blind persons, dependent and crippled children, maternal and child welfare, public health, and the administration of their unemployment compensation laws; to establish a social security board; to raise revenues; and for other purposes" (Nash, Pugach, and Thomasson, 1988, 8). The Social Security Act is a landmark piece of legislation. It established the first federal agency with an elderly constituency and made old-age assistance a right, contingent upon congressional approval. Such a provision invited tinkering by amendment, which would occur first in 1938 and then with increasing frequency after World War II. There was also the risk of reversal, which only recently appears to have receded. All three of these elements contributed to preparing fertile ground for the growth of interest groups.

During and immediately after World War II, a small group of academics, scientists, and physicians formed the Gerontological Society (later the Gerontological Society of America) to research the process and diseases of aging and to seek ways to ameliorate the elderly's plight. This group made the problems of old age a legitimate part of the public agenda when it succeeded in persuading the Social Security Administration to call the National Conference on Aging held in 1950. That conference, entitled "Man and His Years," sparked the formation of congressional and executive committees on aging and alerted the public to the variety of concerns connected with a growing population of dependent elderly. Thereafter, the president convened a White House conference every decade. In 1961, the White House Conference on Aging initiated the move for the establishment of Medicare and the Older Americans Act; to a large extent, the White House Conference of 1971 was the initiator of the Area Agencies on Aging; and the White House Conference of 1981 focused on minority groups and aging as well as the question of mandatory retirement. These conferences focused national attention on the issues of aging and generated the formation of a number of interest groups. In the early 1960s there were very few private interest groups in the field. The Gerontological Society of America (1945), the National Retired Teachers Association (1947), the National Council on the Aging (1950), the Western Gerontological Society (1954, now the American Society on Aging), and the American Association of Retired Persons (1958) were the largest independent associations. The number of these groups jumped rapidly in the 1970s—almost half of the organizations profiled here were founded during that decade (Figure 1). By 1991, when this book was compiled, we identified close to 100 private groups focused on old-age policy and concerns.

These old-age interest groups became known collectively as the gray lobby and have been seen by the media and the public as monolithic in ideology and a very powerful force, called gray power, in Washington. Rather than being uniform in approach or powerful in influence, the gray lobby, in fact, has always reflected the diversity of the elderly and retired population, the varying circumstances of the groups' origins, and the efficacy of their differing structures. All

Figure 1
Founding of Aging Policy Interest Groups by Decade

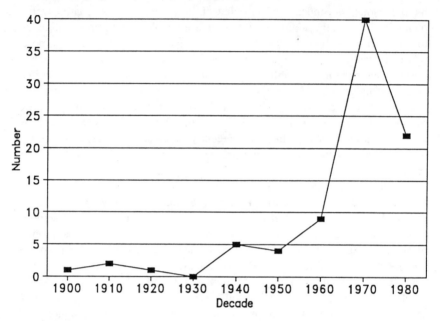

Note: Total number = 84 organizations, including NCOA constituent units and the National Retired
Teachers Association.

old-age interest groups evolved over time, and the differences and similarities
among them become more difficult to sort out as their numbers grow. Political
scientists and sociologists have attempted to account for the varying degrees of
political effectiveness by classifying the groups into different types (Yelaja,
1984). Given the mix represented in this book, however, the attempt to classify
types does not seem to be a fruitful approach. It would be useful at this point
to take a look at the origins and nature of four specific and very different interest
groups—the American Association of Retired Persons, the National Council of
Senior Citizens, the Gray Panthers, and the National Committee to Preserve
Social Security and Medicare—and to assess their efficacy as advocates, analyze
their influence on public policy, and explore their agenda for the 1990s.

Although each of these organizations has a large senior citizen membership
base, each represents a different constituency and often takes opposing positions
on particular issues. The National Council of Senior Citizens (NCSC) had its
roots in the labor-based Senior Citizens for Kennedy in 1960. At the White
House Conference on Aging in 1961, Congressman Aime J. Forand, a Rhode
Island Democrat, initiated an organization of older Americans to work for the
passage of Medicare. Supported by the AFL-CIO with Forand as chairperson,
the new National Council of Senior Citizens for Health Care Through Social

Security began organizing state and local affiliates of blue-collar retirees. After achieving its primary goal—Medicare—in 1965, the organization expanded its objectives and its membership. In 1991, NCSC had 4,800 affiliated clubs with a membership of 4.5 million people, largely representing trade union retirees and ethnic and religious groups. Initially, the unions and the Democratic National Committee supplied approximately two-thirds of the group's operating funds, and membership dues provided one-third. As of 1990, however, with a budget just short of $60 million, NCSC dues constituted less than $3 million. Over 90 percent of the total funding comes from the federal government in restricted grants and contracts from a variety of government agencies. NCSC dispenses a number of services to the elderly, but it also maintains a political action committee that is very active on Capitol Hill, as well as in state and local politics. In 1978, for instance, the NCSC did not stand with virtually all the other elderly organizations to fight mandatory retirement. In the interest of members who have no desire or need to work past the age of 65, NCSC supports the Social Security retirement test that requires beneficiaries to give up a dollar in benefits for every dollar over $9,720 of earned income—putting it at odds with most other old-age interest groups.

Unlike the National Council of Senior Citizens, the American Association of Retired Persons (AARP) had its origins in a retired teachers' insurance organization rather than in political action. In 1947, Ethel Percy Andrus founded the National Retired Teachers Association to obtain inexpensive insurance for retired teachers. Her success attracted retirees from outside education and led her to organize the American Association of Retired Persons in 1958. Andrus, who served as president of NRTA/AARP until her death in July 1967, kept the organization largely out of politics. After her death, NRTA became simply a division of AARP. Membership expanded rapidly through the 1970s and 1980s. In 1991, AARP membership numbered 33 million people, making it one of the largest volunteer organizations in the United States. It publishes position statements on about seventy-five issues, such as long-term care, consumer protection, and housing and energy, in an annual comprehensive legislative manual. AARP's large and diverse membership makes it both easy and difficult to take strong stands on issues. It is easy, since there is always a percentage of the membership that will support any given side of an issue related to old age and retirement. It is difficult, since there is also always a segment of the membership that will oppose such a stand. In fact, a recent membership survey asserts that 40 percent of AARP members are Democrats, 40 percent Republicans, and 20 percent independents. AARP has generally opposed cuts and limits on the Social Security cost-of-living adjustments (COLAs). On the other hand, it has opposed paying higher social security benefits to the so-called notch babies, about seven million people born in the "notch" between 1917 and 1921 who receive proportionately lower Social Security benefits than those born before them, due to a quirk in the benefit formalization process begun in 1972. In 1986 AARP formed the AARP/VOTE, a nonpartisan voter education program active in twenty-nine states in 1990. While not contributing to the campaign coffers of any candidates or party, the program offered free television time for candidates to talk on such issues as health care reform and retirement income security. This is an ongoing, relatively successful effort to force these issues into candidates' electoral platforms.

The AARP nevertheless still draws criticism from the Gray Panthers (the Gray Panthers Project Fund) for not using its membership strength more effectively. The Gray Panthers is a cause-oriented organization working "for a better world for the young to grow old in" through cooperation among generations. It espouses a wide range of causes from civil rights to world peace, reflecting its origins in the social movements of the late 1960s. In 1970, Maggie Kuhn, a retired social worker and activist, convened a group initially called the Coalition of Older and Younger Adults for Social Change. Shortly thereafter the media tagged the group the Gray Panthers, a name it took as its own. Its antiestablishment, anti-institutional stance, reflected in a determinedly democratic structure (no formal membership, no dues, no officers), gradually eroded. In 1977, formal member-ship and dues were instituted. It had already incorporated as a nonprofit orga-nization in 1973 as the Gray Panthers Project Fund. Maggie Kuhn reluctantly accepted the title of National Convener, which she devised presumably as being less autocratic than some other choices. The Gray Panthers symbolically rec-ognized the system (they had, of course, been working within it all along) when they opened an office in Washington, D.C., in 1985. In 1991, the Gray Panthers moved all operations from Philadelphia to the nation's capital.

The group's initial concern was to eliminate ageism in the media and in the workplace, but it soon became involved in a variety of issues, such as nursing home reform and outlawing mandatory retirement. It also joined intergenerational campaigns for gun control and against war toys. The group has, in fact, been a pioneer in the pursuit of a national health service, a position that led it to oppose the Medicare Catastrophic Coverage Act (1988), pitting it against most of the old-age interest groups, including NCSC and AARP.

There was one important ally, however: the National Committee to Preserve Social Security and Medicare (NCPSSM). It joined the Gray Panthers in opposing the catastrophic coverage bill. NCPSSM became the loudest voice in opposition on the grounds that, under the bill's provisions, the elderly alone bear the burden of financing and that the bill did not cover long-term care. The NCPSSM is an advocacy group founded in 1982 by James Roosevelt to mobilize retirees through direct-mail campaigns to defend Social Security against the incursions of budget cutting. It has since taken on the defense of Medicare and Medicaid and the development of a national long-term-care program. In structure it is the antithesis of the Gray Panthers, although both are organized and run from their headquarters in Washington, D.C. Although members are sometimes surveyed about issues that interest them, policy positions are determined by a seven-member Board of Directors elected by the membership.

It is difficult to develop a classification that clearly defines aging-policy groups.

The AARP was initially a service organization, launched to give substantive benefits to retirees such as insurance and prescription drug discounts. Nevertheless, it has developed a strong political arm, although one could speculate that the membership is primarily composed of people who have joined for other than political reasons. The National Committee to Preserve Social Security and Medicare, clearly a cause-oriented group, expanded from one cause to many and now offers member services.

The diversity of focus within the gray lobby makes it seem unlikely that the groups could launch effective cooperative efforts. However, the budget cutting of the 1980s put virtually all welfare interest groups on the defensive and formed an atmosphere conducive to cooperative activity. Also since the 1980s, the elderly have been losing their special place on the public agenda. Recent articles have suggested that the aged are receiving a disproportionate share of the federal budget (Hess, 1990). Many public policy decisions adverse to older persons have proved to be politically feasible, such as changes in the Medicare deductibles, co-payments, and optional supplemental insurance (Part B) premiums, all of which were increased. Old-age insurance benefits have been made subject to taxation, and the cost-of-living adjustments (COLAs) have been decreased. The Tax Reform Act of 1986 eliminated the extra personal exemption that all people 65 and older had been receiving for many years. Some have argued that such a litany of setbacks is testimony to the lack of cohesiveness and lack of influence of the gray lobby. Others argue that the fact that programs for the elderly were not cut even more is a sign of the lobby's strength. Most admit that coalitions are difficult to sustain (O'Donnell, 1987; Binstock, 1989). In fact, the earliest effort at organized coalition of old-age interest groups, the Leadership Council of Aging Organizations (LCAO), was given only a minimal chance of success by Paul Kerschner, one of its founders (Kerschner, 1984).

Coalitions, however, may be the trend of the old-age interest groups in the 1990s. The LCAO, indeed, was little more than a clearinghouse for information and coordination in the 1980s. It began in 1978 as a clearinghouse to develop issues for the 1981 White House Conference on Aging. By 1984, it had twenty-nine member organizations; in 1991, LCAO consisted of thirty-three member organizations and appeared to be a permanently established instrument of the aging network. The Gray Panthers have always stressed the importance of working in coalition and of intergenerational cooperation, arguing that gray lobbies simply perpetuate the conception of separate concerns of the aged and of the young. A new intergenerational coalition, Generations United, was formed in 1986 by the National Council on the Aging and the Child Welfare League. Generations United consists of over 100 organizations that represent children and/or the elderly and works to counter the charge that older people are benefiting from government programs at the expense of children and other groups, a position often propounded by Americans for Generational Equity (Schulder, 1989). It would seem that this sort of coalition would strengthen all groups' positions in an era of budgetary restraints and legislative scrutiny of all welfare programs.

Some of the issues of the rest of the 1990s will encourage cooperative efforts, such as the gathering momentum for a national health care system, affecting all generations. The question is no longer whether there will be a national health care system but how it will be financed and who will control it.

Old-age interest groups will continue to develop as the population increases over the next five decades. Their major contribution will continue to be in the policy area—incremental changes, the administration of programs, and amendments to legislation such as Social Security, Medicare, Medicaid, as well as to the Older Americans Act. This book of institutional profiles, selective as it is, will be useful to a variety of professionals and will serve as a benchmark of some of the major aging-policy interest groups at the beginning of the 1990s.

REFERENCES

Achenbaum, W. Andrew. "Historical Perspectives on Public Policy and Aging." *Generations* (Spring 1983): 27–29.

Binstock, Robert H. "Aging and the Politics of Health Care Reform." In Carl Eisdorfer et al., *Caring for the Elderly*, 422–47. Baltimore: Johns Hopkins University Press, 1989.

Estes, Carroll. *The Aging Enterprise*. San Francisco: Jossey-Bass, 1979.

"Gray Power." *Nation* (May 1990): 727–28.

Hess, John L. "The Catastrophic Health Care Fiasco." *Nation* (May 1990): 698–702.

———. "Confessions of a Greedy Geezer." *Nation* (April 1990): 452–56.

Kerin, Pamela B., Carroll L. Estes, and Elizabeth B. Douglass. "Federal Funding for Aging Education and Research: A Decade Analysis." *Gerontologist* 29 (1989): 606–14.

Kerschner, Paul A. "Advocacy Networks Are Fragile." *Generations* (May 1980): 35, 59.

———. "Aging Network Advocacy at the Crossroads." *Generations* (Fall 1984): 44–46.

Longman, Phillip. "Catastrophic Follies." *New Republic* (August 1989): 16–18.

Nash, Gerald D., Noel H. Pugach, and Richard F. Thomasson, eds. *Social Security: The First Half-Century*. Albuquerque: University of New Mexico Press, 1988.

O'Donnell, James W. "The Rise and Fall of Federal Support." *Provider* 13 (December 1987): 6–8.

Pepper, Claude. "Long Term Care Insurance: The First Step towards Comprehensive Health Insurance." *Journal of Aging and Social Policy* 1 (1989): 9–15.

Pratt, Henry J. "Agitation and Advocacy: Representing Seniors in State Government." *Generations* (May 1980): 33, 55–56.

Riffer, Joyce. "Elderly Twenty-one Percent of the Population by 2040." *Hospitals* 59 (March 1985): 41–44.

Schreter, Carol A., and Steven W. Brummel. "Primer on Private Philanthropy and Aging." *Journal of Applied Gerontology* 7 (December 1988): 530–41.

Schulder, Daniel J. "Public Policy Report." *Perspectives on Aging* (September–October 1989): 30–31.

Torres-Gil, Fernando. "The Politics of Catastrophic and Long-term Care Coverage." *Journal of Aging and Social Policy* 1 (1989): 61–85.

Wyden, Ron. "Inside Congress: A Gray Panther's View." *Generations* (Fall 1984): 31–32.

Yelaja, Shankar A. "A Gray Power: Agenda for Future Research." *Canadian Journal on Aging* 8 (Summer 1984): 118–27.

CHRONOLOGICAL LIST
OF ENACTED
FEDERAL LEGISLATION

———————— / ————————

1935	Social Security Act
1944	GI Bill of Rights (Servicemen's Readjustment Act)
1965	Older Americans Act
1965	Medicare (Health Insurance for the Aged) Act
1965	Higher Education Act
1967	Age Discrimination in Employment Act
1973	Comprehensive Employment and Training Act
1973	Domestic Volunteer Service Act
1974	Employee Retirement Income Security Act (ERISA)
1976	Indian Health Care Improvement Act
1982	Job Training Partnership Act (JTPA)
1984	Environmental Programs Assistance Act
1984	Retirement Equity Act
1984	Carl D. Perkins Vocational Education Act
1985	Gramm-Rudman (Balanced Budget and Emergency Deficit Control) Act
1986	Tax Reform (Private Health Insurance Coverage) Act
1987	Medicare and Medicaid Patient and Program Protection Act
1987	Omnibus Budget Reconciliation Act (OBRA '87)
1987	Stewart B. McKinney Homeless Assistance Act
1988	Medicare Catastrophic Coverage Act
1989	Repeal of Medicare Catastrophic Coverage Act

U.S. AGING POLICY
INTEREST GROUPS

A

AARP
See American Association of Retired Persons.

AARP PUBLIC POLICY INSTITUTE
See American Association of Retired Persons.

AARP/VOTE
See American Association of Retired Persons.

ADOPTED GRANDPARENTS
See Beverly Foundation.

ADVOCATES SENIOR ALERT PROCESS (A.S.A.P.)
See A.S.A.P. (Advocates Senior Alert Process).

AFL-CIO
See National Council of Senior Citizens.

AGING IN AMERICA (AIA)
1500 Pelham Parkway, South
Bronx, New York 10461
(212) 824–4004 or (800) 845–6900   FAX (212) 597–6587
   Aging in America (AIA) is a nonprofit, nonmembership organization providing education and service programs to improve the quality of life and promote independent living for the elderly. It initiates and implements both local and national programs. The organization is affiliated with Morningside House Nurs-

ing Home (MSH), a health care facility for the elderly located at 1000 Pelham Parkway, Bronx, New York 10461, telephone (212) 409–8200.

ORIGIN AND DEVELOPMENT

In 1852, the Reverend Dr. Isaac Tuttle, Rector of St. Luke's Church in New York City, was moved by the plight of a "distressed" woman. Tuttle rented a room for her, and, realizing the number of other people in need, he soon rented the entire building. From this small beginning, St. Luke's Home for Indigent Christian Females was established two years later. In 1966, St. Luke's Home and another institution, the Peabody Home, merged to become Morningside House. In 1972, Morningside House established Morningside House Nursing Home. Morningside House changed its name to Aging in America in 1982.

Aging in America researches and develops social programs on the local and national level for the elderly, provides education for health care providers in the gerontological field, offers employment services and retraining for older adults, and initiates and implements intergenerational programs. It also provides a wide variety of community services, such as Meals-on-Wheels; transportation; senior centers; a respite care center; Pelham House, a residential facility for older adults who do not require medical care; health screening programs; and social services to the elderly and their families.

ORGANIZATION AND FUNDING

AIA and Morningside House Nursing Home are separate corporations with separate boards of directors, although they have in common a minority number of board members, the Chairman of the Board, and the Chief Executive Officer. Each board can have a maximum number of twenty-five members. New members are selected by nominating committees from the boards and are elected by the boards of directors. AIA has a staff of 79 and MSH a staff of 442.

Approximately two-thirds of AIA's budget of just over $3 million is derived from federal, state, and city contracts. The remainder comes from interest on endowments and from grants and foundations. Morningside House Nursing Home has a budget of about $21 million, 98 percent of which is obtained from Medicare and Medicaid.

POLICY CONCERNS AND TACTICS

A planning committee of AIA board members works with the Board of Directors to develop the policies for the organization, which are then implemented by the staff. Several staff members serve on state and national associations that represent the concerns of the elderly, including the American Association of Homes for the Aging[*] and the Greater New York Hospital Association, part of the American Hospital Association.[*] AIA takes positions on public policy only through these other associations. AIA does not have a political action committee.

Issues of concern to AIA include the importance of responsible government reimbursement for health and social service programs and the growing debate over the allocation of resources to the elderly and/or the young. Concerning the latter topic, AIA believes that age should not be a factor that divides people; it should be discarded as a valid argument in support of either the young or the old.

PUBLICATIONS

AIA publishes a newsletter, *Sharing*, three to four times a year, as well as an annual report.

JEAN R. LINDERMAN

ALLIANCE FOR DISPLACED HOMEMAKERS
See National Displaced Homemakers Network.

ALZHEIMER'S ASSOCIATION
919 North Michigan Avenue, Suite 1000
Chicago, Illinois 60611–1676
(312) 335–8700   FAX (312) 335–1110

Roughly 10 percent of the population over age 65 has Alzheimer's disease, the prevalence of which rises with advancing age. The Alzheimer's Association, founded in 1980, is a national voluntary health agency dedicated to researching the prevention, cure, and treatment of Alzheimer's disease and related disorders. The association disseminates information, supports research, and encourages legislative measures on all governmental levels.

ORIGIN AND DEVELOPMENT

Beginning in the mid-1960s, Robert Katzman, of the Albert Einstein College of Medicine in New York, and a team of other biomedical researchers from Great Britain and the United States studied the causes of senile dementia. By 1974, these investigators had discovered that senile dementia was identical to Alzheimer's disease and that it was the fourth leading cause of death in the United States. These conclusions became the catalyst for efforts to increase awareness of the disease as a major health problem and to secure federal funds for biomedical research and patient support.

Late in 1979, with the help of the National Institute of Aging and the National Institute of Neurological and Communicative Disorders and Stroke, representatives from seven lay organizations concerned with the disease met in Washington, D.C., and created a single national Alzheimer's organization. The objectives of the newly formed Alzheimer's Disease and Related Disorders Association (ADRDA) were biomedical research, family support, education, and advocacy. The association elected Jerome Stone, a Chicago businessman, as President of the Board of Directors. Stone attempted to expand the association's resources to reach the widest possible audience, helping those suffering in silence and isolation.

An unexpected impetus came in June 1980 with the publication of the association's address and mission in a "Dear Abby" column in hundreds of newspapers nationwide. Within a month, 25,000 letters poured into the ADRDA's one-room office, staffed entirely by volunteers. At this time, the association had a ten-member Board of Directors, a budget of $85,000, one paid staff person, and 20 local chapters. The association grew quickly. By January 1982, it had a thirty-one-member board, a budget of $650,000, and a staff of four. There were thirty-four chapters in twenty-five states, thirty-four support groups, and 75,000 newsletter recipients. By 1985, the ADRDA had fifty-six board members, a $4.1 million budget, and thirty-five national staff. The organization covered forty states with 125 chapters, over 600 support groups, and 350,000 newsletter recipients. In 1988, ADRDA shortened its name to Alzheimer's Association, to reflect its major focus more accurately.

The Alzheimer's Association lists five principal goals, summarizing them in the acronym RECAP (research, education, chapters, advocacy, patient and family services):

1. Supporting research on the cause, treatment, prevention, and eventual cure of Alzheimer's disease and related disorders

2. Educating the general public and disseminating information about Alzheimer's disease to health professionals

3. Forming chapters to provide a nationwide family support network

4. Advocating for more enlightened public policy and promoting legislation supportive of Alzheimer's patients and families

5. Offering patient and family services

ORGANIZATION AND FUNDING

The national office of the Alzheimer's Association is located in Chicago. On January 2, 1990, the association opened a permanent Washington, D.C., office, to monitor legislation and maintain ties with federal agencies, such as the National Institutes of Health and the U.S. Department of Health and Human Services. In 1990, the Alzheimer's Association had more than 30,000 volunteers in forty-nine states, working in over 200 chapters and 1,600 support groups. Local chapters, chartered by the national board, remit 15 percent of their revenue to the national headquarters, excluding government and research grants. In addition to the work done on a nationwide basis, the Alzheimer's Association helped found and is a member of Alzheimer's Disease International, which pursues the need for research, funding, education, advocacy, support, and information dissemination worldwide.

The Board of Directors, composed of sixty-four working members in addition to several honorary members, governs the association. The board approves annual association goals and actions of association officials. The Alzheimer's Association also utilizes a forty-one-member Medical and Scientific Advisory Board

(MSAB) to review researchers' grant requests. Four MSAB members also serve on the Board of Directors. The Alzheimer's Association has seven major staff officers: the President, four Senior Vice-Presidents, and two Vice-Presidents. In 1990, Edward Truschke was the association's President; staff members numbered 112.

The Alzheimer's Association's 1990 budget was over $15 million. Almost 90 percent of the funding comes from individual and corporate contributions. Sources of the remaining monies include direct mailings, gifts, and foundation donations. In 1989, the Alzheimer's Association spent $10 million for program services, including $4.2 million for research and $3.1 million for education. About $4 million was spent on fund raising.

POLICY CONCERNS AND TACTICS

The Alzheimer's Association provides a forum for federal policy issues; offers key legislative issues pertaining to the funding, research, and reforms needed by those affected by Alzheimer's disease; and furnishes resources to Congress for advancing desired legislation. The national network of Alzheimer's Association representatives and members disseminates information, supports research, encourages legislative measures, helps shape public policies, and assists in federal, state, and local advocacy.

The Alzheimer's Association places heavy emphasis on the need for additional medical research on this disease; funding disparities among the four leading causes of death in the United States (cancer, AIDS/HIV, heart disease, and Alzheimer's disease—$1.5 billion, $958 million, $650 million, and $130 million, respectively); and the need for a national commitment toward the prevention and cure of Alzheimer's disease. The organization also addresses such health insurance issues as eligibility requirements, benefits, services and provisions, research, financing and cost containment, and the assurance of high-quality care. Legislative measures instigated and/or supported by the Alzheimer's Association include task forces to study the disease and its impact, government-sponsored research, funding for respite care, and financial protection for Alzheimer's patients and families.

The Alzheimer's Association produces the annual *Alzheimer's Association Directory of State Alzheimer's Programs and Legislation*, a compendium of programs and legislation aimed at improving public policies for Alzheimer's patients, their families, and other loved ones. The 1990 *Directory* listed over 160 programs and their contact person(s), of which 119 programs are specifically devoted to Alzheimer's disease. The *Directory* noted that more than $25 million was specified for state programs in fiscal year 1990. One hundred sixty-six laws or resolutions were listed in the *Directory* for forty-seven states. New Jersey, California, and Massachusetts were the first states to enact Alzheimer's legislation (1983–84). According to the *Directory*, an average of twenty state laws a year were passed between 1985 and 1988. The peak year was 1987, with nearly thirty laws and resolutions passed; twenty-five more programs were added in 1989. The *Directory* addressed potential challenges to 1990 fiscal year funding for Alzheimer's disease and related disorders and provided advocates with room, building, and telephone numbers for state house and senate representatives.

Future plans for the Alzheimer's Association include training professionals through chapters and expanding information and service to patients and their families. As public awareness of Alzheimer's disease increases, the association is targeting special government and community groups in its educational efforts. The Alzheimer's Association coordinates its actions with groups such as the American Association of Retired Persons[*] (AARP) and the National Citizens' Coalition for Nursing Home Reform.[*]

PUBLICATIONS

Each year the association issues *National Program to Conquer Alzheimer's Disease*, outlining the beginnings and development of the Alzheimer's Association and presenting an overview of knowledge about the disease. It also describes the typical victims of Alzheimer's disease and the future prospects for disease prevention and cure, providing recommendations to help government leaders frame the policies and programs necessary to alleviate the burdens of Alzheimer's disease.

Further Information

Miriam K. Aronson, *Understanding Alzheimer's Disease—What It Is, How to Cope with It, Future Directions.* (New York: Charles Scribner's Sons, 1987); Carroll Estes and E. A. Binney, "The Biomedicalization of Aging," *Gerontologist* 29 (October 1989): 587–96; Patrick Fox, "From Senility to Alzheimer's Disease: The Rise of the Alzheimer's Disease Movement," *Milbank Quarterly* 67 (1989): 58–102; *Losing a Million Minds—Confronting the Tragedy of Alzheimer's Disease and Other Dementias* (Washington, D.C.: U.S. Office of Technology Assessment, 1987); Nancy L. Mace and Peter V. Rabins, *The 36-Hour Day*, rev. ed. (Baltimore: Johns Hopkins University Press, 1991).

ANDREW ACHENBAUM
DONNA POLISAR

ALZHEIMER'S DISEASE AND RELATED DISORDERS ASSOCIATION
See Alzheimer's Association.

ALZHEIMER'S DISEASE INTERNATIONAL
See Alzheimer's Association.

AMERICAN ASSOCIATION FOR CONTINUITY OF CARE (AACC)
720 Light Street
Baltimore, Maryland 21230
(301) 837–1600   FAX (301) 752–8295
The American Association for Continuity of Care (AACC) is a national, professional organization committed to ensuring the availability of continuity of

care for all patients, including the elderly. Continuity of care is defined as "an interdisciplinary process that includes patients/clients, families, and significant others in the development of a coordinated plan of care. This process facilitates the patients'/clients' transition between settings, based on changing needs and available resources."

ORIGIN AND DEVELOPMENT

AACC was founded in 1982 by a group of multidisciplinary health care professionals to provide a national forum for issues around continuity of care and hospital discharge planning. AACC promotes and supports:

- The concept that continuity of care is an essential component of the health care delivery system
- The concept that every patient has the right to quality, coordinated discharge planning, which is an integral part of total patient care
- The philosophy that continuity of care is a holistic health approach that is centered on the patient and family
- The belief that continuity of care encompasses the preventative, therapeutic, rehabilitative, custodial, medical, and nonmedical needs of patients
- The belief that the process of continuity includes assessment of needs and resources to meet needs, planning, implementation, and outcome evaluation
- The concept that professionals responsible for continuity of care should have access to an educational and supportive network

Persons involved in continuity-of-care issues primarily are registered nurses, social workers who work in various settings such as discharge planning in hospitals, case managers, professionals in home care and long-term-care agencies, educational facilities, and government agencies.

ORGANIZATION AND FUNDING

Members of AACC include representatives of health organizations, health care providers, and other persons with a special interest in continuity of care. In 1990, the organization had over 700 members. Membership in AACC can be one of three types: (1) general members— individuals interested in the continuity of care, the only members with the right to vote and hold office on the Board of Directors; (2) sustaining members—firms, partnerships, corporations, or other entities having an interest in continuity of care; and (3) affiliate members—local and state continuity-of-care organizations whose purposes are consistent with AACC's. Membership dues and conference fees comprise the bulk of the $200,000 annual budget.

The American Association for Continuity of Care is managed by a sixteen-member Board of Directors, two paid staff, and sixteen volunteers. The voluntary Board of Directors, elected by the membership, consists of five members of the Executive Committee, five standing-committee chairpersons, and the six Regional Directors. Regional Directors provide the national office with information on needs and issues of the membership. They are also the legislative liaisons between the AACC's Government Relations Committee and their regions. AACC holds an annual conference to address educational needs and provide growth opportunities for its members.

In 1990, AACC formed a separate nonprofit organization, the National Board for Certification in Continuity of Care, to offer certification programs to continuity-of-care professionals, attempting to ensure a common level of expertise. The first certification will be for advanced competency in continuity of care. A test, based on the results of a national analysis of professional functions, will be offered in 1992.

POLICY CONCERNS AND TACTICS

AACC's major policy issues are health concerns of the elderly, abuse of the elderly, transportation alternatives for senior citizens, and long-term home health care. Access to health care for rural residents and for the uninsured or under-insured is another policy concern. The organization has had a significant influence on public policy by testifying before congressional subcommittees, directly informing representatives and senators and their staffs, and through local membership letter-writing efforts. AACC has joined with coalitions of various professional organizations to help effect change in the health care system, such as the Home Care Coalition and the Ad Hoc Committee for the Coordination of Patient Assessment Instruments, led by the National Committee to Preserve Social Security and Medicare*.

AACC established hospital discharge standards of practice to provide safe-guards for both patients and providers, after influencing discharge planning through Medicare. Testifying on Medicare before the House Ways and Means Health Subcommittee in May 1990, the organization's President stated, "The option of caring for the frail elderly and disabled Medicare beneficiaries in their homes will be in great jeopardy if there are more cuts in reimbursement to the home medical equipment industry." The President pointed out that equipment suppliers provide education to patients, family members, and even to home health nurses, as well as delivery of equipment. AACC maintains that the home medical equipment industry is essential to patient welfare, especially for patients no longer in need of the skilled care of a home health agency.

In the late 1980s, AACC members testified before the Senate Committee on Aging concerning Medicare cuts and on discharge planning. AACC provides members with information regarding legislative and regulatory activity in the area of continuity of care. Regional members are encouraged to keep the national office informed of area concerns on continuity-of-care issues.

PUBLICATIONS

Through two newsletters, the association disseminates information to its members. *ACCESS* (quarterly), the official publication of AACC, contains regional and national information beneficial to health care providers. *IMPAACCT* (quarterly) provides members with information on legislative activity in the area of continuity of care. Members and other health care providers can also obtain the *AACC Membership Directory*, published annually to help establish a national network. The *Directory* lists over 700 continuity-of-care professionals.

Further Information

Patricia A. O'Hare and Margaret A. Terry, eds., *Discharge Planning: Strategies for Assuring Continuity of Care* (Rockville, Md.: Aspen Publishers, 1988).

ROBERT ALTMAN

AMERICAN ASSOCIATION FOR INTERNATIONAL AGING (AAIA)
1511 K Street, N.W., Suite 443
Washington, D.C. 20005
(202) 638–6815　　FAX (202) 638–5917

The American Association for International Aging (AAIA) is a private, non-profit, membership organization for groups and individuals concerned with the aged worldwide, especially in Third World countries. Through public education, technical assistance and training, and field project support, AAIA encourages productive aging and strives to respond to the 1982 United Nations International Plan of Action on Aging (IPAA). The IPAA was the result of the first UN World Assembly on Aging and contains twenty-six recommendations endorsed by 125 nations.

ORIGIN AND DEVELOPMENT

The AAIA, a tax-exempt, 501(c)(3) organization, was founded in 1983 in response to the 1982 UN World Assembly on Aging. AAIA superseded Help the Aged, an early U.S. affiliate of the London-based HelpAge International, a worldwide network of twenty-five organizations working to improve the quality of life for poor older persons of all races, sexes, and religions. John McDonald, U.S. Ambassador to the World Assembly on Aging, created AAIA to heighten public awareness of and to respond to the challenges of the IPAA. AAIA claims to be "the only U.S. government-registered private voluntary organization which deals with aging from a global perspective." AAIA's goals are:

1. To educate the American public, corporate, and government sectors about global aging issues and the need for action

2. To develop and implement mechanisms which promote productive aging and exchange

ORGANIZATION AND FUNDING

The twenty-member Board of Directors governs the AAIA. Board members are elected by the previous board. According to AAIA bylaws, the board must represent the public and private sectors and must include persons with geron-tologic, business, philanthropic, media, and/or management experience. A President and Executive Director heads two full-time and three part-time staff. In 1991, Helen K. Kerschner held that position.

AAIA receives its $300,000 annual budget from a variety of sources: private foundations, corporations, and public agencies in addition to membership dues, assessed on a sliding scale. Members of the organization include corporations, foundations, nongovernmental organizations, and individuals from around the world.

POLICY CONCERNS AND TACTICS

AAIA attempts to heighten Americans' awareness of issues related to global aging, to share American expertise and experience worldwide, and to learn from other nations' experience. Working closely with federal agencies and senior-based organizations, AAIA utilizes education and exchange, research, technical assistance and training, and field project support to accomplish these goals. An example of AAIA's education effort, launched in 1988, is the Development Education Program for Retired Americans. The purpose of the program, funded in part by the U.S. Agency for International Development, is to raise the level of awareness of the audience of retired Americans about global concerns, emphasizing international development, developing countries, and world aging. A major activity of the program is to provide assistance and materials to local formal and informal educational entities to facilitate planning and delivery of community-based development education programs for retired Americans. Organizational partners in the educational program include OASIS (Older Adult Services and Information System) and American Association of Retired Persons[*] (AARP). Community colleges and retirement communities also participate in AAIA Development Education Program activities.

AAIA's senior enterprise program, a major research, technical assistance, and training effort, began in 1986 as part of a worldwide action research project, funded by the U.S. Department of Health and Human Services. The project undertook a worldwide survey of income-generating programs for the aging, developed a database of information, initiated demonstrations in the United States, and prepared and disseminated ten publications about senior enterprise, including the option of providing economic support to older workers and organizations serving older people. Today, AAIA responds to requests for information and assistance related to senior enterprises from organizations and groups in the United States and abroad. AAIA is working on several community development efforts in productive aging and economic development, including a multicountry productive aging strategy in the West Indies.

AAIA has supported field projects in a number of countries, with seed money and other assistance. An innovative program model was initiated in 1989 at a home for the destitute elderly in the Dominican Republic. An income-generating self-service laundry and a hydroponic garden project were implemented as part of a country-wide strategy to promote productive aging. In another significant project in 1988, a U.S. senior volunteer program helped to create a partner senior volunteer program in Mexico. Such global sharing of resources and successful models has ramifications for old-age policy, especially in the economic area of productive aging.

In addition to its affiliation with HelpAge International, AAIA is also affiliated with the International Federation on Ageing*.

PUBLICATIONS

AAIA issues a quarterly newsletter for members, *AAIA Reports*. The organization has published two major directories, the *International Directory of Organizations in Aging* (1988) and the *U.S. Directory and Sourcebook on Aging* (1989); a ten-volume series of technical reports on senior economic and enterprise development; and two booklets, *Retired Americans Look at International Development* (1990) and *Retired Americans Ask: "How Can I Be Involved in International Development?"* (1991), which outline ways for older Americans to participate in international development efforts at the local, national, and international levels. AAIA also offers a series of how-to manuals on implementing U.S. model senior volunteer programs. Special reports, such as *Aging and the Global Agenda for Women: Conversations in Nairobi* (1986) and *Aging Populations in Developing Nations: A Strategy for Development Support* (Agency for International Development, 1986), are also available from AAIA.

Further Information

"How Does a Developing Nation Develop?" *Perspective on Aging* 18 (September–October 1989): 12–14; Helen Kershner, and Susan Coombs Ficke, "Senior Enterprise Development: A Strategy for Moving Aging into the Economic Mainstream." *Ageing International* 16 (December 1989): 24–30; "Learning from Each Other: Income-generating Projects," *Perspective on Aging* 18 (September–October 1989): 10–12.

JIMMY E. W. MEYER

AMERICAN ASSOCIATION OF HOMES FOR THE AGED
See American Association of Homes for the Aging.

AMERICAN ASSOCIATION OF HOMES FOR THE AGING (AAHA)
901 E Street, N.W., Suite 500
Washington, D.C. 20004
(202) 783–2242   FAX (202) 638–5917

The American Association of Homes for the Aging (AAHA) is a national trade association representing nonprofit nursing homes, retirement communities, senior housing facilities, and community service organizations for older persons. It promotes the common interests of its members through leadership, advocacy, education, public relations, and other services. The AAHA describes its members as "Communities that Care" and bases its philosophy on the "social components of care": a commitment to the care of the total person, to community involvement, and to a continuum of care, from independent living to nursing home care.

ORIGIN AND DEVELOPMENT

AAHA was founded in 1961 under the auspices of the National Council on the Aging* (NCOA). Concerned with the lack of a united voice for nonprofit nursing homes, NCOA sponsored a conference at Arden House in New York to explore the need for and to found a national association of nonprofit homes for the aged. Ollie Randall of the NCOA secured a grant from the Ford Foundation to fund the 1961 Arden House meeting; she is often referred to as the founder of AAHA. The new American Association of Homes for the Aging encompassed a group already in existence, the West Coast–based American Association of Homes for the Aged. AAHA held its first Board of Directors meeting on January 6, 1962. The first AAHA annual meeting, attracting 300 attendees, was held October 22–24 of the same year. At the end of its first year, AAHA boasted 250 charter members.

For the first few years, AAHA shared office space with NCOA in New York. During this time, members of AAHA held dual membership in NCOA. In 1965, AAHA incorporated as an autonomous organization and in 1971 moved its headquarters to Washington, D.C.

Since its inception, AAHA has addressed policy concerns such as quality care standards for nursing homes, training for administrators, funding for senior housing programs, and Medicare and Medicaid funding. The organization has also emphasized education and the provision of resources in the field of not-for-profit care and services, as well as services such as low-cost insurance and tax-exempt financing for its members. AAHA has led and participated in a variety of public arenas, including White House conferences on aging, Lyndon Johnson's Presidential Task Force on nursing homes (1966), governors' conferences, the Federal Council on Aging (1976), and the launching of the Continuing Care Accreditation Commission (1986). In 1990, AAHA listed the following goals in its long-range plan:

1. Influence national policy pertaining to housing, health, community, and related services to the elderly

2. Enhance members' capability to effectively meet their clients' current and future needs

3. Develop, promote, and maintain a positive image of the American Association of Homes for the Aging and its members

4. Promote the linkages necessary to provide a continuum of services for older adults

5. Develop and maintain an effective relationship between the national and state associations

6. Establish and promote quality in aging services

7. Provide leadership in the field of not-for-profit aging services

8. Represent a broad base of not-for-profit organizations providing aging services
9. Manage effectively AAHA's available resources

ORGANIZATION AND FUNDING

The AAHA includes both corporate members (3,700 facilities providing housing and services to the elderly) and associate members (800 individuals interested in long-term nursing home care of the aging). "Protestant, Catholic, and Jewish organizations sponsor 75% of AAHA's facilities, while private foundations, government agencies, unions, fraternal organizations, and other community groups support 25%." In 1991, there were thirty-seven local and state affiliates.

An eighteen-member Board of Directors governs AAHA, led by the Chair. Members of the board serve staggered three-year terms, with the opportunity to be reelected for one additional term. Representatives from state associations are either elected or appointed (at the state association's discretion) for three-year terms to a House of Delegates, with the option of being elected or appointed to one more consecutive term. Fifteen delegates at large, appointed by the Chair, also serve in this body. The House of Delegates deliberates on key issues, elects the Board of Directors and officers, and approves bylaw changes and dues increases. In 1991, the AAHA House of Delegates numbered about 160.

The AAHA's officers are Chair, Chair-elect, Immediate Past Chair, Secretary, and Treasurer—all elected by the House of Delegates. A staff of sixty-five, headed by Sheldon L. Goldberg, 1991 President, serves the organization. The AAHA utilizes various policy and program committees, which are appointed by the chair and composed of House of Delegate representatives, other members, and/or state association representatives.

AAHA derives its over $5.8 million income from individual and corporate membership dues (46%), foundation grants (3%), and other sources (51%).

AAHA employs a multilevel process of determining policy. The Board of Directors biennially reviews and ratifies general public policy statements, which express AAHA's overall philosophy. More specific than policy statements are long-term public policy objectives, drafted by staff with committee direction and then discussed and ratified by association leadership. Staff continually review the public policy objectives, soliciting information from committees, state association leaders, the House of Delegates, and the membership at large. The Board of Directors approves all public policy objectives. AAHA's annual legislative agenda includes short- and long-term strategies for congressional sessions. Policy committees, the House of Delegates, state association leaders, and other members have input at this level as well. Approval of the legislative agenda rests with the Chair in consultation with the Board of Directors and staff. The final level of policy formulation involves positions on legislative issues. Positions are developed on issues that demand an immediate response, using the policy objectives and legislative agenda as blueprints. State associations and relevant policy committees may participate in developing the positions in consultation with the Senior Vice-President for Policy and Government Affairs.

AAHA holds an annual conference and presents annual awards, including the association's highest award, the Award of Honor, for outstanding contributions to the field of care and service for the aging.

POLICY CONCERNS AND TACTICS

In 1991, AAHA emphasized the major policy areas of nursing home standards, low-income housing for the elderly, continuing-care retirement communities, home health care and other community services, and long-term-care financing. Maintaining tax exemption for nonprofit care providers represents another priority of AAHA.

The organization supplies information to Congress, encourages grass-roots member involvement, and testifies regularly. AAHA also promotes consumer awareness and education through an active national media relations program, consumer publications, and public relations support for AAHA member facilities.

AAHA members and staff testify before various congressional committees, averaging about five appearances per year, and submit written testimony at congressional behest frequently. In March 1991, an AAHA member testified before the House Ways and Means Committee on long-term-care insurance coverage. In 1990, AAHA lobbied and utilized grass-roots and coalition advocacy to encourage the inclusion of amendments related to health care costs in the 1990 Omnibus Budget Reconciliation Act (OBRA '90). The organization also worked for the development and congressional passage of the Cranston-Gonzalez National Affordable Housing Act in 1990.

In 1988, the AAHA successfully advocated for the expanded skilled nursing home coverage provision of the Medicare Catastrophic Coverage Act and in 1989 unsuccessfully opposed the loss of those provisions when the act was repealed. On March 10 and April 20, 1988, AAHA testified, along with the American Health Care Association* (AHCA), before the House Committee on Energy and Commerce on the need for cooperative governmental and private sector long-term-care insurance. AAHA also appears regularly before the Banking Committee in the Senate and the committees and subcommittees on aging in both houses.

AAHA often combines a variety of tactics to reach a policy goal. One 1990 example pertains to an issue unusual in the aging network. Working through Congress, legal channels, and the media, the AAHA entered a ten-year agreement with the major motion picture studios. The agreement allows nursing home residents, as well as residents of other specified health care settings, to view videocassettes of popular films license free. The effort will save AAHA members millions of dollars in license fees.

PUBLICATIONS

The organization publishes a monthly newsletter, *AAHA Provider News*, and a biweekly newsletter, *Washington Report* (for members only). AAHA issues a variety of other literature, including consumer guides and brochures with titles such as *Choosing a Nursing Home* and *Living Independently*. Another publication is *Let's Celebrate: A Public Relations and Special Events Guide for Nonprofit Homes and Services for the Aging* (1988). The first edition of the *National Continuing Care Directory*, produced by AAHA and published and distributed by the American Association of Retired Persons* (AARP) (revised edition, 1988), won accolades as an outstanding reference source. AAHA also makes *Guide to Continuing Care Retirement Communities* available to consumers. The association publishes an annual directory of its members and numerous other resources for aging-service professionals, consumers, and others.

Further Information

American Association of Homes for the Aging: The First 25 Years (Washington, D.C.: AAHA, 1986).

NANCY C. ERDEY

AMERICAN ASSOCIATION OF NURSING HOMES
See American Health Care Association.

AMERICAN ASSOCIATION OF REGISTERED NURSING HOMES
See American Health Care Association.

AMERICAN ASSOCIATION OF RETIRED PERSONS (AARP)
601 E Street, N.W.
Washington, D.C. 20049
(202) 434–2277   FAX (202) 434–6499

The American Association of Retired Persons (AARP) is the largest national organization for the elderly in the United States and the country's second largest mass membership group, next to the Roman Catholic church. The nonprofit association is equally renowned for its wide array of member services and for its power as a federal and state lobbying force. Through education, advocacy, and service, AARP promotes independence, dignity, and purpose, striving to improve the quality of life for older Americans. The membership of AARP reflects a wide cross-section of Americans.

ORIGIN AND DEVELOPMENT

The AARP grew out of the National Retired Teachers Association (NRTA). Both were founded by a retired California teacher, Ethel Percy Andrus (the NRTA in 1947 and the AARP in 1958). Andrus had been a teacher in California and in 1916 became the first female high school principal in the state. After retirement in 1944, she served as the Director of Welfare of the California Retired Teachers Association. Upset by the status of retired teachers—small pensions and nonexistent health coverage—Andrus began a quest to find an insurance company to cover NRTA members. NRTA was founded to advocate for improved teacher pensions. In 1955, a decade before the creation of Medicare, Andrus and insurance broker Leonard Davis instituted the first nationwide group health insurance program for the elderly. This program attracted retirees from outside the teaching profession. Rather than turn them away, Andrus founded the American Association of Retired Persons, with seed money from Davis. Andrus served as President of NRTA/AARP from its incorporation until her death in July 1967.

The AARP and NRTA shared staff and space, although each had a separate Board of Directors, separate local affiliates, and separate membership rosters. A direct-mail marketing campaign spurred initial growth of the organization. In 1959, the AARP had 150,000 members; ten years later, it had 1 million. By 1975, the membership numbered 9 million.

By 1982, the AARP had so outgrown its parent organization that the two groups merged, with NRTA becoming a division within the AARP. The boards of directors of the two groups combined, gradually reducing in size as members' terms expired. In 1983, the age of eligibility for membership was reduced from 55 to 50. Since then, enrollment has increased by more than 80 percent, to 33 million in 1991.

Some observers attribute the phenomenal growth of the AARP to the number of varied, low-priced services available for minimal dues ($5.00 per year in 1991). The association offers not only health and long-term-care insurance but also home owners', auto, and mobile-home insurance to its members. AARP Pharmacy Service, the nation's largest prescription drug mail-order service, is a popular member benefit. Other member services include an investment program, a travel service, a motoring plan, and a purchase privilege program that provides members with discounts at major car rental companies and hotel and motel chains.

Accused in the late 1970s of too close a financial relationship with insurer Colonial Penn, the AARP severed the connection. Prudential Insurance Company of America became the underwriter for AARP's Group Health Insurance Program. Auto/home owners' insurance is offered to members by the Hartford Insurance Group, and insurance for mobile-home owners is provided by the Foremost Insurance Group.

ORGANIZATION AND FUNDING

The membership of AARP grows by approximately 8,000 new members per day. One AARP advertising slogan boasts: "Join the Association that's bigger than most countries." Hundreds of companies present outgoing retirees with lifetime AARP memberships. The amount of mail to AARP necessitates its own Washington, D.C., zip code.

AARP is one of the country's largest volunteer organizations, with a cadre of 360,000 volunteer leaders nationwide. It is governed by a seventeen-person National Board of Directors and a six-member Executive Committee, composed of four elected officers and the Chairman and Vice-Chairman of the board. The national officers are President, President-elect, Immediate Past President, Vice-President, Secretary, and Treasurer. Officers and members of the board are chosen by a nominating committee and then elected by delegates at the association's biennial convention. The board meets quarterly, and board members also serve on a wide range of AARP committees. AARP is staffed by 1,600 employees in Washington, D.C., and Lakewood, California, and ten regional offices across the country. In 1991, the Executive Director was Horace B. Deets.

AARP's National Legislative Council formulates the organization's positions on public policy, with member input and board approval. The AARP President nominates candidates for the council, who are then appointed by the Board of Directors. The twenty-two-member council is composed of two representatives from each of the AARP's ten geographic regions and two representatives at large. National Legislative Council members serve for three years and can be reappointed for a second term.

AARP maintains an extensive local chapter system of 3,700 groups across the United States. First organized in 1960, AARP chapters involve thousands of members in service and advocacy projects, as well as recreational activities. A national volunteer network in ten geographic regions helps maintain local activities. Each region has an Area Vice-President and an Associate Area Vice-President. State Coordinators and Assistant State Directors report to State Directors, who are responsible to the Area Vice-Presidents. Professionally staffed area offices exist in each region, with state offices in Florida and Pennsylvania. Local chapters are incorporated into the national AARP leadership: half of the delegates at AARP conventions must come from chapters. The organization provides free training courses for its volunteers down to the chapter level.

Chapter members and other volunteers are active in a wide range of educational and community service programs on such subjects as consumer affairs, criminal justice services, driver training, health advocacy, housing, tax preparation assistance, and widowed persons counseling. Among other association programs are the AARP Andrus Foundation, which provides grants to colleges and universities throughout the country for research on aging and the Senior Community Service Employment Program, a government-funded program that trains economically disadvantaged older persons and places them in permanent jobs.

AARP operating revenues in 1990 were over $295 million. The largest source of income, 34 percent of the total, was membership dues. Income from the group health insurance program accounted for 25 percent and publication advertising revenue for 14 percent. Other sources included interest income (16%) and royalties and income from programs (9%). In addition to monies obtained through annual revenues, AARP holds assets of over $95 million in undesignated funds.

The largest expenditure in the 1990 AARP budget was for publications (36%). Member services and acquisition comprised 22 percent and programs and field services, 20 percent of expenses. Administration and operation of AARP headquarters involved 16 percent of the budget. Less than 7 percent of AARP's 1990 funds were spent for legislation, research, and development.

One department of AARP closely related to public policy is Legal Counsel for the Elderly (LCE), founded in 1975. LCE is a support center specializing in expanding and improving the availability and quality of legal services for older persons. LCE provides free legal hot lines in a number of states, trains attorneys, paralegals, and other advocates; operates national volunteer programs to assist older people with their financial affairs; and offers a full range of legal services to the District of Columbia's residents aged 60 and over. LCE's major policy concerns are the legal aspects of retirement and welfare benefits, housing, and medical care. LCE provides legislative research and/or technical assistance related to these issues. In addition, LCE engages in impact litigation and legislative advocacy to improve the lives of elderly residents of the District of Columbia.

POLICY CONCERNS AND TACTICS

AARP's National Legislative Council meets with ten of the fifty AARP State Legislative Committee Chairmen in Washington, D.C., each January to set the federal and state legislative agenda for the year. Grass-roots participation in this process includes analysis of correspondence and telephone calls from AARP members and the results of member surveys and field hearings throughout the year on selected issues. After listening to presentations by members of Congress and other policy experts during the week-long meeting, the Legislative Council revises working drafts of policy positions into final form. This work is done in five committees: Economic and Employment Issues, Health Issues, Long-Term Care Issues, Housing and Low-Income Issues, and Consumer and Legal Issues. The full Legislative Council then reviews the final policy statements in a plenary session before submitting them to the Executive Committee and the Board of Directors for final approval.

AARP publishes detailed position statements on about seventy-five issues in a comprehensive legislative manual, *Toward a Just and Caring Society: The AARP Public Policy Agenda*. The 1991 manual, nearly 500 pages long, covered the following areas:

Economic and budget policy

Tax policy

Retirement income security

Employment and worker equity

Human services, education

Personal and legal rights

Protecting government integrity

Consumer protection

Health care costs, quality, and access

Long-term care

Low-income assistance and training

Housing and energy

Concerns for future generations

AARP emphasizes economic and financial concerns across a wide policy spectrum. The manual includes legislative guidelines used by the volunteer AARP state legislative committees in fifty states, Washington, D.C., and Puerto Rico to set their priorities for the year.

The Federal Affairs Department of AARP coordinates federal advocacy activities, with the research support of the organization's in-house think tank, the Public Policy Institute. National officers, board and Legislative Council members, and other volunteer leaders, as well as professional staff, testify before Congress. State-level advocacy is carried out entirely by volunteers, with support from state legislative representatives in each of the ten AARP regional offices.

AARP's focus is broader than that of many other organizations advocating for the elderly, clearly evident in its vision statement: "Bringing lifetimes of experience and leadership to serve all generations." Atypical considerations such as education, utility costs, consumer banking, telephone deregulation, and food labeling appeared along with long-term care and Social Security in the association's policy agenda for 1991. Unlike more activist groups such as the Gray Panthers Project Fund,* AARP does not take positions on issues such as nuclear power or disarmament.

Another unusual feature of AARP's advocacy effort is the attention the organization pays to the regulatory process; i.e., "What happens *after* the bill becomes a law?" Through the years, AARP has monitored the work of federal agencies such as the Federal Trade Commission, the U.S. Food and Drug Administration, and the Equal Employment Opportunity Commission, and it has spoken out successfully in support of regulating the funeral service industry and eliminating prohibitions on price advertising for eyeglasses and prescription drugs.

Although legislative objectives such as improved pensions and tax benefits for retirees were among the original goals of NRTA and AARP, the organization was not founded for political purposes. The early NRTA/AARP placed a higher priority on individual betterment, in keeping with Andrus's motto, "To Serve, Not to Be Served." In the early 1960s, Andrus proposed to Congress—as an alternative to the compulsory Medicare plan—a voluntary health insurance plan with more extensive coverage. However, NRTA/AARP supported final passage of the Medicare program in 1965.

During the same period, Andrus was one of the first to speak out in opposition to mandatory retirement and age discrimination in the workplace. NRTA/AARP pushed for passage of the original Age Discrimination in Employment Act of 1967 (ADEA). And nearly twenty years later, in October 1986, AARP successfully lobbied for an amendment to the ADEA that virtually eliminated mandatory retirement for American workers.

The AARP increased its legislative activities during the 1980s. Between 1983 and 1989, the annual legislation and research budget more than tripled, from $4.2 million to $17.5 million. The organization also became more involved in the courts, first filing a number of amicus curiae briefs and, later, pressing a pension-rights case against du Pont and joining in a nationwide age discrimination suit against State Farm Insurance.

In 1990, at 33 million members, AARP represented an increasingly effective lobby. Although the organization's power may be circumscribed by the diversity of its membership, politicians are wary of AARP's potential as a voting bloc. It is estimated that one of every five U.S. voters belongs to AARP. At least three U.S. Presidents have spoken before the organization.

From its support of Massachusetts senator Edward Kennedy's national health insurance proposal in the late 1970s to its current campaign for comprehensive reform of the nation's health care system, AARP has long emphasized the policy issues of affordable, high-quality health care and long-term care. Indeed, the association has vowed to make health care reform an issue in the 1992 presidential election. In the meantime, AARP has worked with private insurers to formulate long-term-care coverage at reasonable cost.

In 1988 and 1989, AARP was sharply criticized by some of its members and other older persons because of its strong support for the Medicare Catastrophic Coverage Act of 1988, which contained a number of new benefits, including coverage of outpatient prescription drugs. The criticism was directed at the new law's financing mechanism, which placed most of the burden of the cost of the new benefits on higher-income Medicare beneficiaries rather than spreading the cost among all taxpayers. Except for a few provisions, particularly one designed to prevent the impoverishment of the spouses of nursing home residents, the Catastrophic Coverage Act was repealed by Congress in 1989. Despite the controversy, only about 8,000 AARP members canceled their memberships because of the association's position—the same number that join the organization each day.

Throughout the 1980s, AARP generally opposed cuts or limits in Social Security cost-of-living adjustments (COLAs). Indeed, research by AARP showing that a COLA cut would force more than a half-million older people into poverty was cited by the *Los Angeles Times* as the "single most effective weapon" used to defeat a 1985 proposal to cut COLAs.

More recently, the organization has opposed New York Senator Daniel P. Moynihan's proposal for a reduction in Social Security payroll taxes. AARP also disagrees with organizations like the National Committee to Preserve Social Security and Medicare* that want to pay higher Social Security benefits to notch babies—about seven million people born in the "notch" between 1917 and 1921 who receive proportionately lower Social Security benefits than those born before them, due to a quirk in the benefit formalization process begun in 1972. At the same time, AARP has strongly supported improvements in the Supplemental

Security Income (SSI) program to help low-income aged, blind, and disabled Americans.

Many members of Congress, congressional committees, and federal agencies rely on the AARP staff for information. The AARP Public Policy Institute provides detailed research findings on current public issues to key decision makers. This well-documented information is often the only available in the field, as was the case in the spring 1987 debate over reimbursement for outpatient prescription drugs. AARP's cost-analysis predictions helped convince Congress to include an outpatient prescription drug benefit in the 1988 Medicare Catastrophic Coverage Act.

ELECTORAL ACTIVITY

Viewed by some observers during the 1960s as a white-collar, Republican-leaning organization, AARP began to shed that image and gain a reputation as a nonpartisan group in the 1970s. The AARP refuses to endorse candidates or contribute money to political campaigns, and it does not publish ratings of the voting records of members of Congress, as does the National Council of Senior Citizens,* for example.

AARP's strict, nonpartisan stance causes some consternation among other elderly activists. Advocates like the Gray Panthers complain that AARP should put its large number of regular voters to more effective use. AARP responds by noting that, unlike smaller, single-issue groups, it is virtually impossible to get all of AARP's 33 million members to vote as a bloc on any issue. Indeed, recent membership surveys have determined that 40 percent of AARP members describe themselves as Democrats, 40 percent as Republicans, and 20 percent as independents.

While maintaining its nonpartisanship, AARP has become more deeply involved in the electoral process in recent years. In 1986, the organization founded AARP/VOTE, a nonpartisan voter education program designed to "educate and involve voters on issues of concern to older Americans and the community-at-large." Active in twenty-nine states in 1990 with a budget of more than $8 million, AARP/VOTE seeks to inject issues such as health care reform and retirement-income security into political campaigns at the federal and state levels, including presidential election campaigns. Through candidate forums, questionnaires, and personal interviews, AARP volunteers solicit candidates' views on specific issues and share those views with AARP members and the public at large.

In 1990, for example, "AARP/VOTE Voters' Guides," containing the statements of congressional and gubernatorial candidates on issues such as health care reform, Social Security, long-term care, housing, and the budget deficit, were distributed to AARP members statewide. In some cases, such as in New Jersey and Ohio, the guides were inserted in issues of *Modern Maturity* magazine, reaching every AARP household in those states.

Another example of AARP's increased electoral activity began in 1988. In conjunction with the Villers Foundation (now Families U.S.A. Foundation*), the AARP formed Long Term Care '88, forerunner of the Long-Term Care Campaign.* Long Term Care '88 was originally a coalition of eighty organizations aimed at highlighting the issue of long-term care in that year's presidential election. The $2 million crusade, a feature of which was free television time for candidates to address the issue, succeeded in obtaining planks on long-term care in every major candidate's platform. In 1990, the Long-Term Care Campaign was active in state and congressional races and involved 138 cooperating organizations (see Appendix B for a list).

PUBLICATIONS

AARP's bimonthly magazine, *Modern Maturity*, was the nation's largest-circulation magazine in 1991. In addition to general interest articles on a variety of topics, the magazine has recently begun publishing more articles on public policy issues such as health care reform and age discrimination in employment.

All AARP members receive the *AARP Bulletin* eleven times per year; this publication provides information on AARP activities concerning legislation, consumer affairs, volunteerism, and other topics.

AARP publishes three specialized bimonthly newsletters: *Highlights*, for AARP volunteers; *Working Age*, which deals with employment issues; and *Washington Report*, which covers legislative and policy developments. The organization offers more than 800 free publications and a number of audiovisual packages on a wide range of subjects.

In conjunction with the Mutual Broadcasting System, AARP produces *Mature Focus*, a daily news feature radio program aired on more than 160 stations; a Spanish-language version, *Jubilación*, is used by more than 150 stations. AARP's "Maturity Broadcast News" provides weekly news features and in-studio interviews via satellite to television stations across the country.

Begun in 1987 with initial financial support from AARP, the independent Maturity News Service provides weekly news and feature story packages of interest to older readers to more than 200 newspapers through the United Feature Syndicate.

AARP also offers AGELINE, a computerized bibliographic database on aging, available through two commercial vendors: BRS Information Technologies and Dialog Information Services.

Further Information

All About AARP (Washington, D.C.: AARP, 1989); Dorothy Crippen et al., eds., *The Wisdom of Ethel Percy Andrus* (Long Beach, Calif.: AARP/NRTA, 1968); Margaret Hornblower, "Gray Power," *Time*, January 4, 1988: 36–37; Eric Schurenberg and Lani Luciano, "The Empire Called AARP," *Money* 17

(October 1988): 120–46; *Toward a Just and Caring Society: The AARP Public Policy Agenda* (Washington, D.C.: AARP, 1991).

JIMMY E. W. MEYER
RENEE ROMANO

AMERICAN BAR ASSOCIATION (ABA)
COMMISSION ON LEGAL PROBLEMS OF THE ELDERLY (CLPE)

1800 M Street, N.W., 2d Floor, South Lobby
Washington, D.C. 20036
(202) 331–2297   FAX (202) 331–2220

The Commission on Legal Problems of the Elderly (CLPE) is a program of the American Bar Association (ABA), the professional association for American lawyers. The main missions of CLPE are to marshal the thinking and attention of members of the bar on issues affecting the elderly and to provide technical assistance to bar associations and area agencies on aging.

ORIGIN AND DEVELOPMENT

The CLPE was founded in 1978, 100 years after the establishment of the ABA, its parent organization. The commission was created at the suggestion of an ABA task force as a means of focusing ABA's concerns about the needs of the elderly around two clusters of activities: conducting research on legal and policy issues and educating attorneys. Initially, the CLPE concentrated on four major issues: age discrimination, simplification of regulations, long-term care, and legal services for the elderly. The CLPE does not have individual or corporate members. Its constituency is drawn from the 350,000 members of the ABA and ABA's state affiliates, as well as elected officials, other private voluntary organizations, and public policymakers and those influential in public policymaking.

ORGANIZATION AND FUNDING

The CLPE consists of a fifteen-member interdisciplinary commission that functions as a board of directors and a paid staff of ten led by a staff director. Nancy Coleman held this position in 1990. The commission, whose members include attorneys, physicians, academicians, and directors of health centers, sets policy, which is then approved by either the ABA House of Delegates or the ABA Board of Governors. The commission meets three times a year and co-sponsors an annual Joint Conference on Law and Aging (JCLA). Other JCLA sponsors are the Legal Counsel for the Elderly of the American Association of Retired Persons* (AARP), the National Senior Citizens Law Center (NSCLC)*, the National Academy of Elder Law Attorneys, and The Center for Social Gerontology*. This conference is attended by over 500 lawyers and professionals from the network of organizations advocating for the aging. The CLPE also participates in the ABA's annual conference and its midyear meeting.

CLPE's annual budget ranges from $500,000 to $1 million. Funding for the CLPE's activities comes from three major sources: the ABA (33%), foundation grants (17%), and the federal government (50%).

POLICY CONCERNS AND TACTICS

The major priorities of the CLPE are legal problems of the elderly, due process issues related to Social Security benefits, guardianship, surrogate and health care decision making, home health care and long-term care, and nursing home reform. The CLPE uses a variety of techniques to influence public policy, including testifying before Congress, supplying information to members and staff of Congress, and conducting and publishing research on legal issues of concern to the elderly. Research, testimony, and provision of information to legislators are deemed the most successful policy-related activities of the CLPE.

In its more than ten years of existence, CLPE has testified before Congress on numerous occasions. In 1990, testimony on health care powers of attorney was presented to the House Ways and Means and Senate Finance committees in May and July, respectively. Earlier in the year, the CLPE also testified on Social Security before the House Ways and Means Committee. In 1986 and 1988, home care provisions of the Older Americans Act were the focus of CLPE testimony, while board and care regulation issues were the topic of the organization's testimony before the Senate Committee on Aging in September 1989. CLPE coordinates many policy-oriented actions with the NSCLC and the AARP, such as the recent major issues of nursing home reform and the Medicare Catastrophic Coverage Act of 1988.

While CLPE concentrates on issues and concerns of the elderly, legislation affecting the nonelderly, such as the Americans with Disabilities Act and health care decision making, also claims the attention of the organization.

PUBLICATIONS

Educational materials developed by the CLPE include research reports, informational booklets and brochures targeted to attorneys, informational packets, resource manuals, and videos. Two recent publications are *Guardianship of the Elderly: A Primer for Attorneys* (1990) and *Legal Issues and Resources: A Guide for Area Agencies on Aging* (1991) by Stephanie Edelstein. Another useful item, authored by Charles Sabatino, is *Health Care Powers of Attorney: An Introduction and Sample Form* (1990). The CLPE publishes *BIFOCAL*, a quarterly newsletter, jointly with the ABA Young Lawyer Division's Committee on Delivery of Legal Services to the Elderly. In addition, the CLPE publishes a bimonthly bulletin on the elderly for bar groups.

Further Information

"Building Bridges to Bar Associations," *Aging Magazine* 357 (1988): 2–5; Nancy Coleman, "Advocacy for the Elderly," *ABA Journal* 75 (April 1989): 130, and "The Delivery of Legal Assistance to the Elderly in the United States," in *An Aging World: Dilemmas and Challenges for Social Policy*, ed. John Ee-kelaar and David Pearl, 463–77 (Oxford: Clarendon Press, 1989).

PHOEBE S. LIEBIG

AMERICAN COLLEGE OF HEALTH CARE ADMINISTRATORS (ACHCA)

325 South Patrick Street
Alexandria, Virginia 22314–3510
(703) 549–5822   FAX (703) 739–7901

The American College of Health Care Administrators (ACHCA) is a private, nonprofit, professional association of administrators of long-term-care facilities for the aged and chronically ill. The ACHCA and its education and research arm, the Foundation of American College of Health Care Administrators (FACHCA), work to improve the quality of long-term care through the professional advancement and development of long-term-care administrators. ACHCA implements this mission through education, research, information services, and professional representation.

ORIGIN AND DEVELOPMENT

The ACHCA was founded in 1962 as the American College of Nursing Home Administrators. ACHCA members are administrators of or executives affiliated with long-term-care facilities (e.g., skilled nursing homes and intermediate-care facilities, congregate living centers, hospices, adult day care centers, hospital long-term-care units, and retirement communities), academicians interested in the study of long-term care, those in related health care professions, and vendors and suppliers in the long-term health care field. In 1971, ACHCA established a nonprofit foundation to focus on educational research. First called the Foundation of American College of Nursing Home Administrators, the name was later changed to the Foundation of American College of Health Care Administrators (FACHCA).

The ACHCA provides information and consults on long-term-care issues, conducts research and disseminates research findings, administers certification programs and professionalization opportunities, offers national seminars and specialized educational programs, contributes to a central network of health care professionals, and provides an employment and job search referral service. ACHCA maintains Information Central, a large collection of literature on long-term-care administration.

ORGANIZATION AND FUNDING

The ACHCA and the FACHCA share an Executive Vice-President but have separate governing boards. A Board of Governors establishes policy for the ACHCA. The board is composed of the Executive Vice-President, an elected Executive Committee (President, Immediate Past President, President-elect, Secretary, Treasurer, and Governor-at-Large), and the eleven Regional Governors, elected by mail ballot. The organization employs twenty-five professional staff.

Over half of the ACHCA's $2.5 million budget is supplied by member and chapter dues. Revenue from the sale of publications, seminars, and the annual convention provides the remaining funds.

The ACHCA has forty-eight chapters and more than 6,500 members in North America. The organization has eleven regional groups representing forty-eight states. The committees of the ACHCA include: Advancement, Advocacy, Education, Ethics and Standards, and Professional Certification.

A nine-member Board of Directors governs the FACHCA. The board includes two public members (not necessarily ACHCA members) appointed by the foundation and seven elected Directors. Its $250,000 budget is supported by tax-deductible charitable gifts and individual memberships. The foundation also receives grants and contracts that serve three specific activities: (1) research on critical topics, such as nurse recruitment and retention, long-term-care financing, and the impact of new regulations; (2) development and piloting of educational programs; and (3) recognition of professional standards through ACHCA's certification program.

The ACHCA sponsors an annual convocation in the spring and regional seminars periodically. The organization presents several national awards, including the Distinguished Administrator of the Year award, honorary fellowships, and awards in the fields of journalism and education. The FACHCA bestows annual scholarships.

POLICY CONCERNS AND TACTICS

ACHCA attempts to raise and maintain high standards for high-quality long-term care and to heighten consumer consciousness by providing standard guidelines for excellence. ACHCA advocates for health care administrators and their facilities. Media packets stress both marketing (e.g., advertising and networking) and consumer recognition, as well as the need for funding educational programs, training, and research to ensure high-quality long-term care. As part of ACHCA's promotion of high standards, it periodically issues position statements on issues of particular concern, such as: "Advance Directives" (February 1990), "Administrator's Responsibility" (March 1988), "Resolution on Long-Term Care Nursing" (March 1988), and "Licensure of Long-Term Care Administrators" (January 1987). ACHCA does not testify before Congress but occasionally provides information to legislators.

To counteract the negative images of the nursing home industry, ACHCA works to sensitize advocates on aging to the problems of semantics and advertising form, particularly as they affect the substantive content of publications. The self-scrutiny of long-term care that ACHCA tries to instill among administrators is an important step in ensuring high-quality care.

PUBLICATIONS

The ACHCA publishes a monthly newsletter, *Long-Term Care Administrator*, as well as a quarterly journal, *Journal of Long-Term Care Administration*, and assorted consumer publications, such as *Visit a Nursing Home* (1989), the Administrator's Reference series, and self-study programs available in pamphlets, audiotapes, and/or videos. The FACHCA issues a quarterly newsletter, *Foundation Focus*, and an annual research report.

ANDREW ACHENBAUM
DONNA POLISAR

AMERICAN COLLEGE OF NURSING HOME ADMINISTRATORS
See American College of Health Care Administrators.

AMERICAN FEDERATION OF HOME HEALTH AGENCIES (AFHHA)
1320 Fenwick Lane, Suite 100
Silver Springs, Maryland 20910
(301) 588–1454   FAX (301) 588–4732

The American Federation of Home Health Agencies (AFHHA) is a private, nonprofit, trade association of agencies that provide health care services, such as nursing, speech therapy, and physical therapy, to persons in their homes. AFHHA's main goal is to promote home health care through influencing public policy. AFHHA presents information directly to the U.S. Congress and the Health Care Financing Administration and helps member agencies work with third-party payers.

ORIGIN AND DEVELOPMENT

AFHHA was founded in 1981 by a group of free-standing home health care agencies. The original purpose of the group was to preserve the Medicare home health care benefit in response to a proposed limit to such benefits. AFHHA is concerned with keeping its members informed of changes in home health care policy and providing other educational services.

ORGANIZATION AND FUNDING

Two hundred Medicare-certified home health agencies, including several chains, comprise the membership of AFHHA. Additionally, corporations and individuals with an interest in home health care may become associate members. Several state affiliates exist.

The AFHHA is governed by a Board of Directors with thirteen members. AFHHA has an Executive Director and four staff members. Dues and fees from educational seminars support the AFHHA and its activities.

POLICY CONCERNS AND TACTICS

The concerns of the AFHHA relate to home health care and include Medicare benefits and regulations, long-term-care programs, and the development of private home health care agencies. The federation addresses these concerns by supplying information to legislators and their staffs and testifying before congressional committees, including the House Select Committee on Aging and the Senate Committee on Finance. AFHHA offers approximately five seminars each year, open to members and nonmembers alike, on topics related to home health care.

Members of the AFHHA are strongly encouraged to contact their representatives and senators directly to voice their concerns and opinions. AFHHA has also filed friend of the court briefs in response to legal issues of concern.

ELECTORAL ACTIVITY

AFHHA does not contribute to political campaigns but encourages its members to do so.

PUBLICATIONS

AFHHA publishes a biweekly newsletter, *The Insider*, as well as regulatory and legislative alerts.

TAMARA ZURAKOWSKI

AMERICAN FEDERATION OF LABOR–CONGRESS OF INDUSTRIAL ORGANIZATIONS (AFL-CIO)
See National Council of Senior Citizens.

AMERICAN FEDERATION OF STATE, COUNTY, AND MUNICIPAL EMPLOYEES (AFSCME)
RETIREE PROGRAM
1625 L Street, N.W.
Washington, D.C. 20036–5687
(202) 429–1000   FAX (202) 429–1293

The American Federation of State, County, and Municipal Employees (AFSCME) Retiree Program was organized to maintain ties with retired state, county, and municipal workers. The private, nonprofit membership program, a department within AFSCME, promotes the protection of individual employee rights by advocating for improved Social Security, pension, and insurance benefits.

ORIGIN AND DEVELOPMENT

In 1977, at AFSCME's twenty-second international convention, a resolution was passed to establish chapters of retired public employees. The following year, AFSCME's International Executive Board named a retiree committee to establish goals and set a structure. The formal AFSCME Retiree Program began operation in 1980, with the following goals:

1. To maintain and improve pension and health care benefits
2. To develop and support local programs to bring a better life to retired public employees
3. To afford the opportunity for members to maintain the relationships they developed through the union
4. To provide useful social, recreational, and educational opportunities for a rapidly growing senior community
5. To assist locals to develop and support issues that concern all public employees

ORGANIZATION AND FUNDING

AFSCME Retiree Program began as a national organization with only 18,000 members. In 1991, members numbered 135,000, in twenty-five chapters. The minimum retiree dues are $12.00 per member per year, with $10.20 remaining at the local level. Membership is open to all retired public employees; their spouses are also eligible to join. AFSCME locals in states with chartered retirees are urged to pay the first year's dues in the program for retiring members.

Although AFSCME provides the administrative structure, as the parent organization, each retiree chapter sets its own priorities, elects its own officers, and establishes its own budget. Also, each chapter adopts its own constitution and has the same rights of autonomy as does any other affiliate of AFSCME. The national organization receives input from the retiree Council of Presidents.

POLICY CONCERNS AND TACTICS

The AFSCME Retiree Program is concerned with health care costs, serious inadequacies in health care coverages for many public employee retirees, and protecting and improving public sector pensions. Another ongoing national priority is to preserve Social Security and Medicare.

To accomplish these goals, the AFSCME Retiree Program maintains an active presence in Washington, D.C., in state capitals, and in city halls. Grass-roots pressure is utilized when legislation detrimental to public employees is being considered. Write-in campaigns and lobbying days are used to influence legislators and local council members. AFSCME has won cost-of-living adjustments in Illinois, Washington, Ohio, Rhode Island, and Minnesota, to mention only a few. In addition, the AFSCME Retiree Program has won improved employer-paid health insurance coverage for public sector retirees across the United States.

The AFSCME Retiree Program belongs to two senior coalitions, Save Our Security[*] and the Leadership Council of Aging Organizations[*]. The group also coordinates activities with other old-age advocacy organizations, such as the National Council of Senior Citizens[*].

PUBLICATIONS

Retirees receive two publications: AFSCME's *Public Employee* magazine (eight times per year) and the *Retiree Rights* newsletter (quarterly). Other AFSCME retiree publications include *Planning for Your Survivors* (1990) and

Planning for Your Retirement (1991). AFSCME also issues a comprehensive packet of information for retirees.

DONALD SHAFER

AMERICAN GERIATRICS SOCIETY (AGS)
770 Lexington Avenue, Suite 300
New York, New York 10021
(212) 308–1414   FAX (212) 832–8646

The American Geriatrics Society (AGS) was the first organization in the United States focused on geriatric medicine. The nonprofit group has become an international medical and clinical society. AGS promotes the development and dissemination of geriatrics theory and practice and concentrates on policy issues affecting medical care of the elderly.

ORIGIN AND DEVELOPMENT

In 1942, a group of thirty physicians formed the AGS to promote research in geriatric medicine. The initial purposes of the society were to encourage and direct physicians and professional researchers in the field of aging, to develop and expand geriatric training centers, and to establish an educational journal on geriatrics. Founders encouraged the formation of state affiliates; the first state charter was issued in 1952.

AGS strives to increase the awareness and knowledge of physicians and health professionals regarding the diseases and medical conditions of the aged and the aging. The objectives of AGS are to:

• Increase the number of health professionals trained in geriatrics
• Expand and implement geriatric education and training for physicians, nurses, health professionals, and the general public
• Promote effective, high-quality research that addresses health-care problems of older people
• Ensure access to geriatric medical care for the elderly
• Pursue a vigorous public policy effort on the foremost issues that affect the medical care of older persons

ORGANIZATION AND FUNDING

An eighteen-member Board of Directors, elected by members at the society's annual meeting, governs the AGS. Directors serve three-year terms; other officers are elected every year. Sixteen staff persons are employed by AGS nationwide, headed by the Executive Vice-President. In 1991, Linda Hiddemen Barondess held that position. In the same year, the AGS had seventeen state and local affiliates and fourteen student chapters.

The organization maintains twelve standing committees whose work provides a focus and agenda for the society: Clinical Practice, Education, Ethics, Ethnogeriatrics, Finance, Long-range Planning, Membership, Nominations, Publications, Program, Public Policy, and Research. Committee consensus establishes organization policy, with the approval of the Board of Directors.

The 6,000 members of AGS are primarily physicians, with representation among nurses and other health professionals. Member categories are: regular, open to physicians and other health professionals; associate (nonvoting), open to interns, residents, and fellows-in-training; and student (nonvoting), open to medical, nursing, and other students in geriatrics/gerontology. Members joining the society can choose one or more of the following sections: the Section for Teachers of Geriatric Medicine, the Long-Term Care Section, and/or the Section for Fellows-in-Training. The sections work to ensure adequate representation of long-term care and education in the society's overall goals and activities. Each section plans symposia for the annual meeting.

Sources of the society's income are individual membership dues (38%); course registrations, publications, and annual meeting revenue (52%); and foundation grants and additional fund raising (10%). The AGS annual budget ranges between $1.5 million and $2 million.

The society sponsors an annual scientific meeting accredited for continuing medical education (CME). The annual meeting presents recent research developments, workshops, panels, and oral presentations of original research papers. The society also offers symposia, seminars, and other postgraduate educational events, often co-sponsored by hospitals, universities, long-term-care facilities, and other institutions and organizations. The AGS awards several prizes annually to students and other researchers.

The AGS is accredited by the Accreditation Council for Continuing Medical Education to sponsor CME for physicians. AGS focuses a large percentage of its efforts on providing opportunities for health professionals in geriatrics to increase and update their knowledge, developing curriculum guidelines and review materials. AGS offers various CME-accredited courses, including board review courses, throughout the year.

POLICY CONCERNS AND TACTICS

The AGS addresses a variety of policy issues that relate to the medical care of older persons and to the education of professionals in geriatrics. In addition to issues related specifically to the elderly, the society is concerned with other policies, such as physician reimbursement, funding for research and graduate medical education, and access to health care. The AGS affects public policy in these areas by testifying before Congress, providing information to congressional representatives and senators and federal agencies, and filing amicus curiae briefs in the courts. The AGS encourages its members to write to members and committees of Congress and disseminates position statements on pertinent issues.

The AGS presents testimony before Congress several times per session. In April 1990, AGS testified before the Subcommittee on Labor of the Senate Appropriations Committee on fiscal year 1991 funding for the National Institutes of Health (NIH). In January and December of the same year, AGS argued before the Physician Payment Review Commission regarding physician reimbursement issues. In March 1991, AGS testified before the hearing of the House Select Committee on Aging entitled Long-term Care Personnel: Incentives for Training and Career Development. In April, the society submitted written testimony to the Senate Committee on Labor and Human Resources regarding the reauthorization of the geriatric training programs of the Health Resources and Services Administration. The AGS generally supported the 1988 Medicare-Catastrophic Coverage Act (repealed in 1989), though it objected that it overlooked long-term care.

In 1986 and 1987, AGS brought the issue of research and training in geriatrics before the Senate Committee on Labor and Human Resources. The broader issue in 1987 was the reauthorization of the Older Americans Act (OAA); in 1986, it was the Graduate Medical Education Act. Both acts passed.

An example of the society's role as information provider occurred in 1987. The AGS submitted a paper, "Geriatric Expertise in the Context of Critical and Terminal Care," as background for a U.S. Office of Technology Assessment report on life-sustaining treatment and technologies for elderly patients. Occasionally the AGS also files amicus curiae briefs in court cases.

The Public Policy Committee develops position papers for the AGS and submits them to the Board of Directors for approval. The AGS has published position statements on the following issues:

• Care management
• Comprehensive geriatric assessment for the older patient
• Conversion of prescription drugs to over-the-counter designation
• Drug evaluation and surveillance
• Education in geriatric medicine
• Medical treatment decisions concerning elderly persons
• Medicare
• Mental health and the elderly
• Physician reimbursement under Medicare
• Physician's role in the long-term-care facility
• Prevention of nuclear war
• Public financing of catastrophic care for older patients
• Regulations of nursing facilities
• Research and geriatric medicine
• The role of the Veterans Administration in the care of the elderly
• The use of drugs of questionable efficacy with the elderly
• Voluntary active euthanasia

These statements, generally about two pages long, are available from the organization.

The AGS coordinates its actions and maintains liaisons with organizations such as the Gerontological Society of America*, the National Institute on Aging, the American College of Physicians, the American Association of Retired Persons*, the American Federation for Aging Research, the American Academy of Family Physicans, the American Association for Geriatric Psychiatry, the American Academy of Home Care Physicians, the American Medical Directors Association*, and the Joint Commission on Accreditation of Healthcare Organizations.

AGS is a member of the American Medical Association's House of Delegates, the American Association of Medical Colleges' Council of Academic Societies, the International Association of Gerontology*, and Research!America.

Future goals of the AGS include increasing the number of physicians trained in geriatric medicine, improving health care for the elderly, making health care delivery to older persons more equitable and accessible, and educating the public on preventive medicine and healthy aging.

PUBLICATIONS

The *Journal of the American Geriatrics Society* (monthly), first published in 1953, provides a forum for discussion and original articles about developments in this field. The *Journal* is sent to all members; nonmembers can subscribe for $92 per year. The *AGS Newsletter* (bimonthly), sent to all members, covers meetings, seminars, and current events in geriatric medicine. AGS also publishes the *Geriatrics Review Syllabus* (every other year), a two-volume educational program to help physicians and other health professionals evaluate and update their knowledge of geriatric medicine through a comprehensive text, a 200-question self-assessment examination, an annotated bibliography, an appendix of evaluation tools, and answers and referenced critiques for each examination question.

About every two years, AGS publishes an updated edition of the *Directory of Fellowship Programs in Geriatric Medicine*, which includes descriptions of programs in the United States and Canada. AGS also publishes position statements on policy issues and a periodic membership directory, and it offers audio cassettes of annual meeting presentations.

Further Information

Jack Bess, "Geriatric Society President Backs RBRVS Concept," *American Medical News*, November 10, 1989, 17.

JIMMY E. W. MEYER
QIUSHA MA

AMERICAN HEALTH CARE ASSOCIATION (AHCA)
1201 L Street, N.W.
Washington, D.C. 20005
(202) 842–4444   FAX (202) 842–3860

The American Health Care Association (AHCA) is the largest national trade association representing nursing homes in the United States. It is a nonprofit federation of state associations that represent over 10,000 proprietary and non-proprietary long-term health care facilities dedicated to improving the health care of convalescents and chronically ill persons of all ages.

ORIGIN AND DEVELOPMENT

The AHCA was founded in 1949 as the American Nursing Home Association by the merger of the American Association of Nursing Homes and the National Association of Registered Nursing Homes. Prior to World War II, the elderly were generally cared for in private homes; due to changing demographics after the war, however, there was an increase in the demand for public homes and institutions to care for the aging. With the passage of Medicare and Medicaid legislation in 1965, the nursing home industry grew, along with AHCA's membership. In 1975, the American Nursing Home Association changed its name to the American Health Care Association.

ORGANIZATION AND FUNDING

AHCA's membership is composed of owners and operators of nursing home facilities. Facilities belong to one of AHCA's fifty-one state affiliates (including the District of Columbia) and are thereby members of AHCA. The AHCA is governed by a seventy-eight-member Board of Directors, headed in 1991 by Paul Willging, Executive Vice-President. The board includes the sixteen members of the Executive Committee, the thirteen Regional Vice-Presidents, and the fifty-one representatives of the state affiliates. All board positions are elected by the membership. AHCA employs fifty-three professional and support staff in its national office in Washington, D.C.

Approximately two-thirds of AHCA's funding comes from individual membership dues. Each affiliate collects the annual dues according to its bylaws and adds a per-bed fee for AHCA services to a maximum of 200 beds. The remaining one-third of AHCA's 1991 annual budget of $7.4 million is supplied by the sale of professional development materials, audiovisual resources and publications, the revenue from special events, and the annual October convention.

POLICY CONCERNS AND TACTICS

The AHCA promotes standards for professionals and high-quality care for patients and residents in a safe environment in long-term health care facilities. The AHCA focuses on issues of availability, quality, affordability, and fair payment. It conducts seminars that provide continuing education for nursing home personnel and maintains liaison with Congress, governmental agencies, and professional associations such as the American Association of Retired Persons[*], the American Association of Homes for the Aging[*], and the National Citizens Coalition for Nursing Home Reform[*].

One of the main areas of concern for the AHCA is to create a more efficient long-term-care financing system for nursing homes that does not rely so heavily on Medicaid payments. Medicaid, the health care program for the poor, is the largest third-party payer for nursing home care, covering more than 40 percent of all such services. Yet AHCA claims that insufficient Medicaid reimbursement hurts patient care.

In 1991, the AHCA filed suit against the Secretary of the U.S. Department of Health and Human Services to ensure that the Health Care Financing Administration approve state plan amendments offering adequate funding to cover major new rules under the Omnibus Budget Reconciliation Acts of 1987 and 1990. The AHCA has also been investigating private insurance concepts and tax law adjustments as alternative financing of long-term health care to make available private funds for such care.

Another concern of the AHCA is the shortage of nurses in long-term-care facilities. The AHCA testified before the House Energy and Commerce Subcommittee on Health in July 1990 in favor of the Walgren bill, which endorses raising long-term-care nurses' salaries to the level of hospital nurses.

In addition to concerns about long-term-care financing, the AHCA was involved in lobbying Congress for the Omnibus Budget Reconciliation Act of 1990, which sets standards and regulations for nursing homes.

ELECTORAL ACTIVITY

AHCA has a political action committee, registered as AHCA-PAC. In the 1989–90 election cycle, the AHCA-PAC contributed to candidates of both parties.

PUBLICATIONS

AHCA publishes *AHCA Notes*, a biweekly newsletter covering nursing home legislation and regulations. It also publishes *Provider: For Long-Term Care Professionals*, a monthly journal that includes a buyers' guide, reports, an advertisers' index, a listing of new products and services, legal news, and a calendar of events. The association publishes a variety of professional development materials for the long-term-care industry, including training and operational manuals and reference materials, available to both members and nonmembers. The Information Resource Center of the AHCA provides information on new publications and how to order them.

JULIEANNE PHILLIPS

AMERICAN HOSPITAL ASSOCIATION (AHA)
SECTION FOR AGING AND LONG-TERM CARE SERVICES
840 North Lake Shore Drive
Chicago, Illinois 60611
(312) 280–6000 or (312) 280–6372   FAX (312) 280–6252

The Section for Aging and Long-Term Care Services of the American Hospital Association (AHA) provides technical and educational services to member institutions, examines the implications of federal and state health care legislation, and encourages change through advocacy and political action.

ORIGIN AND DEVELOPMENT

The goal of the AHA, a trade organization of 45,000 individuals and health care institutions, is to promote high-quality health care. AHA is "dedicated to promoting the welfare of the public through its leadership and assistance to its members." Its concern with the special needs of the elderly became evident during the 1950s. In 1958, a committee of the AHA Council on Professional Practice Studying the Care of the Chronically Ill and of the Aged targeted the crucial issues of financial strategies, new program implementation, and improvement of health care services for the aged. The AHA helped sponsor the Joint Council to Improve the Health Care of the Aged (1958), as well as a national Conference on the Care of Patients with Long-Term Illness. AHA delegates participated in the 1961 White House Conference on Aging.

In 1969, the AHA created a separate special interest section to address long-term-care issues. A series of name changes suggests a shifting focus from institutional accreditation and services for the elderly into such areas as technical assistance and information dissemination. The Office on Aging and Long-Term Care was established under the Hospital Research and Educational Trust of the AHA in 1983. It channeled relevant research and educational information to member institutions through in-house publications and monographs. Development and implementation of policy issues on a national level were handled informally. Changing demographics and an increased awareness of the importance of political advocacy resulted in the disbanding of the AHA Office on Aging and Long-Term Care in late 1986. It was replaced in 1987 with the Section for Aging and Long-Term Care Services, one of seven special constituency sections in the AHA.

The Section for Aging and Long-Term Care Services moved beyond research and publication to take on active political advocacy. Representing the concerns of member institutions as well as the health care concerns of the elderly, the section actively participates in national policy formulation. It continues to provide research services to its member institutions but has broadened that mandate to include analysis of issues, the implication of pending legislation, and interpretation of policy to its members. The section influences local, regional, state, and national health care policy standards through its institutional membership.

ORGANIZATION AND FUNDING

The AHA Section for Aging and Long-Term Care Services had 2,300 members in 1990. Members of the AHA are eligible to join the section if they provide long-term-care units, community-based special services for the aged, or offer geriatric assessment and/or acute or primary care services. The section is directed by a council of twenty-four members. Any chief executive, operating officer, or director of senior services of a member institution is eligible to serve on the governing council and vote on policy matters. Council representatives are elected from the membership at large. The council is under the direction of the AHA Board of Trustees.

The section has two professional staff members and a representative in Washington, D.C., who allots 25 percent of her time to the interests of this section. Approximately 90 percent of the section's annual budget of $300,000 is obtained from hospital membership dues. The remainder is generated by the annual conference.

POLICY CONCERNS AND TACTICS

The Section for Aging and Long-Term Care Services, along with the AHA Division of Health Policy, Finance, and Data Analysis, monitors health policy issues related to the elderly. In 1990, its focus was on support systems, including funding strategies, coverage, and payment policies. Of particular importance are Medicare and Medicaid programs and funding, nursing home regulation and reform, and home health care issues. The section monitors and interprets legislation and regulation affecting long-term care to its members. It represents the interests of its members and supplies information to congressional leaders and their staff.

The American Hospital Association has testified before Congress on such topics as the Medicare Quality Protection Act of 1986, Catastrophic Illness Expenses (1987), and Rural Health Care Challenges (1989). In the late 1980s, the Section for Aging and Long-Term Care Services informed members of the implications of federal requirements for long-term-care facilities arising from the Omnibus Budget Reconciliation Act of 1987. The section offers suggestions and comments to the federal Health Care Financing Administration (Department of Health and Human Services).

ELECTORAL ACTIVITY

The AHA Section for Aging and Long-Term Care Services tracks the voting position of congressional leaders on key legislation but takes no active role in supporting individual candidates. The section encourages member institutions to write to their representatives as a way to participate in policy decisions.

PUBLICATIONS

The Section for Aging and Long-Term Care Services publishes a quarterly membership briefing, *Case Studies in Aging and Long-Term Development*, and periodic research reports.

                                                    BETH DINATALE JOHNSON

AMERICAN MEDICAL DIRECTORS ASSOCIATION (AMDA)
10480 Little Patuxent Parkway, Suite 760
Columbia, Maryland 21044
(301) 740–9743, (800) 321-AMDA   FAX (301) 740–4572

The American Medical Directors Association (AMDA) is a national, professional, nonprofit organization representing physicians who provide health care in nursing facilities. AMDA works to improve the quality of care in these institutions.

ORIGIN AND DEVELOPMENT

As a result of federal legislation requiring a medical director to serve each nursing home, AMDA was founded in Macon, Georgia, in 1976 by William Dodd. In 1984, the organization moved to Washington, D.C., and established a national headquarters. In 1990, AMDA had approximately 1,280 members and eleven state chapters.

ORGANIZATION AND FUNDING

The state chapters elect one delegate for every fifty members to the House of Delegates. This body nominates and elects all national officers as well as three representatives to sit on the sixteen-member Board of Directors. The House of Delegates meets annually. AMDA has a paid staff of five.

The organization has an annual budget of approximately $250,000. About 75 percent of this amount comes from individual membership dues of $125 and 20 percent from corporate dues, which vary according to the type of corporation. Corporate members include companies that manufacture drugs and durable medical equipment, as well as nursing home conglomerates. The remaining funding comes from educational meetings and private grants. AMDA receives no federal monies.

POLICY CONCERNS AND TACTICS

A public policy committee proposes positions on issues to the Board of Directors. The House of Delegates can also request the board to formulate a policy concerning a specific topic.

AMDA "articulates the views of long-term care physicians and advocates for a stronger role for them." The organization believes that the long-term-care physician should have a leadership role in ensuring high-quality care in nursing homes. AMDA advocates adequate reimbursement for nursing home physicians, supports measures designed to prevent the exodus of physicians from nursing home care, and favors the reduction of physical and chemical restraints for nursing home patients. It announced a certification program for medical directors in January 1990.

To these ends, AMDA testifies before Congress, supplies information to senators, representatives, and staff, and encourages its members to write to legislators about issues that affect nursing home care. Board members of AMDA sit on the advisory committee of the federal Health Care Financing Administration (HCFA) and meet with the HCFA staff. The organization does no lobbying and has no political action committee.

AMDA supports the intent of the Omnibus Budget Reconciliation Act (OBRA) of 1987. AMDA submitted draft language for several technical amendments and has been in constant contact with legislators and regulators since the act was passed, as OBRA continues to be interpreted and amended.

The organization works closely with the American College of Health Care Administrators* and conducts programs about long-term care at meetings of the American Geriatrics Society* and other organizations.

PUBLICATIONS

AMDA publishes a quarterly newsletter, *AMDA Reports*, and a professional journal, the *Annual of Medical Direction*.

Further Information

Ron Rajecki, "Medical Directors to Carry More Weight," *Contemporary Long-Term Care* (October 1990): 42.

JEAN R. LINDERMAN

AMERICAN NURSING HOME ASSOCIATION
See American Health Care Association.

AMERICANS FOR GENERATIONAL EQUITY (AGE)
3231 Beech Street, N.W.
Washington, D.C. 20015–2207
(202) 686–4196

Americans for Generational Equity (AGE) is a nonprofit, nonpartisan research and education organization urging U.S. fiscal reform in the interests of the future elderly and their children. Through information dissemination, congressional testimony, and widespread use of the media, AGE attempts to warn policymakers and the general public of the perceived threat to the American economic lifestyle posed by the aging of the population, low productivity growth, and increasing national indebtedness.

ORIGIN AND DEVELOPMENT

AGE was founded in 1984 by two members of Congress, Republican Senator David Durenberger of Minnesota and Democratic Congressman James Jones from Oklahoma. Paul Hewitt, who served as staff director of the Senate Subcommittee on Intergovernmental Relations, was hired as Executive Director and Philip Longman as Research Director. AGE founders perceived a growing economic gulf between generations and established the organization to address and promote the cause of the young, whom they saw as the least represented. Calling itself the "lobby of the future," AGE believes that the economic prospects are bleak for the baby-boom generation and their children. Citing higher poverty levels, AGE claims that "the downward mobility of the baby boomers has compounded with a vengeance on their children."

AGE promoted its ideas widely in the media, marshaling the research support of conservative think tanks and the financial support of like-minded corporations and foundations. As a result of AGE's media efforts, "generational equity" has been widely argued within the aging network. For example, at a standing-room-only debate at a meeting of the American Society on Aging* in 1986, Hewitt opposed Ron Pollack, of the Villers Foundation (now Families U.S.A. Foundation*).

AGE held its first annual national conference in Washington, D.C., only a few days later. The conference was entitled Tomorrow's Elderly: Planning for the Baby Boom Generation's Retirement. The House Select Committee on Aging held a one-day hearing at the same time, called Investing in America's Families: The Common Bond of Generations. Organizations and coalitions, such as Generations United*, formed to counteract AGE's message.

ORGANIZATION AND FUNDING

AGE had 700 members in 1991 and a budget of over $300,000. It is governed by an advisory board and headed by an Executive Director. In 1991, J. J. Wuerthner held that position. AGE is a designated tax-exempt, 501(c)(3) organization.

POLICY CONCERNS AND TACTICS

As a means of restoring generational equity, AGE recommends taxing Social Security benefits; subjecting Social Security cost-of-living increases to a means test disqualifying retirees with higher pensions; and raising the benefit eligibility age. AGE encourages private retirement plans rather than governmental entitlement programs.

In addition to media promotion, AGE utilizes research as an educational tool. In 1987, the group compiled a statistical abstract, *The Challenge of An Aging Society: Planning for the Baby Boom Generation's Retirement*. AGE has presented testimony before congressional committees, opposing such legislation as the 1988 Medicare Catastrophic Coverage Act. AGE holds public forums and regional conferences featuring health experts and policymakers addressing issues such as generational conflict and Medicare reform.

PUBLICATIONS

AGE issues The *Generational Journal* (quarterly) and periodic conference proceedings.

Further Information

Amitai Etzioni, "Spare the Old, Save the Young, Health-Care Generation War." *Nation*, June 11, 1988, 818–22; Edwin Kiester, Jr., "Young vs. Old: The War We Must Never Allow to Happen," *50 Plus* (August 1986): 40–45;

Philip Longman, *Born to Pay: The New Politics of Aging* (Boston: Houghton Mifflin, 1987).

JIMMY E. W. MEYER

AMERICAN SOCIETY OF PROFESSIONAL ADMINISTRATORS
See Society of Professional Benefit Administrators.

AMERICAN SOCIETY ON AGING (ASA)
833 Market Street, Suite 512
San Francisco, California 94103
(415) 882–2910   FAX (415) 882–4280

The American Society on Aging (ASA) is one of the largest professional associations in the United States in the field of aging. The organization provides continuing education and training for a wide cross-section of gerontology professionals and practitioners. The ASA usually influences policy indirectly, through conferences, education and training seminars, and publications, but occasionally the group utilizes the more direct approach of congressional testimony.

ORIGIN AND DEVELOPMENT

ASA was founded in 1954 in San Francisco as the Western Gerontological Society (WGS). Co-founders Oscar Kaplan and Louis Kuplan formed the organization to promote the well-being of the elderly and to foster unity among those working with and for the elderly in the western United States. For over twenty years, the informal, loosely structured group maintained a regional focus. The small membership represented primarily academic and research interests.

Between 1973 and 1977, WGS strengthened its organizational framework, hiring an Executive Director and creating an official membership structure. WGS widened its membership base, including practitioners as well as academicians. The WGS board also decided to take a more active part in policymaking, voting unanimously "that the organization had the responsibility to utilize knowledge to advocate on behalf of issues significant to the aging community."

The regional geographic focus broadened to a national one in 1985, when the Western Gerontological Society changed its name to the American Society on Aging. With the expansion, the size of the membership increased from 3,000 (1985) to 8,000 (1990). In addition, the amount of programming and staff size more than doubled.

The society has always provided continuing education and training in aging-related fields, at first only through an annual conference. Beginning in 1980, the organization instituted multiple regional seminars, fall/winter conferences, a summer series on aging, and special programs targeted at specific audiences, in addition to the yearly event. Topics emphasize current developments in research, practice, policy, and theory.

ORGANIZATION AND FUNDING

"ASA's members are a national, multi-disciplinary coalition that includes public- and private-sector administrators and executives, service providers and researchers, educators and advocates, health and social service professionals, students and the retired." Membership is open to individuals and organizations with concerns in the field of aging. In 1990, ASA's individual members numbered more than 7,000 and organizational members more than 1,000. The ASA is governed by a twenty-eight-member Board of Directors and run by twenty-six professional staff. The board sets policy on the basis of recommendations by committees such as Public Policy, Minority Concerns, Research, and Education.

ASA offers two membership affiliations for additional fees: the Forum on Religion and Aging and the Business Forum on Aging. The Forum on Religion and Aging is an interfaith organization for individuals or groups concerned with the spiritual needs of older persons, promoting "programs, policies, and educational opportunities which empower the experience and expression of religion and spirituality in later life." The Business Forum on Aging, open to organizational members only, "provides a framework for businesses to address the issues and opportunities associated with . . . aging." Forum members create networks and share models, experience, and information. Each of the forums publishes a newsletter and issues periodic White Papers on critical topics.

The ASA obtains its budget, over $2 million per year, from a variety of sources: approximately 45 percent from conference fees, 32 percent from membership dues, 13 percent from publications, and 10 percent from additional fund raising.

POLICY CONCERNS AND TACTICS

ASA has consistently emphasized educating its members about current and developing policy matters pertinent to the elderly. The organization publishes research, provides opportunities for informed policy debates, and disseminates information through its conferences and seminars. ASA also supplies data to members of Congress on issues such as financial appropriations for needs of the elderly.

In 1976, the Western Gerontological Society created a legislative-policy committee focusing on the broad spectrum of aging policy, with special attention to issues affecting westerners such as distribution of government surplus food to rural areas. The WGS joined with other organizations in 1976 to advocate successfully for the retention of the Senate Special Committee on Aging.

Occasionally the Western Gerontological Society scheduled annual meetings to coincide with congressional briefings and hearings. For example, in March

1977, the society's twenty-third annual meeting took place in Denver, where the Senate Special Committee on Aging continued hearings on the nation's rural elderly. WGS Past-President W. Roy Van Orman testified. The Older Americans Act in the context of fiscal constraint was the topic of a House Select Committee on Aging briefing, held in April 1981 in conjunction with WGS meetings. Carl Eisdorfer, WGS President, testified in behalf of community-based services to the elderly. In 1984, the society arranged its annual meeting in Anaheim, California, to coincide with a House Select Committee on Aging hearing on the future of elderly health care. The WGS President, Carroll Estes, presented an introductory statement; the Public Policy Committee Chairperson, Charlene Harrington, was a witness.

A WGS board member testified in May 1982 before the Senate Committee on Appropriations recommending that funding levels of the Older Americans Act (OAA) be maintained and opposing cuts in Title IV of OAA and Title XX of Social Security. Title IV provides funds for research, training, and special projects; Title XX, a block grant program, provides states with funding for services for poor residents of all ages. Other organizations advocating for the elderly at this hearing included the Association for Gerontology in Higher Education*.

The ASA worked closely with other agencies in planning a series of public forums beginning in 1989. The forums involved such cooperating organizations as the Alzheimer's Association*, the Associacion Nacional Pro Personas Mayores*, the Older Women's League*, the Gray Panthers*, and the American Association of Retired Persons*. In 1990, ASA, a member of the Leadership Council of Aging Organizations*, joined that organization in proposing a basis for a national health care plan. The principal components of the proposal are universal access, comprehensive benefits, cost containment, equitable financing, quality control, and consumer rights.

The American Society on Aging created the staff position of Director of Public Policy in 1990. The post was half-time for the first year and full-time thereafter. Plans were for the Director of Public Policy to work together with the Public Policy Committee and the ASA board to identify critical political issues and to formulate policy statements on those issues, informing both the membership and the general public. Initially, ASA focused on income security, national health and social services policy, and the concerns of caregivers in the work force.

PUBLICATIONS

The society has two major publications: the journal *Generations* (quarterly) and the newspaper *Aging Today* (bimonthly) (formerly the *Aging Connection*). Each issue of *Generations* offers diverse perspectives from researchers, policymakers, theorists, and practitioners on a single theme. *Aging Today* provides national coverage of developments in practice, research, and policy and keeps members up-to-date on activities of the ASA.

JIMMY E. W. MEYER
QIUSHA MA

AMERICAN VETERANS OF FOREIGN SERVICE
See Veterans of Foreign Wars of the United States.

ARTIST RESOURCE PROGRAM
See Generations Together.

A.S.A.P. (ADVOCATES SENIOR ALERT PROCESS)
1334 G Street, N.W.
Washington, D.C. 20005
(202) 737–6340   FAX (202) 347–2417

A.S.A.P. (Advocates Senior Alert Process) is a national "legislative information and action network for politically active seniors and senior advocates" designed to mobilize individuals and aging-advocacy organizations "to fight legislative battles" for improving the quality of life for older Americans, especially those of low income.

ORIGIN AND DEVELOPMENT

A.S.A.P. was organized in 1985. The project grew out of the activities of the Villers Foundation and its advocacy arm, Villers Advocacy Associates, now Families U.S.A. Foundation*. Villers Advocacy Associates, founded in 1981, surveyed the networks representing the elderly and saw the need for a multiorganizational pool for action in the federal legislative arena of policy on aging, especially in the areas of health care and income security. A.S.A.P.'s motto states "Together, we *can* make a difference!"

ORGANIZATION AND FUNDING

A.S.A.P. is sponsored by Families U.S.A., where its offices are located. In 1991, seventeen advocacy organizations cooperated in the A.S.A.P. network (see Appendix B for a list). To join A.S.A.P., each of these organizations must also belong to the Leadership Council of Aging Organizations* and have an office in Washington, D.C.

Representatives of cooperating organizations establish policy for A.S.A.P; there is no formal governing board. All policy statements and publications are reviewed by representatives of all seventeen participating groups; A.S.A.P. must have the consensus of all the representatives before taking a public stand on a policy issue. Two staff members manage the organization. Families U.S.A. underwrites all costs.

There are nearly 10,000 participants in A.S.A.P., drawn from the membership of the cooperating organizations and other members of the public. A.S.A.P does not charge participants but requires a commitment: "mobilizing at least five other people to take action." A pledge to that effect is included on the membership sign-up form.

POLICY CONCERNS AND TACTICS

A.S.A.P. focuses on federal policy, particularly the issues of a national long-term-care program within a national health care system, the protection of Social Security, the continuation of Older Americans Act programs, the control of the private health insurance industry, and the expansion of employment and/or volunteer opportunities for older persons. A.S.A.P. does not testify or advocate directly but rather mobilizes its participants and other advocates. The organization alerts members to pending congressional actions and encourages them to call or write to pertinent legislators and to hold meetings with elected officials, urges members to write letters to the editors of local and national newspapers, and publishes research. A.S.A.P. educates its members in methods of effective advocacy and provides background information on upcoming legislative issues, such as "The Medigap Mess" (*A.S.A.P. Special Report*, May 1990).

In 1990, A.S.A.P. sponsored an "Open Letter to Congress" supporting the passage of five Medicaid bills, including one to expand Medicaid coverage of home care for older people. Through A.S.A.P. efforts, over 600 grass-roots groups signed the letter to the Senate Finance Committee, and 300 signed the letter to the House Energy and Commerce Committee. The signers represented thirty-three states and a variety of associations, including local senior centers, area agencies on aging, and state, county, and local advocacy associations— inside and outside the field of aging—as well as branches of national organizations. The Frail Elderly Home Care provisions were passed, with limitations, as amendments to the 1991 Omnibus Budget Reconciliation Act.

PUBLICATIONS

During sessions of Congress, A.S.A.P. publishes *Update*, a periodic legislative newsletter. The organization issues Special Reports occasionally, providing background information on key topics, and Action Alerts, requesting calls and letters to legislators on impending congressional actions. Advocacy Tips, distributed to members, describes the legislative process and suggests ways for individuals to participate. A.S.A.P. participants also receive the *Families U.S.A. Guide to the U.S. Congress,* a two-part brochure detailing key committee personnel in Congress (part I) and the names, addresses, telephone numbers, and committee assignments of the member's particular state delegation to Congress (part II).

JIMMY E. W. MEYER

ASOCIACION NACIONAL PRO PERSONAS MAYORES (ANPPM)/NA-TIONAL ASSOCIATION FOR HISPANIC ELDERLY

3325 Wilshire Boulevard, Suite 800
Los Angeles, California 90010
(213) 487–1922   FAX (213) 385–3014

The Asociacion Nacional Pro Personas Mayores (ANPPM), or National Association for Hispanic Elderly, is a national, nonprofit membership association. One of the most broad-based Hispanic organizations in the United States, ANPPM works to increase awareness of and encourage positive response to the needs and concerns of Hispanic and other low-income older persons. ANPPM sponsors research and data collection, develops and manages model projects, and performs specialized work in media and communications on behalf of low-income and/or Hispanic elderly.

ORIGIN AND DEVELOPMENT

ANPPM was founded in 1975 to give voice to the needs of the 2 million Hispanic elderly in the United States. "Special concerns" sessions following the 1971 White House Conference on Aging illuminated problems specific to minority older persons, such as the prevalence of poverty and shorter life expectancy. Carmela G. Lacayo, ANPPM President/CEO since the organization's inception, founded the Asociacion Pro Personas Mayores to address the concerns of Hispanic older persons. The U.S. Administration on Aging (AoA) provided start-up funds for the ANPPM, incorporated as a tax-exempt, 501(c)(3) organization on April 28, 1975.

In 1977, the association created the Resource Center on Hispanic Data and Information (later called the National Hispanic Research Center) and the next year received funding for its first research project, A National Study to Assess the Service Needs of Hispanic Elderly. The organization initiated a Senior Community Service Employment Program (SCSEP) in 1978 with a grant from the U.S. Department of Labor. In its early stages, Project Ayuda served older workers in California, Kansas, Louisiana, Oklahoma, and Texas.

Throughout the 1980s, the ANPPM conducted further research and surveys, sponsored numerous conferences and meetings, including the 1981 White House Mini-Conference on Hispanic Aging in Los Angeles, expanded Project Ayuda, and originated another AoA-funded program, Project Respeto. This intergenerational support project for low-income and minority older people received the Voluntarism in Action Award from the National Council on the Aging* in 1986. Also during the 1980s, ANPPM started the Hispanic Gerontological Internship Program designed to train Hispanics for administrative and managerial careers in aging and established El Pueblo Community Development Corporation, which focuses on low-income housing and economic development in the Hispanic community. Aware of the importance of media, the ANPPM developed the National Hispanic Media Center, or Rainbow Communications. ANPPM has consistently created and distributed filmstrips and videotapes as educational tools.

ORGANIZATION AND FUNDING

The members of ANPPM represent the nation's varied Hispanic communities: Mexican, Puerto Rican, Cuban, and Central and South American. ANPPM recognizes the separate cultural heritage and special needs of each group and works to bond them together. ANPPM offers both individual and corporate memberships to older persons, organizations, and social service groups concerned with aging. In 1991, individual members numbered 5,000 and corporate members 100.

ANPPM maintains ten regional offices across the United States and a liaison office in Washington, D.C. The national headquarters is located in Los Angeles. ANPPM has a thirteen-member Board of Directors, which sets policy. Board members serve three-year terms and choose the members for the next board. A staff of forty-three manages the organization, led by the President/CEO. In 1991, ANPPM founder Carmela G. Lacayo held that office.

The major income source of the ANPPM is federal government funds (90%). Other monies are derived from grants (almost 10%) and membership dues (less than 1%). The ANPPM budget exceeds $15 million.

ANPPM manages several projects that benefit Hispanic and other low-income elderly. Project Ayuda, an SCSEP administered by the association, provides working opportunities to more than 1,800 low-income older persons in ten states and the District of Columbia. El Pueblo Community Development Corporation (CDC) embodies another ANPPM vision—that of public and private sector cooperation to provide community-based economic development. El Pueblo CDC has developed low-income housing projects worth $26 million, which were financed in part by the Community Redevelopment Agency of the city of Los Angeles. El Pueblo CDC serves as a prototype for other nonprofit, community-based development corporations. Established as a subsidiary of ANPPM, El Pueblo CDC is governed by a separate board and has its own status as a separate tax-exempt, 501(c)(3) organization.

The ANPPM's extensive research component, represented by the National Hispanic Research Center, makes ANPPM unique among American Hispanic organizations. The association supports the National Hispanic Media Center, maintains a 2,500-volume library, and sponsors the Arthur S. Flemming Hispanics in Human Services Scholarship Fund. ANPPM holds a national conference every two or three years and publishes the proceedings.

POLICY CONCERNS AND TACTICS

ANPPM focuses on "Improving the Quality of Life for Aged Hispanics and Other Older Americans," as the title of a 1987 policy statement proclaims. The comprehensive thirty-five-page document highlights the following areas: income, employment, health, long term care, housing, services, budget, civil rights, and crime. ANPPM's many recommendations include the following:

- Updating of the poverty definition for older Americans
- Continuing to target low-income older minorities for SCSEP enrollment
- Researching race- and ethnic-related life expectancy differences
- Establishing a community-based long-term-care system.
- Constructing more Section 202 [subsidized] housing units for the elderly
- Increasing Older Americans Act (OAA) provisions for minority older persons
- Reducing the federal deficit without cutting services to the poor
- Assessing OAA programs as to their compliance with civil rights laws
- Replicating successful crime prevention programs across the country

ANPPM frequently testifies before congressional committees, regularly appearing before Congress to promote the reauthorization of the OAA and extensions and amendments to it. In April 1991, ANPPM's President/CEO testified on 1991 reauthorization of the OAA before the Subcommittee on Human Resources of the House Education and Labor Committee. She strongly recommended continued support for the AoA's Hispanic initiative and increased emphasis on research on and training for minority populations. ANPPM testified before the Senate Select Committee on Aging in July 1988 on the subject of minority elderly mental health, as well as before other House and Senate committees in the 1980s on SCSEP reauthorization and the OAA Nutrition Program.

The ANPPM emphasizes employment and services for Hispanic and low-income elderly. Businesses and other organizations often consult with ANPPM over marketing and employment concerns. ANPPM has served on advisory committees and panels for businesses such as Allstate and ITT. ANPPM assists grass-roots groups in fund raising and helps other organizations decide about services to the Hispanic community.

ANPPM is a charter member of the Leadership Council of Aging Organizations[*] and coordinates efforts with other groups serving elderly minority populations, such as the National Indian Council on Aging[*], the National Pacific/Asian Resource Center on Aging[*], and the National Caucus and Center on Black Aged[*].

Future priorities for ANPPM include national health insurance with provision for long-term care, national housing policy emphasizing affordable housing for the elderly, and increased focus on research and service regarding the needs of minority older persons.

PUBLICATIONS

ANPPM publishes a quarterly newsletter, *Que Pasa?*. Other publications include *A Research, Bibliographic and Resource Guide on the Hispanic Elderly* (1981), videotapes such as *"Valemos La Pena!" "We're Worth It!"* (1990), *Triple Jeopardy: The Hispanic Elderly in the U.S.* (1981), and *Barriers: Service Delivery to the Hispanic Elderly of the U.S.* (1983). ANPPM also makes available English- and Spanish-language brochures on Social Security, Medicare, health-related topics, and starting volunteer groups; and publishes occasional public policy statements, such as "Improving the Quality of Life for Aged Hispanics and Other Older Americans" (1987).

Further Information

Carmela Lacayo, "The Asociacion Nacional Pro Personas Mayores: Responding to the 'Decade of the Hispanic,' " *Aging*, nos. 305–306 (March–April 1980): 12–13.

JIMMY E. W. MEYER

QIUSHA MA

ASSOCIATION FOR GERONTOLOGY IN HIGHER EDUCATION (AGHE)

1001 Connecticut Avenue, N.W., Suite 410

Washington, D.C. 20036–5504

(202) 429–9277   FAX (202) 429–6097

The Association for Gerontology in Higher Education (AGHE) is a national, nonprofit, membership organization of educational institutions striving to advance gerontology as a field of study. AGHE's missions are to foster gerontological training, research, and instruction and to heighten public awareness about the field. AGHE advocates through education, research, and congressional testimony to influence public policy, especially in the area of federal support for research and education on aging.

ORIGIN AND DEVELOPMENT

Professional gerontological research and instruction came of age during the late 1960s and the early 1970s. The AGHE developed out of the work of the Ad Hoc Committee on the Development of Gerontology Resources at Brandeis University from 1972 to 1973. The committee was formed to respond to a proposal by the U.S. Administration on Aging (AoA) to establish regional gerontology centers and was composed mainly of educators and training program directors from AoA- and Older Americans Act (OAA)-funded programs. AGHE was formally incorporated in 1974, growing out of the Gerontological Society of America[*] (GSA). Its purpose was to facilitate institutional communication regarding the development of gerontology instruction programs.

In the 1970s and early 1980s, the AGHE not only built its membership and strengthened its organizational structure but also laid the basis for much of its future emphasis. The organization secured AoA funding to help publish the *National Directory of Educational Programs in Gerontology* in 1976. In cooperation with the GSA, AGHE initiated a proposal for establishing gerontology program guidelines, forming the basis for the ongoing project establishing standards and guidelines for gerontological instruction.

In 1985–86, the AGHE undertook a national data collection project, Enhancing the Quality of Gerontology Instruction. The AoA funded the project, and educators from the universities of Southern California, Oregon, and Utah cooperated in its execution. The survey was intended to determine the extent and character of gerontology higher education across the United States. Over 3,000 accredited institutions of higher learning offering gerontological instruction were asked to provide information on funding, curriculum, structure, and faculty preparation. Survey results formed the basis for the AGHE's National Database on Gerontology in Higher Education and the fourth edition of the *National Directory of Educational Programs in Gerontology* (1987).

In 1989–90, the AGHE worked jointly with University Microfilms, Inc. (UMI) to collect and evaluate unpublished training materials in the field of aging. This project resulted in the publication of a UMI series, the Microfiche Library of Gerontology and Geriatrics. Reviews of training materials continue to be published in AGHE's newsletter.

AGHE's major missions are to provide:

• Unity through common organization.

• A forum for debate of issues regarding the advancement of gerontology, educational opportunities for older people, and the education of society about aging.

• A network base for communication, inter-organizational cooperation, and leadership with associations of higher education, public officials, volunteers, and others interested in aging and education.

• Leadership on policies and issues related to higher education for institutions, organizations, and individuals concerned about aging

ORGANIZATION AND FUNDING

The AGHE is managed by an Executive Committee, consisting of nine elected officers, who also serve as the Board of Directors, and no more than eight appointed committee chairs. The board, elected by the membership, is composed of the President, President-elect, immediate Past-President, Secretary, Treasurer, and four members at large. The elected officers serve two-year terms, with the exception of the President, who serves a three-year term, first as President-elect, then President, and then Past-President. Committee chairs are appointed for one year to the Executive Committee. AGHE employs a professional staff of three, including the Executive Director. In 1991, Elizabeth Douglass held this position.

AGHE's twenty committees include Public Policy, Research, and Long-range Planning. The AGHE sponsors four study sections: Older Adult Learners, Interdisciplinary Education, Community Colleges, and Religion and Aging. Anyone on AGHE's mailing list can select one or more study sections; membership is also available to individual subscribers outside the AGHE membership.

The Executive Committee establishes operating and management policies within the organization. Institutional representatives vote on bylaw changes. The Public Policy committee, with the approval of the Executive Committee, makes key decisions about policy. Generally, the AGHE endorses policy positions taken by the Leadership Council of Aging Organizations[*] (LCAO).

In 1990, AGHE member institutions numbered 325. Membership is open to two-year and four-year colleges, professional schools, and universities "with a demonstrated interest in initiating, developing, and expanding education, research, or training programs in gerontology." The Board of Directors approves all new-member applications. Each member institution designates a representative to AGHE meetings. Nonvoting affiliate membership is available to interested organizations outside higher education. Dues are assessed on a sliding scale, according to type of school or organization. A special membership recognition exists for Sustaining Affiliate Members, schools and organizations that contribute funds and services "over and above the regular membership dues." In 1990–91, the ten Sustaining Affiliate Members included the American Association of Retired Persons[*], the National Council on the Aging[*], and eight universities.

AGHE's budget is approximately $200,000, unless the organization holds an outside grant. Sources of AGHE's funds, though varying from year to year, are corporate membership dues (44%), conferences (31%), project grants (12%), and publication sales (6%). The remaining monies come from additional fundraising and interest income.

The AGHE maintains the National Database on Gerontology in Higher Education, developed in 1985–86 in conjunction with the AoA-funded survey of gerontological instruction. This computerized database provides access to information about 800 programs of instruction on more than 400 campuses, representing over seventy disciplines. AGHE performs database searches for a fee.

AGHE sponsors an annual meeting, workshops, and seminars where ideas and information are shared on curriculum development, faculty training, and other issues. Each year the organization presents the Clark Tibbitts Award, supported by an endowment fund, to an individual or organization for significant contributions to gerontological education.

POLICY CONCERNS AND TACTICS

AGHE advocates and promotes the interests of gerontological education, training, and research. The AGHE testifies before Congress; supplies information to representatives, senators, and their staffs; and conducts and publishes research on related issues. It annually submits budget testimony to both the House and the Senate appropriations committees, as well as the committees on aging in both houses, supporting federal funding for gerontological research, training, and education. A related AGHE policy concern is the appropriations level for Title IV of the Older Americans Act (OAA), funding research and training. The AGHE had considerable input into the language contained in the 1984 OAA amendments. The organization testifies before the Senate Labor and Human Resources Committee and House Education and Labor Committee when the

OAA is up for reauthorization. The AGHE supports the continued reauthorization of the Higher Education Act.

AGHE promotes academic research as a means of heightening public awareness and modifying public policy. In 1990, AGHE focused on three major research areas:

- Present and future personnel needs in the field of aging.
- Guidelines and standards for academic gerontology programs.
- The impact of federal policy changes and funding reductions on academic gerontology programs

In the first area, AGHE sponsored a research project from 1989 to 1991, Determining the Impact of Gerontology Preparation on Personnel in the Aging Network. Funded by the AoA, the study surveyed area agencies and state units on aging to determine the characteristics of professionals in the AoA-funded aging network. Cooperating agencies in this project were the National Association of State Units on Aging[*], the National Association of Area Agencies on Aging[*], and the Ethel Percy Andrus Gerontology Center at the University of Southern California.

In the late 1980s, the AGHE began to work on ensuring consistency in gerontology instruction. In 1989, the organization issued the first report of its ongoing project, *Standards and Guidelines for Gerontology Programs*. Funded in part by an AoA grant, the standards project is the result of the combined efforts of many AGHE institutions. The second edition, issued in 1990, includes recommendations for program development appropriate to any level or type of gerontology education and a chapter about doctoral degrees in the field.

In cooperation with other organizations like the Gerontological Society of America[*] (GSA), the AGHE works to implement programs and to strengthen its influence. The AGHE has sponsored symposia at recent GSA conferences. AGHE represents the interests of its members in coalitions such as the LCAO and A.S.A.P.[*] (Advocates Senior Alert Process).

PUBLICATIONS

AGHE's quarterly newsletter, *AGHE Exchange*, sent to everyone on AGHE's mailing list, contains information about educational practices and programs, public policy issues, and member news. The newsletter also provides an opportunity for members to market their programs, publications, and job openings. Nonmember subscriptions are available. AGHE's study sections produce newsletters periodically: Interdisciplinary Education's *Forum*, Religion and Aging's *The Message*, Community Colleges' *The Notebook*, and the Older Adult Learner's *Newsletter*.

Since 1976, the AGHE has published the *National Directory of Educational Programs in Gerontology*, revised biennially. The fifth edition (Joy Lobenstine, ed., 1991) includes information on gerontology instruction at over 300 AGHE member institutions. Another important publication is the *Standards and Guidelines for Gerontology Programs* (Thomas A. Rich, J. Richard Connelly, and Elizabeth B. Douglass, eds., 1990).

The AGHE also offers research reports, proceedings of conferences, and Brief Bibliographies, a series of occasional publications listing resources on certain topics, such as "Public Policy and Aging," "Older Persons and the Family," and "Interdisciplinary Aging Education." The AGHE makes its mailing list available for purchase, in label format.

Further Information

Thomas Hickey, "The Association for Gerontology in Higher Education—A Brief History," in Mildred Seltzer, Thomas Hickey, and Harvey Sterns, eds., *Gerontology in Higher Education: Perspectives and Issues*, 2–11. (Belmont, Calif.: Wadsworth, 1978).

JIMMY E.W. MEYER
QIUSHA MA

B

/

BENJAMIN ROSE HOSPITAL
See Benjamin Rose Institute.

BENJAMIN ROSE INSTITUTE (BRI)
500 Hanna Building
1422 Euclid Avenue
Cleveland, Ohio 44115–1989
(216) 621–7201   FAX (216) 621–7201 ex.217

The Benjamin Rose Institute (BRI) is a voluntary, nonprofit, nonsectarian service and research organization. The first U.S. foundation to concentrate solely on the elderly, its goal is to encourage independent living for the elderly within the community through high-quality, affordable services.

ORIGIN AND DEVELOPMENT

The Benjamin Rose Institute was founded in Cleveland in 1908 out of concern for the city's elderly poor. Benjamin Rose, a local businessman, stipulated that, upon his death, his $3.4 million estate and the income generated by the Rose office building be used to establish an agency to help the elderly and crippled children. The goal of the institute has remained constant: to help the elderly maintain independence in their homes and self-respect in the community. The institute demonstrates its commitment to the elderly through health and social service programs, service-related gerontological research, and a residential facility.

Under the directorship of Margaret Wagner, Executive Secretary from 1930 to 1959, the Benjamin Rose Institute added research and advocacy for the elderly to its service role. Projects included a study of area nursing homes in the 1930s,

the founding of the first Golden Age Club (1937), and a survey of needs of the
chronically ill elderly (1944). In 1943, the BRI discontinued children's services
and focused entirely on the elderly.

During the 1940s, the BRI acquired three residential homes, ultimately con-
solidated into the Margaret Wagner House. This short- and long-term-care facility
was built in 1961 and continues to provide care for the elderly. In 1953, the
BRI opened the Benjamin Rose Hospital, a sixty-three-bed facility affiliated with
University Hospitals of Case Western Reserve University. The hospital's function
was the diagnosis and rehabilitation of the chronically ill aged. In 1968, University Hospitals took over operation of the hospital and renamed it Abington
House.

ORGANIZATION AND FUNDING

One unique stipulation of the Benjamin Rose estate was that the BRI's Board
of Trustees consist solely of women. Consequently, although the board membership has grown from fifteen to thirty, the all-woman composition of the board
has not changed. In 1990, the institute had 376 employees and more than 140
volunteers. The Executive Director oversees three separate sections within the
Benjamin Rose Institute. The Margaret Blenker Research Center works with
clinical in-house staff to plan, implement, and evaluate current and future programs. It serves as a catalyst to encourage service-related research, publishes
its findings, and maintains a gerontological library. The Residential and Rehabilitation Services section operates the Margaret Wagner House. The Community
Services Division directs three neighborhood offices that offer information and
home services to the elderly. Their goal is to enable the elderly to live
independently.

In 1910, the Benjamin Rose Institute spent $7,998 to help eighty-one elderly
Clevelanders. By 1989, those figures had grown to more than $10 million and
2,200 older individuals. Income from trusts, interest, and dividends accounts
for 35 percent of the institute's support. An additional 10 percent is received in
contributions, grants, and community service fees. The remainder is derived
from residential service fees. Residential and Community Service costs account
for 81 percent of BRI's annual expenditures. The remaining funds are appro-
priated to administration (12%), research (4%), and affiliated organizations (3%).

POLICY CONCERNS AND TACTICS

Serving the needs of the elderly in the Cleveland and Cuyahoga County
community remains the primary policy objective of the Benjamin Rose Institute.
A pioneer in the field, the institute became a nationally recognized model for
service and research. Innovative leadership, strategic planning, commitment,
and cooperative community involvement characterize the foundation as a leader
in issue identification and prescriptive programs.

In addition to the health and social services offered to the elderly, the BRI maintains a local, national, and international leadership role. Education, information dissemination, and research are important policy tactics of the agency. It sponsors workshops, training programs, and research projects and provides students and professionals with educational experiences in applied research on aging. In 1990, the BRI, along with twenty-five local organizations, was planning a regional resource center to consolidate health information materials.

PUBLICATIONS

The Benjamin Rose Institute publishes the *Benjamin Rose Institute Bulletin* (three times per year) and occasional research reports, such as *Caregiving for the Elderly: Recognizing Your Strengths and Weaknesses* (1986).

BETH DINATALE JOHNSON

BEVERLY ENTERPRISES
See Beverly Foundation.

BEVERLY FOUNDATION
70 South Lake Avenue, Suite 750
Pasadena, California 91101
(818) 792–2292

The Beverly Foundation is a nonprofit, nonmembership organization seeking to advance autonomy, optimal functioning, and well-being of older adults through research, public education, and publication of resources for long-term-care providers.

ORIGIN AND DEVELOPMENT

The Beverly Foundation was established as an independent organization in 1978 by Beverly Enterprises, a proprietary long-term-care provider. Beverly Enterprises, founded in 1963, is the endowment sponsor of the Beverly Foundation. Beverly Foundation was established to advance the well-being of older adults and foster progress of long-term care as a vital segment in the continuum of health care services. Beverly Foundation also seeks to build public awareness of issues that focus on the autonomy of older people. Research and demonstration projects of the foundation expand knowledge relating to aging and long-term care.

ORGANIZATION AND FUNDING

The Beverly Foundation has a Board of Trustees and a professional staff headed by Carroll J. Wendland, President. In 1991, Robert Van Tuyle, former Chairman and CEO of Beverly Enterprises, was Chairman of the foundation Board of Trustees. Beverly Foundation operates an Institutional Review Board for Research (IRB) to review research proposals involving human subjects to ensure informed consent, confidentiality, and privacy and that the benefits of the proposed research outweigh its risks. Foundation funding derives from endowment income, supplemented by restricted and unrestricted contributions from individuals and corporations, grants from other foundations and government agencies, and program revenues and educational materials sales income. In 1990, the Beverly Foundation's assets (prior to audit) were over $6 million, and its expenses were over $600,000.

POLICY CONCERNS AND TACTICS

Among the programs developed and sponsored by the Beverly Foundation are the Adopted Grandparents program, a shared-housing program for seniors, and long-term-care staff development and continuing-education programs. Primary issues of concern to the Beverly Foundation in the area of policy on aging include home health care and nursing home long-term care, health care financing, coordinated or managed long-term-care concepts, ethical issues relating to research and life sustainment, and autonomy and the rights of older people. The Beverly Foundation is also interested in the role of long-term-care services for the non-elderly with chronic or progressive, disabling illnesses. In addition to directing its communications to the general public and long-term-care providers, the Beverly Foundation provides information to policymakers on community, state, and federal levels.

The Beverly Foundation has worked cooperatively with many other organizations with similar interests, including the American Health Care Association*, the Gerontological Society of America*, and the National Institute on Aging.

PUBLICATIONS

Two publications of the foundation are *The Teaching Nursing Home: A New Approach to Geriatric Research, Education and Clinical Care* (1984), developed in conjunction with the National Institute on Aging, and *What Legislators Need to Know About Long-Term Care Insurance* (1987), co-developed and sponsored with the National Conference of State Legislatures, the Health Insurance Association of America, and the American Association of Retired Persons*.

The Beverly Foundation also has published the following long-term-care staff development materials: *Pharmacy Manual: Policies, Procedures, and Quality Assurances Provisions for Long-term Care Facilities* (revised through 1990), *Geriatric Nutrition: Patient Assessment and Care Planning Reconsidered* (1989), *The Art of the Possible: Rehabilitating for Continency in Long-Term Care* (1987), and *Nurse Assistant Video Theater* (1984).

Further Information

Thomas C. Boyle, "Beverly Enterprises: From David to Goliath in Long Term Care," *Consultant Pharmacist* 2 (1987): 33–42.

NANCY C. ERDEY

BUSINESS FORUM ON AGING
See American Society on Aging.

C

/

CAMPAIGN FOR QUALITY CARE
See National Citizens' Coalition for Nursing Home Reform.

CAPS
See Children of Aging Parents.

CARING INSTITUTE
See Foundation for Hospice and Homecare.

THE CENTER FOR SOCIAL GERONTOLOGY (TCSG)
117 North First Street, Suite 204
Ann Arbor, Michigan 48104
(313) 665–1126   FAX (313) 665–2071
   The Center for Social Gerontology (TCSG) is a nonprofit organization working to advance the well-being of older people in the United States through research, education, technical assistance, and training. TCSG focuses primarily on legal rights and delivery of legal services, guardianship and alternative protective services, and the right to refuse medical treatment and the use of advance directives to protect that right.

ORIGIN AND DEVELOPMENT

   Established by Wilma Donahue in 1971 as the International Center for Social Gerontology, TCSG adopted its current name in 1985 to reflect a shift of focus from international to national activities and moved its headquarters from Washington, D.C., to Ann Arbor, Michigan.
   Its general purpose is to advance the well-being of the growing population of

older people in the United States by encouraging and conducting research in social gerontology, conducting training programs to prepare and advance the skills of professional and technical workers in the field of aging, and working directly with older persons to ensure that they are aware of their legal rights.

Since its beginnings, TCSG has successfully conducted national support projects in law and aging and national research and demonstration projects; sponsored international and national symposia; published numerous articles; produced training materials, films, and legal videotapes; and provided consultation to the private, public, and voluntary sectors. Of special importance is TCSG's research and development of standards for the provision of guardianship services for older people, its work to improve the court process for determining the need for guardianship through development and evaluation of a new model, and its periodic training and newsletters on legal rights and legal resources for legal advocates, nonlegal service providers who work with the elderly, and older consumers. TCSG's library includes extensive standing files on substantive legal issues and delivery of legal services to older persons.

ORGANIZATION AND FUNDING

Since 1985, TCSG has served as a national support center in law and aging through grants from the U.S. Administration on Aging (AoA). Its staff includes pioneers in the field of law and aging, who have substantial skill and experience working with all levels of the aging network, legal providers in programs funded by the Older Americans Act (OAA), continuing legal education programs, law schools and their clinical programs, and private bar groups. TCSG's staff has conducted numerous legal training programs and developed and disseminated substantive legal materials, as well as materials on evaluating the delivery of legal assistance to the elderly.

TCSG has a staff of eight persons. In 1991, the President was John Martin, the President Emeritus was Wilma T. Donahue, and the Executive Director was Penelope A. Hommel. TCSG sponsors periodic national conferences as well as regional conferences and state-specific programs. Primary funding sources are federal and state grants.

POLICY CONCERNS AND TACTICS

Under its 1985–86 grant from the AoA, TCSG prepared substantive legal materials in three areas affecting older persons: guardianship and alternative protective services, age discrimination in employment, and Social Security disability. In addition, TCSG developed guidelines for planning and evaluating OAA legal assistance providers.

Under its 1986–1987 grant from the AoA, TCSG published twelve issues of a newsletter, *Best Practice Notes*, which addressed concerns of legal providers and area agencies and offered examples of best-practice models. TCSG also sponsored a national conference on delivery of legal assistance to older persons.

In 1988, again with the AoA, TCSG published a *Comprehensive Guide to Delivery of Legal Assistance to Older Persons*, conducted eight regional workshops, published quarterly issues of *Best Practice Notes*, and provided technical assistance to legal services developers, ombudsmen, state and area agencies, and legal providers.

As part of its 1989–90 grant from AoA, TCSG worked with individual states in addressing issues related to the state's delivery system, legal training, and selected substantive areas of law. At the national level, TCSG continues to publish quarterly issues of *Best Practice Notes* and *Headnotes on Critical Legal Issues Affecting Older Persons* and co-sponsors the annual Joint Conference on Law and Aging.

Working jointly with the Michigan Office of Services to the Aging through a grant from AoA, TCSG also developed standards and monitoring mechanisms to ensure the quality of guardianship service programs for needy older persons and disseminated the standards for use throughout Michigan.

TCSG has conducted a model guardianship project, Facilitating the Use of Alternatives to Guardianship, funded under a subgrant from the Michigan Office of Services to the Aging. In 1991, TCSG was conducting national research on the guardianship system.

PUBLICATIONS

Besides its two newsletters, *Best Practice Notes on Delivery of Legal Assistance* and *Headnotes on Critical Legal Issues Affecting Older Persons*, TCSG has also published *Social Security Disability Law: A Compendium for Training and Practice* (1986) and *A Comprehensive Guide to Delivery of Legal Assistance to Older Persons* (1988).

JOAN ORGAN

CHILDREN OF AGING PARENTS (CAPS)
Woodbourne Office Campus, Suite 302-A
1609 Woodbourne Road
Levittown, Pennsylvania 19057
(215) 945–6900

Children of Aging Parents (CAPS) is a nonprofit organization working to develop a national system of support groups to serve caregivers of the elderly more effectively. CAPS utilizes education and networking to increase local and national awareness of the needs of caregivers and their elderly charges.

ORIGIN AND DEVELOPMENT

CAPS was organized in 1977 in Bucks County, Pennsylvania. Founders Mirca Liberti and Louise Fradkin were concerned with helping families of aging parents and relatives cope with the stress of daily caregiving. CAPS states that "approximately eighty percent of all services provided to the elderly come from the family." Yet most people arrive at the caregiving role unprepared, without knowledge of services available. CAPS was established to provide support and guidance to spouse and adult-children caregivers.

For the first few years, CAPS remained predominantly a local group, defining goals and securing support and media coverage. In 1980, CAPS registered as a tax-exempt, 501(c)(3), organization and secured a volunteer Board of Directors. In the next decade, CAPS developed national support groups and expanded educational efforts and information and referral services.

The major goals and services of the organization are to provide resource information and referral services throughout the country, to help increase community awareness of the challenges of aging and caregiving, and to act as a clearinghouse for individuals and organizations serving families with aging parents or relatives. CAPS also provides individual peer counseling and employee assistance programs.

CAPS sponsors workshops and seminars for caregivers and professionals; inservice training programs for hospitals, long-term-care facilities, and rehabilitation and home care agencies; educational presentations to schools, service organizations, senior centers, and religious organizations; and consultation about programs and services to the elderly.

ORGANIZATION AND FUNDING

CAPS maintains eleven regional groups in southeastern Pennsylvania and provides advice to groups throughout the United States. Membership is open to all individuals, professionals, and organizations who have an interest in elder care. In 1990, CAPS consisted of about 850 individual members and 200 corporate members. The group is run by co-directors Mirca Liberti and Louise Fradkin and governed by a twelve-member Board of Directors.

The operating budget is approximately $30,000 per year. Major sources of funds are membership dues, honoraria, receipts from the sale of publications, and contributions.

POLICY CONCERNS AND TACTICS

Within its central policy concern of long-term care, CAPS concentrates on intergenerational relations and respite for the caregiver. The group influences policy mainly through education and media promotion, drawing attention to the special issues of elder care. The directors have appeared on nationwide and local television and radio programs.

Occasionally CAPS appears in Congress on behalf of caregivers. In 1986, a CAPS representative testified before a House subcommittee hearing on the issue of long-term care. CAPS has also furnished caregivers to testify before the Pepper commission, established in 1988 to study long-term care and headed by Representative Claude Pepper of Florida. At times, the group provides reference and information services to legislators. For example, in 1990 Fradkin reviewed the content of a new brochure, geared toward caregivers, for the House Committee on Aging.

PUBLICATIONS

CAPS issues the *CAPSule*, a bimonthly newsletter, and publishes resource and educational materials such as the manual *Starting a Self-Help Group for Caregivers of the Elderly* (1984); *Instant Aging, Sensitivity Training* (1984) (also a manual); and *Care Sharing Directory* (1991), a national directory of private geriatric case managers, caregiver support groups, and related services. The organization offers a variety of informational pamphlets.

JIMMY E. W. MEYER

COALITION TO PROTECT SOCIAL SECURITY
See Save Our Security.

COMMISSION ON LEGAL PROBLEMS OF THE ELDERLY
See American Bar Association Commission on Legal Problems of the Elderly.

COMMITTEE FOR NATIONAL HEALTH INSURANCE (CNHI)
1757 N Street, N.W., Suite 500
Washington, D.C. 20036
(202) 223–9685   FAX (202) 293–3457

Since its founding in 1968, the Committee for National Health Insurance (CNHI) and its associated lobbying group, the Health Security Action Council (HSAC), have sought to reform the structure and organization of health care delivery. Although CNHI continues to support Medicare reform, it believes that only universal, comprehensive health insurance will guarantee adequate health care to all Americans. In 1989, CNHI introduced the Health Security Partnership Plan, a program for national health insurance based on cost-containment policies. If adopted, the plan would initially continue Medicare ''as a separate and parallel program,'' featuring expanded benefits and mandatory assignment for physician payments.

ORIGIN AND DEVELOPMENT

CNHI was founded on a belief that American ''ingenuity and social inventiveness'' could be marshaled to create a distinctive national health care system, rooted in consumer free choice. The committee's formation was announced by Walter P. Reuther, then president of the United Auto Workers* (UAW). Speaking before the American Public Health Association in the fall of 1968, Reuther enumerated the problems Americans confronted in obtaining ''access to decent health care.'' Confident that a solution existed, Reuther announced that a Committee of 100 for National Health Insurance would be established the following day in Washington, D.C. Reuther served as the committee's Chairman and was joined by Michael E. de Bakey as Vice-Chairman. Other original members included Whitney M. Young, Jr., leader of the National Urban League, and Mary Lasker.

The Committee of 100 was the initial step toward the formation of two new policy groups that would execute the committee's mission. By 1969, the Committee of 100 had evolved into the Committee for National Health Insurance (CNHI) and the Health Security Action Council (HSAC). Each group possesses a separate function. The Committee for National Health Insurance is a lobbying group; the Health Security Action Council is an educational group. Their responsibilities often overlap, however, and they are governed by the same Chair and Director.

ORGANIZATION AND FUNDING

CNHI's Expert Committee, headed by Harvard Medical School economist Rashi Fein, assists in policy development for the organization. All policy issues are voted on by the CNHI's twenty-three-member board. These board members belong to national associations representing senior citizens, women, youth, education, business, labor, farm, and religious groups. Representing interests of the aging on the CNHI board in 1991 were Arthur S. Flemming, Chair, Save Our Security*; Lawrence Smedley, Executive Director, National Council of Senior Citizens;* and Daniel Thursz, President, the National Council on the Aging* (NCOA). The CNHI has over forty member organizations, invited by the board; there are no individual memberships. The Board of Directors elects new board members as well as the organization's officers. No minimum tenure is required for board memberships or offices. The board's 1991 Chair was Douglas A. Fraser. At the time of his election in 1977, Fraser was also President of the UAW. The CNHI's 1991 Director was Melvin A. Glasser, former Director of the UAW's Social Security Department. CNHI has three staff members.

Voluntary contributions from member organizations comprise the majority of CNHI's revenue. Since the committee does not require minimum fees from its members, its operating budget is variable. Bequests are accepted, though they generally comprise a minimal percentage of its budget.

POLICY CONCERNS AND TACTICS

The committee allocates approximately a third of its resources to aging issues. Central to these issues are Medicare and Medicaid programs and funding. Other issues include home health care, long-term care, and nursing home reform. The CNHI coordinates its actions with other organizations, especially the NCSC, the NCOA, the National Education Association, and the AFL-CIO (American Federation of Labor–Congress of Industrial Organizations).

Medicare reform has been a basic feature of CNHI programs for national health insurance. Since the committee's founding, it has designed three programs for health insurance: the Health Security Program, the Health Care for

All Americans Act, and the Health Security Partnership Program. The committee's first two programs, created in the early and late 1970s, respectively, required that Medicare be integrated into the national health system. Under the more recent partnership, however, Medicare would initially remain in its present form, as a distinct program, for a trial period. Such inclusion is designed to allay fears among some senior citizens of any program that modifies Medicare's structure.

In 1989–90, CNHI and HSAC presented their programs for national health insurance before Congress, and they have testified on behalf of similar bills for universal medical coverage. In addition, the organization testifies on Medicare reform and cost-containment issues. In September 1983, the HSAC testified in favor of the Health Care Cost Control Act of 1983 before the House Ways and Means Subcommittee on Health. The following September, HSAC offered support for the Medicare Solvency and Health Care Financing Reform Act of 1984, again before the House Subcommittee on Health.

Testifying before congressional committees is only one method CNHI and HSAC utilize to influence policy. Each organization also encourages its members to write to legislators and committees. Leaders of member organizations promote CNHI and HSAC programs through television and radio appearances.

In addition, CNHI and HSAC speak before various citizen groups on the quality and cost of medical care. In 1991, they presented the Health Security Partnership before citizen and state groups, state legislatures, and federal congressional committees.

PUBLICATIONS

CNHI and HSAC have published a variety of educational materials on health care and health insurance. Both organizations provide brochures, and the HSAC publishes a bimonthly newsletter, *Health Security Action News*. The newsletter lists current activities within CNHI and HSAC and reports on topics pertaining to the quality, utilization, and cost of health care. Past issues of *Health Security Action News* have featured articles ranging from the causes of prescription drug inflation to potential retirement risks for Americans enrolled in company health plans.

Further Information

David C. Jacobs. "The UAW and the Committee for National Health Insurance: The Contours of Social Unionism," in *Advances in Industrial and Labor Relations*, edited by David Lipsky and Joel M. Douglas. (Greenwich, Conn.: Jai Press, 1987.)

JANICE A. CAFARO

COMMITTEE OF 100 FOR NATIONAL HEALTH INSURANCE
See Committee for National Health Insurance.

CONCERNED RELATIVES OF NURSING HOME PATIENTS
See Nursing Home Advisory and Research Council.

CONSULTATION OF OLDER AND YOUNGER ADULTS FOR SOCIAL CHANGE
See Gray Panthers Project Fund.

COUNCIL OF HOME HEALTH AGENCIES
See Foundation for Hospice and Homecare.

D

DISPLACED HOMEMAKERS NETWORK
See National Displaced Homemakers Network.

E
/

EDUCATION AND RESEARCH FUND
See Employee Benefit Research Institute.

EL PUEBLO COMMUNITY DEVELOPMENT CORPORATION
See Asociacion Nacional Pro Personas Mayores.

EMPLOYEE BENEFIT RESEARCH INSTITUTE (EBRI)
2121 K Street N.W., Suite 600
Washington, D.C. 20037–1896
(202) 659–0670   FAX (202) 775–6312

The Employee Benefit Research Institute (EBRI) is a nonprofit, nonpartisan organization sponsored by corporations, labor groups, financial institutions, pension plans, and service organizatons such as law and accounting firms and money managment groups. EBRI gathers, analyzes, and disseminates "sound, relevant information" on employee benefits to employers, policymakers, and the general public. It claims to be the only organization in the United States solely committed to policy research and education on economic security and employee benefits.

ORIGIN AND DEVELOPMENT

EBRI was conceived in 1977 and founded in 1978 to address the perceived need for a think tank focusing on employee benefits and economic security. Major corporations underwrote the initial costs. Dallas Salisbury, 1991 EBRI President, was hired to organize the institute. He had been active in benefit issues through positions with the U.S. Department of Labor and the Pension Benefit Administration. The institute and its tax-exempt arm, the Education and Research Fund (ERF), founded in 1980, were created to collect and publish data on health, welfare, and retirement concerns and to promote the development of soundly conceived private and public employee benefit plans. By the mid to late 1980s, information gathered by the EBRI was being used by the President's Commission on Pension Policy.

ORGANIZATION AND FUNDING

EBRI had almost 300 members in 1991. The organization maintains two divisions: education and communication, and research. The ERF performs the charitable, educational, and scientific functions of the institute. Its activities are supported by tax-deductible contributions and grants. The institute is run by a staff of thirty, headed by the President. Policy is established by a forty-two-member Board of Trustees, appointed by corporations contributing to EBRI at the sustaining-membership level.

EBRI's 1990 budget was $2 million. Corporations and businesses provide most of the support through membership dues. Costs for the varying levels of membership range from $1,500 to over $20,000.

POLICY CONCERNS AND TACTICS

Employee benefits, retirement, long-term care, health care, Social Security, and pension issues represent the primary policy concerns of EBRI. As a policy research organization and think tank, EBRI responds to requests for information from the media, the federal government, and its corporate members. It collects and analyzes data on legislation, fiscal trends, and public opinion pertaining to employees, benefit plans, taxes, and the business environment. EBRI's research "strives to anticipate emerging benefit issues and to develop objective data relating to those issues before policy decisions are made." For example, EBRI researched individuals' use of preretirement pension distributions before legislation appeared in this area.

ERF interprets and makes this information available through policy forums, monthly meetings, an annual membership meeting, press statements, and seminars. Its outreach extends as far as Europe and Asia. Policy forums presented in 1990 included "Pension Portability and Preservation: Assuring Adequate Retirement Income in the 21st Century" and "Retirement Security in a Post-FASB Environment."

EBRI provides an online information service, EBRI-NET, and supports research in areas such as financing health care for the elderly, financial aspects of pension plans, tax policy, employee benefits, and retirement income. EBRI holds briefings for members of Congress and staff to educate and promote awareness of employee benefit and retirement issues. It has presented testimony before congressional committees but does not lobby. It conducts monthly EBRI/Gallup polls on public attitudes and since 1988 has sponsored Fellows opportunities for in-depth study of economic security and work force issues by selected individuals.

PUBLICATIONS

EBRI publishes a monthly newsletter, *Employee Benefit Notes*; *Issue Briefs*, research reports on individual topics; and the *Quarterly Pension Investment Report*. The organization has also issued the following monographs, among others: *Fundamentals of Employee Benefit Programs* (1987) and *Financing the Elderly's Health Care* by Deborah Chollet (1987).

KIMBERLY S. LENAHAN

F

/

FAMILIES U.S.A. (UNITED FOR SENIOR ACTION) FOUNDATION
1334 G Street, N.W.
Washington, D.C. 20005
(202) 628–3030   FAX (202) 347–2417

Families U.S.A. (United for Senior Action) Foundation is an independent, nonprofit, nonmembership organization that seeks to nurture through legislative means a movement of empowerment among elders, especially those of low income. Generally called Families U.S.A., its goal is to strengthen, preserve, and expand the dignity of older Americans, their security, and their continuing contributions to society. Its name reflects the centrality of family in the lives of seniors and of parents and grandparents in the lives of American families. Through grants, educational activities, research, and advocacy, the organization works to foster fundamental changes in societal attitudes that affect the elderly. Its major focus is the intergenerational problem of access to affordable and high-quality health care. Other major concerns include the development of a social insurance program for long-term care, income security for poor and near-poor elders, and opportunities for productive aging in paid work and voluntarism.

ORIGIN AND DEVELOPMENT

The Families U.S.A. Foundation was founded in 1981 as the Villers Foundation, Inc. by Philippe and Katherine Villers to counter negative stereotypes about the elderly. In 1984, through its advocacy arm, Villers Advocacy Associates, its primary functions were public policy formulation and information dissemination. Since 1986, the foundation has been engaged in an extensive program of grant making to projects that affect public policy and raise levels of public consciousness about the economic problems and potential productivity of older persons. One of its major projects has been the creation, with the collaboration of sixteen other organizations, of A.S.A.P.* (Advocates Senior Alert Process), a national legislative information and action network for politically active seniors and senior advocates. In 1989, Villers Advocacy Associates and the Villers Foundation became Families U.S.A. Foundation.

ORGANIZATION AND FUNDING

Families U.S.A. is governed by an eight-member Board of Directors, augmented by a three-member Executive Committee. The board membership is drawn from university-based research programs in aging, those influential in policymaking at the national and state levels, and organizations that deliver services to the elderly. The board sets and establishes policy based on staff recommendations that it has approved. The staff numbers twenty-five persons—nineteen in the national office in Washington and six in Boston. They are assigned to several functions: community resources, lobbying and policy coordination, legal counseling, grants, employment and voluntarism coordination, and media and public affairs.

Philippe Villers has served as the President of the foundation since its inception and in 1991 was a member of the Executive Committee, as was Katherine Villers. Katherine Villers also served as the Director of the Massachusetts office in 1991, and in the same year Ronald F. Pollack was the Executive Director of Families U.S.A.

POLICY CONCERNS AND TACTICS

Families U.S.A. utilizes a variety of methods to influence policy in the area of aging, including grass-roots advocacy and congressional testimony. As a grass-roots coalition effort, the 20,000 A.S.A.P. members are encouraged to write to their representatives. Families U.S.A. frequently presents testimony on a number of issues such as Medigap insurance (policies issued by private insurers to fill the "gaps" in Medicare coverage) and long-term-care insurance problems, as it did in May 1990 before the House Committee on Energy and Commerce. Other tactics include direct action or protest activities, the commissioning of national public opinion polls, and the provision of grants, training, and technical assistance to grass-roots organizations for elders.

In addition to A.S.A.P., many of the other activities of Families U.S.A. are conducted in cooperation with other organizations. Families U.S.A. is a member of the Leadership Council of Aging Organizations* and frequently collaborates with the Children's Defense Fund, the National Council of Senior Citizens*, and the Older Women's League*. On occasion, it takes on specific projects with other organizations, as it did with the American Association of Retired Persons* on Long Term Care '88 (now the Long Term Care Campaign*), a public information campaign to encourage candidates for federal office, especially the candidates in the presidential primaries, to address the issues of long-term care. To increase public awareness, Families U.S.A. has created an awards program to recognize exceptional accomplishments in areas that benefit the low-income aged. It also holds occasional conferences and meetings on specific issues.

ELECTORAL ACTIVITY

Families U.S.A. does not endorse candidates. The strategy used in Long Term Care '88 has been continued at the grass-roots level to ensure that candidates for national and state offices address the long-term-care issue at community forums.

PUBLICATIONS

Most of the publications produced and disseminated by Families U.S.A. are monographs, such as *The Best Medicine: Organizing Local Health Care Campaigns* (1984), *The ABCs of DRGs: How to Protect and Expand Medicare Patients' Rights* (1988), and *On the Other Side of Easy Street: Myths and Facts about the Economics of Old Age* (1987). Audiovisual productions include a videotape on long-term care, produced in conjunction with the Long-Term Care Campaign, *Our Parents, Our Children, Ourselves* (1987), and a slide/tape, *Off Our Rockers: Seniors Organizing in the 80's* (1986).

Further Information

Christine Day, *What Older Americans Think: Interest Groups and Aging Policy* (Princeton, N.J.: Princeton University Press, 1990). Mary Jane Fisher, "Health Care Costs Expected to Skyrocket to $1.47 Trillion," *National Underwriter* 46 (November 12, 1990): 52.

PHOEBE S. LIEBIG

FAMILY FRIENDS PROGRAM
See National Council on the Aging.

FEDERATION OF JEWISH PHILANTHROPIES OF NEW YORK
See Jewish Association for Services for the Aged.

FORUM ON RELIGION AND AGING
See American Society on Aging.

FOUNDATION FOR HOSPICE AND HOMECARE (FHH)
519 C Street, N.E.
Washington, DC 20002
(202) 547–6586   FAX (202) 546–8968
The Foundation for Hospice and Homecare (FHH) is a nonprofit organization dedicated to improving the quality of life for the dying, disabled, disadvantaged,

and elderly. It promotes hospice and home care services and education, research, and policy development in these specialized areas.

ORIGIN AND DEVELOPMENT

FHH was organized in 1978 as a companion agency to the National Association of Home Health Agencies (NAHA). It was constituted as a nonprofit corporation to provide education, conduct research, and promote policy development in the areas of hospice, home care, and aging. In 1982, NAHA merged with the Council of Home Health Agencies to become the National Association for Home Care* (NAHC), a trade association that represents home health agencies, hospices, and homemaker–home health aide services. FHH was structurally unaffected by the merger and continued its affiliation with the newly created NAHC.

Every year FHH establishes a policy focus for research, education, and policy development. In 1985, it established the National Caring Awards, which included an Art of Caring National Photography Contest, and the national newsletter *Caring People,* to initiate, reinforce, and recognize the activities of individuals and organizations that care for the dying, disabled, and disadvantaged. The expansion of activities in this area has resulted in the Caring Institute's becoming an independent entity in 1990. Other policy initiatives have included a pediatric home care emphasis in 1986 and a national AIDS community survey in 1988. In 1990, FHH began revising its model curriculum for home health aide certification and promoting consumer usage of home health aide services.

During 1986–87, FHH absorbed the National HomeCaring Council (NHC) as a semi-independent division. The NHC, established in New York in 1962 to coordinate services, disseminate information, and develop standards for accreditation of home health care, retains its name and manages the FHH accreditation programs. NHC also sponsors training programs for homemaker–home health aides. Research and publication resources of NHC were combined with the FHH's projects.

ORGANIZATION AND FUNDING

The Foundation for Hospice and Homecare's Board of Directors is appointed by the NAHC Board of Directors. FHH is administered by its own Executive Director and staff. The Executive Director of FHH in 1991 was Bill Halamandaris, the brother of the President of NAHC, Val Halamandaris. FHH is primarily supported by individual and corporate contributions. It receives income from accreditation programs, publications, and training events. Special projects are funded by grants from private foundations and the federal government. FHH's annual budget generally totals $500,000.

POLICY CONCERNS AND TACTICS

The Foundation for Hospice and Homecare works to influence and inform public opinion and educate government leaders. Its mission is to improve the quality of life for American citizens, emphasizing the needs of the dying, the disabled, the disadvantaged, and the elderly. To accomplish this end, the FHH sponsors training and accreditation programs for homemaker–home health aides and conducts research related to health services, aging, and social policies.

Most of FHH's policy initiatives, public presentations, and political endeavors, such as testifying before Congress, presentations at the White House Conferences on Aging, and legislative lobbying, are done in conjunction with the NAHC.

PUBLICATIONS

FHH issues an annual report and a biweekly newsletter of the NHC, *HomeCare News*. It produces a wide range of educational materials, such as the 1986 documentary on chronically ill children, *Suffer Not the Little Children*; training manuals for homemaker–home health aide programs; specialized care guides; management and statistical studies; and video and audio instructional tapes.

Further Information

E. Ginzberg, W. Balinsky, and M. Ostow, *Home Health Care*: *Its role in the Changing Health Services Market* (Totowa, N.J.: Romand and Allanheld, 1984), and Joan Quinn, et al., *Coordinating Community Services for the Elderly* (New York: Springer, 1982).

KIMBERLY S. LENAHAN

FOUNDATION OF AMERICAN COLLEGE OF HEALTH CARE ADMINISTRATORS
See American College of Health Care Administrators.

FOUNDATION OF AMERICAN COLLEGE OF NURSING HOME ADMINISTRATORS
See American College of Health Care Administrators.

G

/

GENERATIONS TOGETHER
121 University Place, Suite 300
Pittsburgh, Pennsylvania 15260
(412) 648–7150   FAX (412) 624–4810

Generations Together is a nonprofit, nonmembership, educational networking and research organization that serves children and youth, educators, elderly persons, and public policymakers. To promote positive interactions between the young and the elderly, Generations Together develops programs that link human service agencies working with these populations, researches the effects of intergenerational programs on the participants and their communities, and disseminates information on intergenerational program models locally and nationally.

ORIGIN AND DEVELOPMENT

Generations Together was established in 1978 to promote mutually beneficial interactions between the young and old. The University of Pittsburgh's Center for Social and Urban Research is home to Generations Together. The mission of Generations Together is to develop innovative intergenerational programs and models, to research the impact of these models on the participants and the community, and to disseminate information on program development and research through teaching, conferences, technical assistance, and interaction with other human service agencies and educational institutions.

From a single program model, the Senior Citizen School Volunteer Program, which involved elders and youth in 1978, Generations Together has spawned a variety of models that bring together agencies serving children and youth, the aged, and special needs populations. The intergenerational approach has combined high school and college youth with frail elders in the Youth in Service to

Elders (YISTE) model, senior artists with elementary and high school youth in the Artist Resource Program (ARP), low- and middle-income senior citizens with preschoolers and infants in the Intergenerational Early Childhood Program (IECP), and senior citizens with vulnerable, at-risk children in the Mentors in Service to Youth Program (MISTY). These program models and others involve over 10,000 children and youth and 1,000 elders annually.

ORGANIZATION AND FUNDING

Generations Together is led by its Executive Director, an administrative officer, and other professional staff, including a librarian and program coordinators. In 1990, Sally Newman was the Executive Director. The Board of Directors is composed of twenty-five professionals and laypersons from the greater Pittsburgh area. The leadership of the board comes from its executive committee. The Board of Directors has historically been an advisory body; rarely has it shifted the policy direction of the executive staff. The board meets every other month, and there are frequent informal meetings with the executive staff.

The annual budget, including the space, is over $600,000, with 20 percent provided by the University of Pittsburgh. Of the remaining monies, 45 percent comes from foundation grants and corporate contributions and another 30 percent from local, state, and federal agencies. Other sources of revenue are individual donations, sales of publications, and fund-raising activities. There are no individual or corporate memberships.

POLICY CONCERNS AND TACTICS

As an information resource and as part of an advisory task force, Generations Together has been influential in drafting legislation at the national, state, and local levels. For example, in 1984–85, Generations Together was instrumental in shaping Senate bill 2310, sponsored by U.S. Senator Carl Levin (D, Michigan), designed to bring together disadvantaged children and senior citizen tutors as part of a volunteer network. A similar bill was introduced in the House, and both measures were on the legislative agenda of the Ninety-eighth Congress.

More recently, Generations Together in 1990 supplied key information in the shaping of a child care law that included a role for older adults as nurturing resources. Intergenerational education was a part of this measure; high school academic credit was granted to students providing service to elders. Minority elderly women were highlighted as nurturing resources, as part of the National Community Service Act co-sponsored by Senators Orrin Hatch of Utah and Ted Kennedy of Massachusetts.

At the state level, Generations Together participated in a recent Pennsylvania Governor's Commission on community within families, recommending a series of initiatives on family needs that included an intergenerational component. These recommendations were endorsed by the governor and submitted to the Pennsylvania legislature in 1991. Locally, Generations Together is part of the Mayor's

Council of Pittsburgh, focusing on intergenerational needs and programs within an urban setting.

PUBLICATIONS

An important communication link and network tool of Generations Together is the newsletter *Exchange*. Published annually, it has a national readership of 4,000. The group has also produced a curriculum, *Share It with the Children*, that includes a handbook, guide, and video (1988).

Further Information

David Diamond, "The Pittsburgh Story: Filling the Grandparent Gap," *50 Plus*. (May 1988): 42–51; Charles W. Lyons, "Interagency Alliances Link Young and Old," *Children Today* 15 (September–October 1986): 21–25; Sally Newman and Kathleen Bocian, "Connecting the Generations," *Ageing International* 13, no. 3 (Autumn 1986): 13–15; Sally Newman and S. Brummel, eds., *Intergenerational Programs: Imperatives, Strategies, Impacts, Trends* (New York: Haworth Press, 1989).

JAMES BANKS

GENERATIONS UNITED
440 First Street, N.W. Suite 310
Washington, D.C. 20001–2085
(202) 638–2952   FAX (202) 638–4004

Generations United is a coalition of national organizations designed to promote cross-generational understanding and cooperative action. The goals of this coalition are to advocate for public policies and programs that recognize the interdependence of children, youth, families, and the elderly and to promote awareness and understanding of the value of fostering intergenerational harmony and organizational cooperation at every level.

ORIGIN AND DEVELOPMENT

In 1986, the National Council on the Aging* (NCOA), the Child Welfare League of America, and thirty other groups representing the young and the old formed Generations United to emphasize the issues that unite old-age advocacy groups, groups advocating for the rights of the young, and other interested organizations. In October 1988, Generations United sponsored the first national conference on intergenerational issues in Washington, D.C. In conjunction with NCOA and the Child Welfare League, Generations United organized the conference to establish a network among organizations interested or involved in intergenerational programs and/or policies.

ORGANIZATION AND FUNDING

As a coalition, Generations United differs from the usual nonprofit group—for example, there is no separate 501(c)(3), tax-exempt designation. Over 100 national agencies participated in Generations United in 1991. The Child Welfare League and NCOA have shared the staffing of Generations United since its inception. The Executive Director of the Child Welfare League and the President of NCOA are co-chairs of the coalition. Generations United has a voluntary steering committee; anyone who belongs to a participating organization can be a steering committee member. Generations United has no separate budget but has received grant support from such sources as the Ittleson, Skillman, and Mott foundations. The coalition has also received in-kind services from such organizations as the Red Cross and the American Association of Retired Persons[*] (AARP). In addition, Generations United requests voluntary contributions from its participants.

POLICY CONCERNS AND TACTICS

Generations United favors increased aid to poor families, elders, and children but opposes the call for cuts in Social Security by groups such as Americans for Generational Equity[*]. Generations United maintains that tension between the young and the old is unnecessary, as is withdrawal of government assistance from any one age group. In fact, the coalition believes that such tension exists only in the media and challenges the groups trying to divide the generations. Generations United argues for policies indicative of a caring society, characterized by intergenerational exchange, problem solving, and program opportunities.

Generations United utilizes education and occasional congressional testimony to achieve its objectives. In the summer of 1991, the coalition sponsored Beyond Medicaid: Building a Health Care System for All Ages, a conference to discuss present and future health policy options. AARP funded the conference, which involved the four leading members of Generations United: the Child Welfare League, NCOA, AARP, and the Children's Defense Fund. Coalition participants testify before Congress, on issues pertinent to their own agenda, such as the Older Americans Act or the Claude Pepper Young Americans Act (1990), as well as on issues universal to human welfare, such as Title XX of Social Security, a block-grant program giving states money for programs and services for the poor.

PUBLICATIONS

Generations United issues a periodic newsletter, *Newsline*.

JOAN ORGAN
JIMMY E. W. MEYER

GERONTOLOGICAL SOCIETY OF AMERICA (GSA)
1275 K Street, N.W., Suite 350
Washington, D.C. 20005–4006
(202) 842–1275

The Gerontological Society of America (GSA) is a national, nonprofit, professional organization. One of the oldest gerontological associations, it develops multidisciplinary research agendas, curricula, and training programs. The society emphasizes the modification of gerontological research policy in the public and private sectors through education, congressional briefings, and research rather than direct lobbying.

ORIGIN AND DEVELOPMENT

The GSA organized in 1945 to promote the fledgling field of gerontology and to advocate for the elderly through research. Private associations such as the Josiah Macy, Jr., the Glendorn, and the Forest Park foundations supported the original effort. The founding of GSA, coupled with the founding of the American Geriatrics Society* by physicians in 1942, represents a watershed in the history of structured efforts to examine aging. "Establishing gerontology as an important field of scientific study," the GSA's original purpose, provided a basis for encouraging interdisciplinary exchange among researchers, practitioners, and educators and later for applying gerontological research to policy formation.

The eighty original members of the GSA represented primarily the biological, medical, and behavioral sciences. Gradually the society broadened its scope to include scholars in the social sciences and humanities, administrators, policy analysts, educators, and practitioners. Professionals such as social workers, nurses, program planners, administrators, and educators, as well as physicians and scientists, belong to the association.

The GSA helped to found such related organizations as the Association for Gerontology in Higher Education* and the International Association of Gerontology*. The GSA is one of only two official U.S. members of the international group.

ORGANIZATION AND FUNDING

The GSA is divided into four sections: Biological Sciences; Clinical Medicine; Behavioral and Social Sciences; and Social Research, Planning and Practice. A Student Organization completes the internal structure. Each section maintains its own bylaws, officers, committees, and activities and holds equal representation on standing committees of the whole and on the governing council.

The budget of the Gerontological Society is approximately $2 million. GSA receives about a quarter of its revenues from each of the following: grants, dues, publications, and other sources. The organization spends its income in four roughly equal categories: membership, publications, information, and management.

The Society offers various informational programs. Emerging Issues in Aging (a series of reports and presentations) and Aging Policy Seminars educate decision makers as well as researchers and practitioners. GSA maintains Information Service, a computerized database of over 3,000 experts in the field. In 1988, the organization produced a brief public information video, *Travelers in Time*, which "illustrates how the scientific pursuit of theory, research, education and practice . . . all merge in the multi-disciplinary study of gerontology."

Each November, the Gerontological Society sponsors a four-day scientific meeting that attracts an average of 3,500 participants. GSA offers several awards to encourage the development of gerontological research and practice, as well as to draw attention to new developments in the field. Since 1974, the society has provided more than 250 postdoctoral research opportunities through its Fellowship Program in Applied Gerontology; a similar effort was begun in the 1980s on the predoctoral level.

POLICY CONCERNS AND TACTICS

Although its organizing charter stipulated that no activities of the corporation would attempt to influence legislation, the Gerontological Society was never totally removed from the policy arena. The lead article in the first issue (1946) of the *Journal of Gerontology* clearly stated, "We need a national policy to guide our social, political and especially our economic activities . . . to replace the present, almost brutal, neglect or callous dismissal of the aged." In 1956 and 1957, the Biology and Medicine Subcommittee of GSA developed guidelines used to shape federal and private policies supporting gerontological research. Individual GSA members such as Clark Tibbitts and Wilma Donahue were early federal and state policy activists; other GSA officers served as consultants to the White House Conference on Aging in 1961.

It was not until the mid-1960s, however, that GSA formally created the Policy Liaison Committee (later called the Public Policy Committee). The committee concentrated especially on governmental research policy, responding to requests for congressional testimony and advising federal committees on aging. In 1970, GSA moved its headquarters to Washington, D.C., to concentrate and strengthen its influence on federal policy.

The politicization of the Gerontological Society became a controversial issue in the 1970s. Members complained about the increasing political activity of an organization designed as a scientific forum while activists such as Maggie Kuhn of the Gray Panthers Project Fund* argued for radicalization of GSA and of social gerontology policy in general. The Public Policy Committee continued to be active in the 1980s. For example, the committee provided the 101st Congress with a position paper on methods of approaching current aging-policy issues. The GSA's methods continue to be indirect: briefing the related congressional committees and executive branch offices and educating through formal and informal interest groups.

The future direction of the Gerontological Society focuses on continuing its original mission of linking research and practice through education and information exchange across disciplinary lines. The GSA's Task Force on Minority Issues, formed in the late 1980s, represents an ongoing effort to remain in close contact with the needs and policy issues of the American aging community.

PUBLICATIONS

In 1946, GSA began publishing the *Journal of Gerontology*, which emphasized basic research and soon became an important forum for discussing and exchanging ideas, information, and issues in the field. Reorganized in 1988, the bimonthly *Journals of Gerontology* contains four independent refereed research journals: *Journal of Gerontology: Biological Sciences*, *Journal of Gerontology: Medical Sciences*, *Journal of Gerontology: Psychological Sciences*, and *Journal of Gerontology: Social Sciences*. Their publication reflects the unique emphasis of the Gerontological Society on multidisciplinary study and practice. The *Gerontologist*, another refereed journal, has been published by the GSA since 1961. This bimonthly publication (with a special issue in October) stresses applied research, policy analysis, and practice concepts, and reviews pertinent books and films.

Further Information

W. Andrew Achenbaum, ''Reconstructing GSA's History,'' *Gerontologist* 27 (1987): 21–29; Robert Binstock, ''The Gerontological Society and Public Policy: A Report,'' *Gerontologist*. 9 (1969): 69; Herman Blumenthal, ''The Politicization of the Gerontological Society,'' *Gerontologist* 11 (1971): 2–3; Lawrence K. Frank, ''Gerontology.'' *Journal of Gerontology* 1 (1946): 1–11; Margaret Kuhn, ''Open Letter,'' *Gerontologist* 18 (1978): 422–24; Robert Morris, ''Reality or Illusion: The Gerontological Society's Contribution to Public Policy,'' *Gerontologist* 7 (1967): 229–33.

JIMMY E. W. MEYER
RENEE ROMANO

GERONTOLOGY IN SEMINARY TRAINING
See National Coalition on the Aging Constituent Unit: National Interfaith Coalition on Aging.

GLOBAL LINK FOR MIDLIFE AND OLDER WOMEN
See International Federation on Ageing.

GRAY PANTHERS PROJECT FUND
1424 16th Street, N.W., Suite 602
Washington, D.C. 20036
(202) 387–3111   FAX (202) 387–2492
The Gray Panthers Project Fund, better known as the Gray Panthers, is a private, nonprofit coalition of older and younger Americans, ''working together

for a better world for the young to grow old in.'' The Gray Panthers strive for social justice, advocate for civil rights, and champion world peace through congressional testimony, research and education, direct action, and empowerment of the grass roots.

ORIGIN AND DEVELOPMENT

Maggie Kuhn founded the Gray Panthers in Philadelphia in 1970. Kuhn, then 65 years old, had been forced to retire from her job as editor of *Social Progress: The Presbyterian Action Journal*. With a few friends in similar situations, Kuhn established the Consultation of Older and Younger Adults for Social Change and became its first national convener. In 1972, the media dubbed the group the Gray Panthers; the name quickly became official. With the motto, ''Age and Youth in Action,'' the Gray Panthers opposed mandatory retirement, ageism, and the Vietnam War. A 1991 membership brochure contained this description: ''We are colorful, assertive, dynamic, working for change, raising hell. We're activists of all ages.''

Incorporated in the spirit of the civil rights, antiwar, and feminist movements, the Gray Panthers avoided a hierarchical structure. Initially there were neither formal membership nor dues. A network of community groups, coordinated by a central steering committee, soon spread to several states. In 1973, the Gray Panthers and Ralph Nader's Retired Professional Action Group merged, forming the Gray Panthers Project Fund. Formal dues were established in 1977. From 1976 to 1979, the National Gray Panthers, an IRS-designated 501(c)(4) group, conducted most of the organization's activities, permitting political action and lobbying. Since 1979, the Gray Panthers Project Fund has conducted all activities under the 501 (c)(3) IRS designation, permitting tax-deductible donations but limiting lobbying. In 1991, the 501(c)(4) group still existed but was inactive.

In 1985, the Gray Panthers opened an office in Washington, D.C. The national headquarters remained in Philadelphia until April 1990, when all operations relocated to Washington, D.C.

ORGANIZATION AND FUNDING

In 1991, the Gray Panthers had 70,000 national members at large. In a network representing twenty-four states, 8,000 chapter members belonged to more than eighty local groups. Local networks have autonomy in issue emphasis and decision making but are expected to work on at least one national issue. A twenty-five-member National Board of Directors guides the organization. In 1991, founder Maggie Kuhn held the title of National Convener. Officers and committee chairpersons form the Executive Committee, which handles business affairs between board meetings. Local network delegates elect the National Board of Directors, amend the Articles of Agreements (stating the group's goals and purposes), and adopt the Gray Panther Resolutions (policy guidelines) at the biennial convention. The Gray Panthers also maintains a forty-four-member

Advisory Committee, composed of such public figures as Harry Belafonte, Bella Abzug, and Benjamin Spock.

Annual dues were $15 in 1991. Local networks retain 60 percent of that amount; the remainder goes to the Gray Panthers Project Fund. There are no corporate or organizational members. The major source of the Gray Panthers' $608,175 budget in 1989 was individual contributions (82%). Other sources of revenue, all less than 5 percent of the total, included federal campaign monies, foundation grants and corporate donations, membership dues, and sales and publications. Expenses are divided into two major categories: program services, comprising network support and public education and publications ($484,467), and supporting services, comprising management and general expenses and fund raising ($113,740).

The Gray Panthers Project Fund operates the Margaret S. Mahler Institute, funded by a bequest from the estate of psychologist Margaret S. Mahler. The institute awards funds twice a year to scholars over age 70 for educational, research, or media projects.

Groups have organized on the Gray Panthers' model in two foreign countries, Japan and Germany. The Gray Panthers have accreditation with the United Nations (UN) Department of Public Information, and in 1981, the group received consultative status to the UN Economic and Social Council. This recognition provides the Gray Panthers the opportunity to participate in the international community.

POLICY CONCERNS AND TACTICS

The Gray Panthers bring a holistic perspective to a wide spectrum of issues. Their goals are:

- To foster the concept of aging as growth during the total life span from birth to death

- To challenge and help eliminate ageism

- To advocate for fundamental social change that would eliminate injustice, discrimination, and oppression in our society, help create a humane society, and heighten opportunities for people to realize their full potential

- To act independently and in coalition with other movements to build a new power base to achieve short-term social change and ultimately a society which will put the needs of people above profits, eliminate the concentration of corporate power, and serve human needs through democratic means

The organization works on national, state, and local levels to promote a variety of concerns: world peace, women's right to choose, government-sponsored housing for low-income Americans of all ages, and handgun control, among others. A primary concern has consistently been the need for affordable health care, in the form of a national health service. The Gray Panthers utilizes tactics such as education, congressional testimony, direct action protests, and networking.

Initially, the Gray Panthers concentrated on diminishing cultural and symbolic ageism. In 1974, the group established the Gray Panther Media Watch National Committee to undertake the elimination of ageism on television. Members submitted reports of programs portraying a negative stereotype of the elderly or ignoring the elderly. When the group presented its findings to the National Association of Broadcasters Code Board, the board voted to include age in its sensitivity guidelines.

In the later 1970s, the Gray Panthers became involved in congressional politics. *Nursing Homes: A Citizens' Action Guide*, published by the group in 1977, led to Senate hearings and nursing home reforms. The Gray Panthers claim to have played a large role in the 1978 legislation outlawing mandatory retirement on many federal jobs and raising the retirement age to 70 for most nongovernment workers. The group sent questionnaires concerning mandatory retirement to congressional representatives, collected cases of forced retirement to take to the courts if necessary, and attempted to gain support on college campuses and among religious groups.

Protest activities have included performing street theater about heartlessness and greed within the health care industry outside the 1974 Chicago convention of the American Medical Association. More recently, a 1990 local campaign against war toys in Washington, D.C., in conjunction with the DC Area Toys of Peace Campaign, involved the Gray Panthers in an intergenerational march, a teach-in, and passing out leaflets to holiday shoppers.

In the late 1980s, the Gray Panthers came out strongly against the financing plan of the Medicare Catastrophic Coverage Act because of fundamental problems with the Medicare system. The Gray Panthers would prefer to dismantle Medicaid and Medicare completely and establish a national health service featuring universal coverage, funded by general tax revenues, and regulated by consumers. During the 1989 repeal process of the Catastropic Coverage Act, the Gray Panthers successfully campaigned for retention of provisions for low-income families, women, and children and against the act's financing plan, which "ignored the principles of social insurance."

The Gray Panthers are convinced that the battle for national health care must be fought on the state level. They are prepared to go state by state if necessary. Initiatives are in progress in Florida, Massachusetts, Oregon, Minnesota, Michigan, Texas, and New Jersey. The group is confident that national legislation will follow the states' lead.

The Gray Panthers have consistently focused on world peace as an imperative. In 1991, the national organization publicly opposed the Persian Gulf War, while local networks in cities such as Seattle, Boston, and New York mounted demonstrations, encouraged letter-writing campaigns, and advocated a revised national energy policy.

One of the Gray Panthers' basic tenets is the need to work in coalition with other advocacy groups. For example, in the National Health Care Campaign, the Gray Panthers have allied themselves with several other organizations, including the Coalition for a National Health System. Aging organizations involved in this effort include the American Society on Aging* and the National Council on the Aging*. Other groups with which the Gray Panthers have worked in coalition on a wide variety of topics are the Leadership Council of Aging Organizations*, the major peace and disarmament groups, Ralph Nader's the Public Citizen, and the National Citizens' Coalition for Nursing Home Reform*, a spinoff of the Gray Panthers.

As an intergenerational group, the Gray Panthers sometimes find themselves at odds with other organizations in the field. The group believes that advocating only for elderly issues is nonproductive and divisive. The Gray Panthers see all ages and all of society's problems as interrelated, arguing that gray lobbies perpetuate the misconception of separate concerns of the aged and the young. The Gray Panthers especially opposes groups such as Americans for Generational Equity*, which contend that increased benefits to the elderly imperil the fiscal future for younger baby boomers.

The Gray Panthers and other groups also disagree on services. Provision of a variety of services is a trademark of such organizations as the American Association of Retired Persons*. Emphasizing the need for social change, the Gray Panthers believe that their most important service is empowering the grass roots.

ELECTORAL ACTIVITIES

The Gray Panthers do not support individual candidates; however, the group, in coalition with eighty other organizations, has worked for the reform of campaign finances.

PUBLICATIONS

The Gray Panthers' newspaper is entitled the *Gray Panther Network* (quarterly). Subscription is included in members' dues. Individuals who are not members may subscribe for $15 per year; the price for organizations is $30 per year. The organization publishes the bimonthly *HealthWatch* ($12), a health issues newsletter mailed free to board members and members of the Gray Panther National Health Task Force. *WashingtonWatch* ($12) is a bimonthly newsletter focusing on legislative advocacy.

Further Information

Jan Fisher, "Maggie Kuhn's Vision: Young and Old Together," *50 Plus* 26 (July 1986): 22; Dieter Hessel, ed., *Maggie Kuhn on Aging* (Philadelphia, Westminster Press, 1977); Ruth Harriet Jacobs and Beth Hess, "Panther Power: Symbol and Substance," *Long-Term Care and Health Services Administration Quarterly* (Fall 1978): 238–43; Maggie Kuhn, with Christina Long and Laura Quinn, *No Stone Unturned: The Life and Times of Maggie Kuhn* (New York:

Ballantine Books, 1991); John Zinsser, ''Gray Panthers: Fighting the Good Fight for 15 Years,'' *50 Plus* 26 (March 1986).

JIMMY E. W. MEYER
QIUSHA MA

H
/

HEALTH PROMOTION INSTITUTE
See National Council on the Aging Constituent Unit: Health Promotion Institute.

HEALTH SECURITY ACTION COUNCIL
See Committee for National Health Insurance.

HELPAGE INTERNATIONAL
See American Association for International Aging.

HELP THE AGED
See American Association for International Aging.

HISPANIC AGING IN LOS ANGELES
See Asociacion Nacional Pro Personas Mayores.

HISPANIC GERONTOLOGICAL INTERNSHIP PROGRAM
See Asociacion Nacional Pro Personas Mayores.

HOME HEALTH SERVICES AND STAFFING ASSOCIATION
See National Association for Home Care.

HOUSING MANAGEMENT CORPORATION
See National Council of Senior Citizens.

I
/

INSTITUTE OF LIFETIME LEARNING
See American Association of Retired Persons.

INTERGENERATIONAL EARLY CHILDHOOD PROGRAM
See Generations Together.

INTERNATIONAL ACTION FORUM FOR MIDLIFE AND OLDER WOMEN
See National Action Forum for Midlife and Older Women.

INTERNATIONAL ASSOCIATION OF GERONTOLOGICAL SOCIETIES
See International Association of Gerontology.

INTERNATIONAL ASSOCIATION OF GERONTOLOGY (IAG)
c/o Dr. Samuel Bravo Williams, President
Jojutla #91
Tlalpan CP. 14090
Mexico D.F., Mexico

   The International Association of Gerontology (IAG) is a federation of national gerontological societies that promotes cross-cultural exchange of biomedical research and professional training in the variety of scientific fields concerned with aging. One of the oldest international organizations in the field, the IAG works to improve communication within and across various disciplines among scientists and scholars throughout the world.

ORIGIN AND DEVELOPMENT

The IAG was founded as the International Association of Gerontological Societies on July 10, 1950, at the first International Congress of Gerontology convened at Liège, Belgium. The prime motivator was V. Korenchevsky, the founder of the British Aging Club (1938). He encouraged scientists and other professionals in aging from many countries to establish their own national gerontological societies. At Korenchevsky's suggestion, L. Brull, professor of medicine at the University of Liège, called the Liège meeting. Almost 100 official delegates from sixteen gerontological societies in thirteen countries attended.

The IAG held a second international congress, in St. Louis, Missouri, in 1951. The association's name was changed to the International Association of Gerontology, reflecting the problems of associating societies with no legal standing outside their own countries. Since 1951, the international meetings have been held every three or four years. Fourteen congresses have been held since 1950. The 1985 International Congress was held in New York City; more than 3,000 representatives from fifty-two countries attended. In 1989, the International Congress was held in Acapulco, Mexico, with the theme, The Old in the New World. The 1993 congress is scheduled for Budapest. The proceedings of these multidisciplinary scientific meetings provide an overview of gerontological theory and research worldwide.

The major purposes of the IAG, as stated in the constitution and bylaws, revised in 1985, are:

- To promote gerontological research in the biological, medical, behavioral, and social fields (social psychological fields) by member organizations and to promote cooperation among those organizations

- To promote the training of highly qualified professionals in the field of aging

- To protect the interests of gerontological societies, associations or groups in all questions pertaining to foreign or international matters

- To promote and assist in the arrangements for holding the International Congress of Gerontology at intervals determined by the Council

From the beginning, the IAG has emphasized research and training in gerontology and geriatrics. Organizations that focused exclusively on social or medical services were not eligible to join. The second admission qualification was that the joining organization be multidisciplinary in nature and have a membership of at least ten (later fifty) investigators, from the scientific disciplines of biology, medicine, and sociology or psychology. A third stipulation was that the organization be national in scope, although as of 1990 persons who reside in nations without a member society can be granted individual memberships. The first U.S. members were the Gerontological Society of America* and the American Geriatrics Society*. These became the only U.S. members, when it was decided to limit future IAG membership to one society per country, with the exceptions of the United Kingdom (two), Japan (three), France (two), and the United States.

ORGANIZATION AND FUNDING

In 1990, the IAG included fifty constituent societies. The governing body is the Council, elected at the congress and composed of the Executive Committee and representatives from each member society. The number of Council representatives is based on the number of members of each society. The Council generally manages the association, electing officers, admitting new members, approving the budget, and determining the time and place for each international congress. The President of the association chairs the Council.

The Executive Committee is composed of the President, Immediate Past-President, the President-elect, Secretary General/Vice-President, and Treasurer. All hold office for three years, from the end of one congress to the beginning of the next. The President-elect is elected by a majority of votes of Council members. Duties assigned to the Executive Committee include handling the IAG's daily affairs, representing the IAG before outside groups, and coordinating committee and regional activities. The President-elect organizes the next congress.

The IAG is divided into four regions: Asia/Oceania, Europe, Latin America, and North America. Regional meetings are held in the years between congresses. Such meetings have taken place in Budapest, Singapore, Brighton (UK), and Bangkok. Between congresses, regional committees handle IAG matters within their geographic areas.

Funds of the IAG are allocated by the group's President. Financial sources for the IAG's annual budget of under $50,000 include membership dues, miscellaneous gifts, and grants from private and/or public organizations. The largest member groups pay the bulk of the IAG's support, since dues are assessed per person, based on the number of enrolled members in each society.

Since its formation, the IAG has paid dues to the Council for the Coordination of International Congresses of Medical Sciences and has thus been consistently affiliated with the United Nations (UN) and WHO (World Health Organization). The IAG works closely with these and other international groups, such as the Pan American Health Organization.

Every two years since 1983, the IAG has awarded the Sandoz Prize, which recognizes an outstanding contribution to gerontology, emphasizing interdisciplinary study.

POLICY CONCERNS AND TACTICS

The IAG heightens public awareness of the need for gerontological research and stimulates that research worldwide. By organizing regional and international scientific meetings on the biological and clinical aspects of aging, the IAG instigates international study in these areas. Often the congresses provide the stimulus and vehicle for collaborative, cross-cultural, comparative research on topics such as patterns of work and retirement. The IAG emphasizes the normality of the biological aging process, refuting the misconception of aging as a disease.

In the late 1970s, the IAG's congresses became more oriented toward the politics of social welfare and social service. Symbolic of this shift, the IAG in 1978 sponsored a UN proposal to hold a World Assembly on Aging in 1982. The overriding purpose of the world assembly was to guarantee economic security to older people, a goal unrelated to the strictly biomedical research goals of the early IAG. Much of the 1981 International Congress was devoted to support for the upcoming assembly. In 1982, H. Thomae and G. L. Maddox were authorized by IAG's governing body to publish an edited volume, *New Perspectives on Old Age: A Message to Decision Makers* (1982), which included a policy statement for transmittal to the World Assembly, held in Vienna, July 26 to August 6, 1982.

The outcome of the UN World Assembly on Aging was a broad statement, the International Plan of Action on Aging (IPAA). Endorsed by 125 nations, the plan contains twenty-six recommendations and an introduction summarizing the status of knowledge and research about the aging process. Members of the IAG helped to formulate this document.

Much of the emphasis of the IAG in the 1980s was on the challenges developing countries faced in providing services to their older citizens. The IAG stresses the potential mutual benefits of information exchange between First and Third World countries.

PUBLICATIONS

The IAG publishes the *IAG Newsletter* (twice a year) and the *IAG Newsletter for Developing Nations* (quarterly). Other publications include *Aging: The Universal Human Experience* (1987), co-edited by George Maddox and E. F. Busse, and *The Role of Hospitals in Geriatric Care* (1988), edited by George Maddox and Carl Eisdorfer. Proceedings of the Fourteenth International Congress of IAG in Acapulco, Mexico, were published in *Old in a New World* (n.d.).

Further Information

Aging in All the Nations: A Special Report on the United Nations World Assembly on Aging (Washington, D.C.: National Council on the Aging, 1982); Bernice L. Neugarten, "The XIIIth Congress of the IAG: A Postscript," in George Maddox and E. W. Busse, eds., *Aging: The Universal Human Experience*, (New York: Springer, 1985); Nathan Shock, *The International Association of Gerontology: A Chronicle—1950–1986* (New York: Springer, 1988).

JIMMY E. W. MEYER
QIUSHA MA

INTERNATIONAL FEDERATION ON AGEING (IFA)

601 E Street, N.W., Building A, Floor 10, Room 200
Washington, D.C. 20049
(202) 434–2430   FAX (202) 434–6494

The International Federation on Ageing (IFA) is a nonprofit, nongovernmental federation of national and regional voluntary organizations representing the elderly. The IFA is an authoritative source of information on worldwide service and policy developments affecting the status and well-being of the elderly.

ORIGIN AND DEVELOPMENT

In 1973, delegates from seventeen national voluntary organizations on four continents met in London to discuss the formation of a new international organization on aging. Asserting the importance of voluntary organizations in the field of aging, the founders formed the IFA to strengthen the effectiveness of such groups around the world and to share the diversity of national experiences. The IFA provides an international forum for exchange of opinions, ideas, and possible solutions to the dilemmas of aging, disseminating the information and knowledge among the elderly, scientists, and practitioners worldwide.

The IFA holds triennial conferences, open to all members, and annual meetings of the Executive Board. It also sponsors a number of symposia and workshops, usually held in conjunction with other international conferences on gerontology or social welfare. The first IFA global conference will take place August 30 to September 3, 1992, in Bombay and Pune, India. Such meetings provide for exchange of ideas and viewpoints between researchers and practitioners.

ORGANIZATION AND FUNDING

A fifteen-member Board of Directors, elected by the membership, governs the IFA. Policies are set at the annual meeting of the Executive Board and at the triennial members' conference. Full membership is open to nongovernmental, national, voluntary organizations that either represent or serve the elderly. Associate memberships are available to regional and provincial organizations, professional societies, for-profit groups, governmental groups, and national groups wishing nonvoting status. In 1990, 106 national and regional voluntary organizations belonged to the IAG, from over fifty countries on every continent. Regional offices are located in the United States, Mexico, England, India, and Hong Kong.

IFA's annual budget ranges between $250,000 and $350,000; 5 percent of it comes from membership dues, 85 percent from fund raising, and 10 percent from publication sales.

POLICY CONCERNS AND TACTICS

The IFA is concerned with a wide spectrum of issues on aging, all from a comparative, cross-national perspective. The IFA emphasizes communication between and among the elderly, practitioners, specialists, and organizations in the field. Advocacy at the international level and the global exchange of information on the humanitarian and developmental issues and policies related to aging, through publications and education, represent the missions of this federation.

In 1982, the first United Nations (UN) World Assembly on Aging met at Vienna and formulated the International Plan of Action on Aging (IPAA), endorsed by 125 nations. The IFA is committed to implementing the recommendations of the plan, the first comprehensive international instrument in the field. The IFA works as a catalyst, pursuing the IPAA's primary goal of improving the socioeconomic status and the health of older citizens worldwide.

An example of this effort has been the Skills Exchange Programme. IFA experts provided on-site consultation upon the request of countries needing assistance with local projects, such as day centers for care of the elderly. The IFA prepared a manual for establishing such care centers, *An Ageing Population: Focus on Day Centres* (1984), and has published it in four languages. A second manual, *Children Growing Up* (1987), is a guide for teaching older persons about child development.

In preparation for the tenth anniversary (1992) of the World Assembly on Aging and the IPAA, the IFA promoted the UN's adoption of a Universal Declaration of the Rights and Responsibilities for Older Persons. The IFA published a draft of such a declaration in the winter 1990 issue of *Ageing International*. The UN Social Development Commission approved a set of UN Principles for Older Persons largely based on the IFA draft. The principles were submitted to the General Assembly for final approval in 1991.

With the American Association of Retired Persons[*] (AARP), the IFA jointly sponsors the Global Link for Midlife and Older Women. Funded by the Women's Initiative of AARP, the Global Link is a network of researchers, planners, practitioners, and activists that was organized in 1985; it emphasizes information exchange, data collection and publication, and advocacy on behalf of the world's older women. Among its activities has been the organization of two meetings in cooperation with the Pan American Health Organization, focusing on research knowledge and gaps and model programs serving older women in the Americas. The Global Link planned to hold an expert group meeting in 1991 on the contribution of older women to national development, with the UN Division on the Advancement of Women as joint sponsor.

A second international network, the International Network for Older Persons in Employment, explores work-related issues that affect older persons. AARP's Worker Equity program and the IFA co-sponsor this network. Through publications and meetings, the network examines employment-related issues from an international perspective. Among the uses of this data is to inform the IFA's advocacy positions with the International Labor Organization (ILO).

IFA maintains close contact and often coordinates its actions with other international organizations, such as the London-based HelpAge International, the International Association of Gerontology*, the International Federation of Associations for the Elderly, and the International Council on Social Welfare. The IFA holds consultative status with the World Health Organization, the Economic and Social Council of the UN, the ILO, UNESCO, and the International Social Security Association. The IFA provides testimony and information to the UN and other international groups. Occasionally the IFA testifies before U.S. congressional committees, as it did before the House Select Committee on Aging in 1988 when it supplied an international perspective on family support for the elderly.

PUBLICATIONS

The IFA seeks to keep its membership informed about the latest research results, as well as developments in public policy around the world. *Ageing International*, the biannual journal of the IFA, publishes information about program innovations and new ideas in service delivery, research results in social gerontology, developments in aging policy, and actions by the elderly on their own behalf. Published in English with abbreviated French and Spanish editions, the journal encourages cross-cultural, cross-national adaptation to ensure the relevance of ideas, programs, and policies in more than one country. *Network News*, the newsletter of Global Link for Midlife and Older Women, is issued semiannually in conjunction with the AARP.

The IFA also publishes monographs and special reports, including: *Older Women around the World*, by Mary Jo Gibson (1985); *The International Directory of Research and Researchers in Comparative Gerontology*, edited by Charlotte Nusberg and Jay Sokolovsky (1990); the *International Glossary of Social Gerontology*, edited by Mary Jo Gibson and Charlotte Nusberg (1988); and *Rethinking Worklife Options for Older Persons*, edited by Jack Halib and Charlotte Nusberg (1990).

Further Information

David Hobman, "An Aging World," *World Health* (March 1985): 21; "Keeping Worldwide Watch: *Ageing International*," *Perspective on Aging* 18 (September–October 1989): 17–18; Charlotte Nusberg, "A Declaration of Rights and Responsibilities of Older Persons?" *Ageing International* 17 (Winter 1990): 23–25; "Seven Years Later, the World Assembly Remains a Landmark," *Perspective on Aging* 18 (September–October 1989): 8–9.

JIMMY E. W. MEYER

INTERNATIONAL FOUNDATION OF EMPLOYEE BENEFIT PLANS
See Society of Professional Benefit Administrators.

INTERNATIONAL NETWORK FOR OLDER PERSONS IN EMPLOYMENT
See International Federation on Ageing.

INTERNATIONAL RETIRED AND OLDER WORKERS
See United Auto Workers Retired and Older Workers Department.

INTERNATIONAL RETIRED WORKERS ADVISORY COUNCIL
See United Auto Workers Retired and Older Workers Department.

INTERNATIONAL RETIRED WORKERS DEPARTMENT
See United Auto Workers Retired and Older Workers Department.

J /

JEWISH ASSOCIATION FOR SERVICES FOR THE AGED (JASA)
40 West 68th Street
New York, New York 10023
(212) 724–3200   FAX (212) 769–1218

Jewish Association for Services for the Aged (JASA), with its housing company and home care subsidiaries, is a social agency operated under Jewish auspices in New York City and Nassau and Suffolk counties of New York State. Its purpose is to provide a network of services and facilities to enable older adults to function with dignity and autonomy while remaining in their local communities. JASA affects policy through the advocacy efforts of its Joint Public Affairs Committee.

ORIGIN AND DEVELOPMENT

JASA was founded in 1968 by the Communal Planning Committee of the Federation of Jewish Philanthropies of New York. Based on the results of a two-year study and a set of conferences investigating the needs of the elderly and the best means of addressing those needs, the purpose of JASA is to assist older persons in coping with the challenges of aging while remaining in their homes. JASA provides a network of multifunctional services through community-based offices, local senior citizen centers, and senior clubs. The association has constructed, developed, and manages senior citizen housing facilities. It supplies home care services, maintains training programs, and provides intergenerational programs, volunteer services, legal and protective services, Meals-on-Wheels, transportation, financial assistance, and a public information service. JASA estimates that it serves over 51,000 people per year. JASA's services emphasize Jewish elders but are open to older persons without regard to race, creed, or ethnicity.

ORGANIZATION AND FUNDING

JASA's programming is supported largely by federal and state government funds. Contributions from the Federation of Jewish Philanthropies, United Jewish Appeal, United Way, private foundations, individuals, and program fees make up the balance of its income. JASA is administered by a Board of Trustees and an Executive Vice-President. JASA employs a large staff of about 150 professionals (social workers, lawyers, nurses, physicians, and interns) and an additional 2,150 clerical, administrative, food service, maintenance, and support persons. Volunteers are also a vital force in the operation of JASA. An Advisory Committee of older adults composed of delegates from the senior clubs meets quarterly to provide advice and information to the organization.

POLICY CONCERNS AND TACTICS

Concerns of JASA center on issues of service and provision for senior citizens: health care reform, housing, income maintenance, and prevention of elder abuse. Education and communication on policy concerns are based in the local network of senior citizen centers and clubs. Advocacy is conducted primarily by the Joint Public Affairs Committee (JPAC), a coalition of JASA senior citizen centers, clubs, housing complexes, and affiliates representing 11,000 persons. Each year the JPAC Central Committee sets a legislative agenda for local, state, and national advocacy, although it is most active and effective on the state level. The JPAC sponsors monthly meetings and annual legislative trips to Albany, New York; organizes social action committees; initiates letter-writing campaigns; arranges rallies and public hearings; educates groups on legislative issues and elected officials on current senior citizen concerns; provides information and referral services; and testifies before local, state, and national committees on behalf of older Americans.

On the state level, JPAC helped to establish New York State legislation for medical insurance, the EPIC Program (1986), and promoted its reform in 1990. JPAC also worked on state Health Care Proxy legislation, which allows a competent adult to appoint an agent to make health care decisions. Another success was JPAC's endeavor to help pass the Mandatory Medicare Assignment in the 1990 New York State Legislature. The committee co-sponsored the National Conference of Jewish Community Senior Advocacy Groups in Washington, D.C., during 1984 and in 1987 testified before the House and Senate committees on aging regarding the maintenance of Social Security and Medicaid Catastrophic Coverage.

PUBLICATIONS

JPAC publishes *Action Memo/Senior Citizens Advocate* periodically, which notifies constituents of pending legislation and other policymaking activities. The *JASA Progress Report* (published biennially), the *Senior Citizens Advocate* newsletter (quarterly), and the *Aspects of Aging* newsletter (quarterly) give specific current information on the organization.

KIMBERLY S. LENAHAN

JOINT COUNCIL TO IMPROVE THE HEALTH CARE OF THE AGED
See American Hospital Association Section for Aging and Long-Term Care Services.

L

/

LA CLINICA CENTRAL DEL PUEBLO
See Asociacion Nacional Pro Personas Mayores.

LEADERSHIP COUNCIL OF AGING ORGANIZATIONS (LCAO)
1331 F Street, N.W.
Washington, D.C. 20004–1171
(202) 347–8800   FAX (202) 624–9595

The Leadership Council of Aging Organizations (LCAO) is a coalition of nonprofit associations that have the welfare of older persons as their central purpose. The LCAO serves as an information source, encourages communication and resource sharing, and initiates joint advocacy on behalf of its participants. LCAO strives ''to provide leadership and vision as America meets the challenges and opportunities presented by its aging society.''

ORIGIN AND DEVELOPMENT

The Leadership Council of Aging Organizations began in 1978 as a clearinghouse designed to strengthen and unify the aging network. In the months of planning preceding the 1981 White House Conference on Aging (WHCOA), the council took on a more formal role. A committee of about a dozen LCAO representatives drafted an eight-point policy agenda, ''8 for the 80's,'' recommendations for consideration at the WHCOA. Twenty-three organizations adopted the agenda in November 1981. The proposals were discussed and expanded in the fourteen WHCOA committees. During the conference, the LCAO convened an open session where representatives of a wide variety of advocacy groups aired their views.

ORGANIZATION AND FUNDING

In order to join LCAO, an organization must be approved by the Executive Committee and the council itself. The potential member group must meet the following criteria:

1. The organization must have as its central purpose the welfare of older persons.

2. The organization must be national in scope and/or membership, must have a presence in Washington, D.C., and participate in LCAO activities.

3. The organization must be comprised of: (a) older persons, OR (b) individuals/groups whose primary function is to serve older persons, either directly or indirectly, OR (c) individuals/groups whose primary function is to generate or advance knowledge of older persons and aging.

4. The organization must have an identified unit concerned with national policy affecting older persons.

5. The organization must be nonprofit, shall not be a subunit or affiliated entity of a for-profit enterprise, and the organization's membership must be composed predominantly of individuals or nonprofit organizations.

6. The organization must embrace the mission and purpose of LCAO.

LCAO does not have dues or other funding sources. The LCAO Chair rotates among the three largest members: the American Association of Retired Persons* (AARP), the National Council on the Aging*, and the National Council of Senior Citizens* (NCSC). The Chair of each of those three organizations heads the LCAO in turn for one year, and LCAO shares space at that group's headquarters for the period. In 1991–92, LCAO was located at NCSC headquarters, and Lawrence Smedley held the position of Chair. Thirty-two organizations comprised the LCAO in 1991. At monthly meetings, LCAO representatives set organization policy and plan public policy initiatives. In 1992, LCAO will move to AARP.

According to the Leadership Council's statement of mission and purpose, revised in May 1991, LCAO is dedicated to:

1. Strengthening both the public and private sector response to meeting the needs of America's older population

2. Promoting thoughtful and rational policy changes where such changes are necessary, recognizing that state and local level activities are important both to the generation and implementation of public policy

3. Seeking dialogue with responsible leaders of both the public and private sector

4. Working with all of society's institutions—political, social, economic, religious—to ensure that they welcome and support full participation by America's older population

5. Working to ensure that no older person is a victim of discrimination based on age, gender, race, or ethnic origin

6. Recognizing the diversity of America's older population, which includes the most vulnerable and frail elderly in need of a range of services, as well as older persons who are contributing to their communities through work-related pursuits and volunteer service

POLICY CONCERNS AND TACTICS

The main policy concerns of LCAO revolve around the health of and health care for older persons: Medicare and Medicaid programs and funding, home health care and long-term care, and nursing home quality and reform. LCAO also seeks to improve the economic situation of older persons, as represented in the questions of Social Security increases and benefits, maintenance and guarantee of pensions, and employment for the elderly. Additionally, LCAO is concerned with the topics of affordable housing, family and medical leave, transportation alternatives, age discrimination, and intergenerational relations.

The role of the Leadership Council on Aging is to initiate and coordinate joint action in the policy arena among its membership. Although the LCAO Chair occasionally testifies on an issue, most of the LCAO members' appearances before Congress are on behalf of their own organizations. LCAO representatives provide information to Congress on pertinent topics and write letters to members of congressional committees. During the 1980s, LCAO carried out and published research, especially on the provisions in the federal budget pertaining to older persons. In 1991, research was not a major emphasis.

PUBLICATIONS

LCAO publishes occasional research reports.

Further Information

Martha Baum and Bennett M. Rich, *The Aging: A Guide to Public Policy* (Pittsburgh: University of Pittsburgh Press, 1984); Linda Marie Delloff, "Democracy in Action and Inaction," *Christian Century*, December 16, 1981, 98: no. 41, 1299–1300; Paul Kershner, "Advocacy at the Crossroads," *Generations* (Fall 1984): 44–45.

JIMMY E. W. MEYER

LEGAL COUNSEL FOR THE ELDERLY
See American Association of Retired Persons.

LIGHTHOUSE NATIONAL CENTER FOR VISION AND AGING (NCVA)
The Lighthouse Inc.
800 Second Avenue
New York, New York 10017
(212) 808–0077 or (800) 334–5497 (V/TDD)   FAX (212) 808–0110

The Lighthouse National Center for Vision and Aging (NCVA) is a division of The Lighthouse Inc., a private, nonprofit, nonmembership, education, research, and advocacy organization promoting the interests of persons who incur or are at the risk of incurring a vision loss. NCVA educates policymakers and increases public awareness regarding needs, benefits, and services for older persons with vision loss.

ORIGIN AND DEVELOPMENT

NCVA was organized in 1985 as a division of The Lighthouse Inc. Organization goals include involvement of visually impaired older persons in existing community services, recognition of the specialty of low vision, and research on the implications of sensory changes in later life. In 1988, the Lighthouse marked the thirty-fifth anniversary of its low-vision services with a major interdisciplinary symposium, Age-Related Vision Loss. Leading authorities in medicine, optometry, vision science, gerontology, and rehabilitation came together to share information and exchange views and ideas. One key speaker, T. Franklin Williams, in a speech entitled "Research Needs in Aging and Vision," emphasized the lack of existing research on the effects of low vision on the full range of life.

ORGANIZATION AND FUNDING

The Lighthouse NCVA has no individual or corporate members and no local or state affiliates. Four staff members and a fourteen-member Advisory Board meet in an annual planning process to set center policy. The appointed Advisory Board is composed of professionals from the aging and the vision fields. A biannual symposium is held that addresses some area of low-vision services. In 1991, Director of the Lighthouse NCVA was Cynthia Stuen.

The annual budget for the group ranges between $250,000 and $350,000. Funding sources include fund raising (50%), foundation grants (30%), government funding (10%), and Lighthouse endowment monies (10%).

POLICY CONCERNS AND TACTICS

The Lighthouse NCVA emphasizes the need for "accessibility to the mainstream of gerontological services for visually-impaired older adults." Other issues, such as general health, Medicare and Medicaid funding, Social Security benefit increases, independent living, and employment, also concern the organization. The Lighthouse NCVA does not testify before Congress but does encourage its constituents to contact members of Congress on critical topics. One such grass-roots effort supported the Americans with Disabilities Act (1990) with letters and telegrams. In addition, the Lighthouse NCVA supplies information to members of Congress and conducts and publishes research. The center also serves a networking function, maintaining a list of programs around the country devoted to vision loss.

The Lighthouse NCVA coordinates actions with other interest groups, such as the American Foundation for the Blind, the Association of Private Agencies Serving the Blind, the National Association of Public Agencies Serving the Blind, the American Society on Aging[*], the Gerontological Society of America[*], and the National Council on the Aging[*].

Educational material from the NCVA includes publications and multimedia presentations. The newsletter *Aging and Vision News*, published three times a year, is free to professionals engaged in research, education, and/or practice in the area of eye/vision care and aging. Three multimedia packages offered by NCVA are *A Better View of You*, a consumer education presentation geared to older people that covers age-related vision changes and treatment and rehabilitation options; *Work sight*, which educates employers and employees about vision loss and the workplace; and *Look Out for Annie*, to help older persons and professionals understand the personal and social consequences of age-related eye diseases and diminished vision. Each media package includes a presenter's guide, brochures, and a video and/or slide presentation.

MARIS J. DENEKE

LONG TERM CARE CAMPAIGN
1334 G Street, N.W., Suite 500
Washington, D.C. 20005
(202) 393–2092   FAX (202) 393–2109

The Long Term Care Campaign is a coalition of national organizations ''dedicated to enacting comprehensive legislation to protect American families against the devastating costs of long-term care.'' The Long Term Care Campaign works on the federal, state, and local levels to educate the general public, legislators, and other policymakers and to press for comprehensive, national long-term-care financing.

ORIGIN AND DEVELOPMENT

The Long Term Care Campaign was organized in 1988 as Long Term Care '88, a joint effort of the Villers Foundation and its advocacy arm, Villers Advocacy Associates (now Families U.S.A. Foundation*), the Alzheimer's Disease and Related Disorders Association (now the Alzheimer's Association*), and the American Association of Retired Persons* (AARP). Long Term Care '88 successfully brought the issue of long-term-care financing to the attention of the electorate and the 1988 candidates for the U.S. presidency. The $2 million crusade, a feature of which was free television time for candidates to address the issue, succeeded in obtaining planks on long-term care in every major presidential candidate's platform.

The Long Term Care Campaign grew out of the increasing concern with the financial demands of long-term care on American families. Three key legislative principles form the basis for the Long Term Care Campaign's activities:

• Long Term Care services should be available to all who need them, regardless of age or income.
• A national Long Term Care program should provide a comprehensive range of facility-based and community-based health, social, and support services to maintain and enhance personal independence.

• Long Term Care should be financed through a social insurance program similar to Social Security or Medicare, financed by all generations.

The campaign claims that a designated tax of approximately five dollars per week could provide long-term-care protection for all Americans.

ORGANIZATION AND FUNDING

In 1991, almost 140 organizations belonged to the Long Term Care Campaign across a wide spectrum of religious groups, labor unions, associations focused on women's and children's interests, and ethnic associations, in addition to more typical health, law, and aging advocacy groups. (See Appendix B for a list.) The combined memberships of these groups total more than 60 million Americans.

Major financial sponsors for the Long Term Care Campaign are three organizations: the AARP, Families U.S.A., and the Alzheimer's Association. There is no formal governing body; the executive directors of these three groups comprise the de facto board and set campaign policy. All of the member organizations offer advice and information on legislative decisions, such as congressional testimony. Four staff members serve the organization.

POLICY CONCERNS AND TACTICS

The Long Term Care Campaign focuses on policy issues directly connected to public assistance for the care of the chronically ill, severely disabled, and/or the frail elderly, whether the care is institutional or home based. The campaign utilizes congressional testimony and public education to accomplish its goal of national coverage of long-term-care costs. As a broad-based, multiorganizational effort, the Long Term Care Campaign also emphasizes grass-roots involvement. Individuals representing their own organizations and the Long Term Care Campaign testified at every hearing of the Pepper Commission established in 1988 to study long-term care and chaired by Representative Claude Pepper of Florida. Grass-roots work of the campaign includes gathering signatures on petitions pledging support for a federal social insurance program, sponsoring town meetings, debates, and rallies, and holding house parties to view the video *Third Step to Dignity*.

The campaign sponsors educational events for policymakers, called Family Caregiver Days. In 1989, one such program involved seventy-five federal lawmakers in one-day, one-to-one caretaking experiences for the severely disabled across the country.

PUBLICATIONS

The Long Term Care Campaign publishes a bimonthly newsletter, the *Long Term Care Campaign Insider's Update*, which is sent to all national members, as well as state and local groups. The campaign offers brief fact sheets about long-term care, caregivers, and financing resources, for example. The organization issues a brief bibliography of key sources and a background paper of ten long-term-care legislative principles. The campaign has produced and distributes a video, *Third Step to Dignity* (1988).

JIMMY E. W. MEYER

LONG-TERM CARE CHOICES

See National Council on the Aging Constituent Unit: National Institute on Community-Based Long-Term Care.

M

MARGARET BLENKER RESEARCH CENTER
See Benjamin Rose Institute.

MARGARET S. MAHLER INSTITUTE
See Gray Panthers Project Fund.

MARGARET WAGNER HOUSE
See Benjamin Rose Institute.

MATURITY NEWS SERVICE
See American Association of Retired Persons.

MENTORS IN SERVICE TO YOUTH PROGRAM
See Generations Together.

MID-AMERICA CONGRESS ON AGING (MACA)
P.O. Box 99
Blue Springs, Missouri 64013
(816) 229–5078   FAX (816) 229–1676
   Mid-America Congress on Aging (MACA) is a nonprofit organization dedicated to increasing the quality of life for older Americans. It is an alliance of service providers, health care professionals, educators, students, older adults, and state and area agencies on aging personnel, primarily from Illinois, Iowa, Kansas, Missouri, Nebraska, and Wisconsin. Since 1977, MACA has served as a network of information and a training resource for interested persons, professionals, and organizations in the multidisciplinary field of aging.

ORGANIZATION AND FUNDING

The Mid-America Congress on Aging is composed of approximately 600 members and is governed by a Board of Directors. The elected board includes an Executive Committee, composed of the President, Past-President, Vice-President, Secretary, Treasurer, and two Administrative Chairs. The group's central office in Kansas City, Kansas, is staffed by one administrative assistant.

Members of the organization contribute time and resources to help carry out the organization's activities. Funding is derived from membership dues, publication sales, and conference and workshop income. The organization receives no public monies.

Membership in MACA can be one of five types: life ($200), three year ($100), individual ($40), student ($25), or senior ($25). Most members are people in occupations and organizations that serve an elderly clientele. For example, most of the nutrition directors (in charge of Meals on Wheels types of programs), community senior center directors, and area agency staff members in the core six-state area have MACA memberships. MACA members receive a listing in the MACA directory, a complimentary copy of the directory, and a bimonthly newsletter. They are entitled to discounts on conference and workshop fees, MACA publications, American Society on Aging* publications, and Terra Nova Film videotapes and films on aging.

The Mid-America Congress on Aging offers conferences and workshops for its members and others interested in aging. These activities help to maintain the network, inculcate new members, disseminate information, and provide training for people working in the field. Most important is the annual conference designed and conducted by MACA members. The annual conference site alternates among midwestern cities. Recent conferences have been held in St. Louis, Omaha, Chicago, and Kansas City. Between annual conferences, MACA offers shorter meetings at various times and locations in the Midwest, typically focusing on a single issue of interest and concern to those involved in service or advocacy for the elderly.

POLICY CONCERNS AND TACTICS

MACA focuses on affecting state policy in the Midwest. Issues of major concern to the organization are catastrophic-care insurance, nursing home reform, and reauthorization of the Older Americans Act. MACA attempts to influence policy mainly through networking and publications.

PUBLICATIONS

The *MACA Exchange* is a newsletter published six times a year and sent to every member. In addition to a calendar of conferences, meetings, and events of interest to those in the aging field, the newsletter provides information on current topics and issues of local, regional, and national concern. Through this publication, members share information, ideas, and accomplishments. Program innovations, grants, new publications, and audiovisuals relevant to aging are announced and discussed. Reaching a large and diverse membership, the *MACA Exchange* conveys to its subscribers a sense of belonging to a closely knit community whose common bond is involvement and interest in the field of aging.

MACA also publishes for its members a *Membership Resource and Networking Directory* (which can be obtained by nonmembers for $35). Members' names, areas of expertise, addresses, and telephone numbers are included in the directory, which provides access to a large number of agencies, organizations, and individuals connected with the field of aging in the central states.

GRETCHEN J. HILL

MORNINGSIDE HOUSE
See Aging in America.

MORNINGSIDE HOUSE NURSING HOME
See Aging in America.

N
——————— / ———————

NATIONAL ACTION FORUM FOR MIDLIFE AND OLDER WOMEN (NAFOW)

c/o Jane Porcino
P.O. Box 816
Stony Brook, New York 11790–0609

The National Action Forum for Midlife and Older Women (NAFOW) is a nonprofit organization founded to further the interests of midlife and older women in the United States and abroad. It serves as a resource center for the information needs of individual women, the professionals working with them, organizations, and the media, focusing on new developments and research in the field of aging women.

ORIGIN AND DEVELOPMENT

NAFOW was created in 1981 when founder Jane Porcino organized a questionable claim conference on the unique health concerns of older women. The three-day meeting, funded by the U.S. Administration on Aging, was held at the State University of New York, Stony Brook. Participants wanted to continue the dialogue and exchange of information; the result was the formation of NAFOW.

NAFOW's primary goals are information dissemination and public education to heighten awareness of the concerns of midlife and older women. These functions are accomplished through lectures, seminars, and especially the quarterly publication of its newsletter, *Hot Flash*. NAFOW encourages research in the field of aging and supports the development of pertinent community resources such as hospice programs and cooperative housing.

In 1987, NAFOW created the International Action Forum for Midlife and Older Women, a network for information exchange. The international component includes members from Australia, Canada, Great Britain, France, Israel, Japan, and Sweden.

ORGANIZATION AND FUNDING

NAFOW has a seventeen-member editorial board, with Jane Porcino as the Editor-in-Chief and Gunilla Myrberg as the European coordinator. The organization relies totally on its volunteer force. Funding comes from contributions and membership dues. An individual membership is $25 per year and includes a subscription to the newsletter. In 1991, NAFOW had about 1,500 members.

POLICY CONCERNS AND TACTICS

NAFOW affects policy chiefly through education, networking, and resource sharing via its newsletter. Each issue of *Hot Flash* presents the "Action Agenda," outlining current legislation and its relevance to older women and often naming a contact person for more information. Readers are encouraged to write to their representatives to voice opinions on specific bills.

PUBLICATIONS

NAFOW's major publication is *Hot Flash: Newsletter for Midlife and Older Women*, disseminated to members four times a year and focusing on the health, legal, social, and personal concerns of aging women. This publication reports on current legislation of interest to older women and on topics such as health care issues, housing, and bereavement, as well as book and literature reviews in related fields. Jane Porcino's two books, *Growing Older, Getting Better; A Handbook for the Second Half of Life* (1983) and *Living Longer, Living Better: Adventures in Community Housing for People in the Second Half of Life* (1991), are also offered through the organization.

SUSAN ABRAHAM

NATIONAL ACTION FORUM FOR OLDER WOMEN
See National Action Forum for Midlife and Older Women.

NATIONAL ALLIANCE OF SENIOR CITIZENS (NASC)
1700 18th Street, N.W., Suite 401
Washington, D.C. 20009
(202) 986–0117   FAX (202) 986–2974

The National Alliance of Senior Citizens (NASC) is a private, nonprofit organization with over 2 million members throughout the United States. Its purpose is to provide a voice for "responsible seniors" on national, state, and local policy issues, advocating a sound fiscal policy and emphasizing the values of individuality and personal freedom.

ORIGIN AND DEVELOPMENT

Founded in 1974, NASC has an interest in long-term care and health care, in Social Security and pension policy, and in elderly crime-protection issues. Priorities for the 1990s and beyond are to eliminate government impediments to good health care, require firms to fund pensions fully, and require mandatory Individual Retirement Accounts for young persons in lieu of Social Security.

ORGANIZATION AND FUNDING

NASC has a professional staff of three, a membership of 105,000, and an annual operating budget of over $500,000. Seven members serve as the Board of Directors; this body is responsible for organizational policy. Lawrence Bivins was the group's Executive Director in 1991. NASC carries out a direct-mail membership campaign, acquiring new members, dues, and contributions.

The organization accepts no government funds. Income is generated from individual membership dues (70%), additional fund raising (25%), and foundation grants (5%).

NASC's focus is broad; the organization maintains Advisory Council Chairs in such areas as Adult Education, Budgeting, Consumerism, Crime, Economics, Election Laws, Employment Security, Family Life, Gerontology, Health Care, Housing, Nursing Homes, Nutrition, Pension and Retirement Benefits, Political Action, Productivity, Retirement Centers, Social Security, Taxation, Veterans Affairs, Volunteerism, and Welfare.

NASC has a library for political and general research and sponsors a Person of the Year and Lifetime Achievement awards honoring individuals for outstanding service to the senior community.

POLICY CONCERNS AND TACTICS

NASC advocates for the advancement of senior Americans through control of government spending, even for old-age programs. NASC's purpose is to inform its membership and the American public of the needs of senior citizens and of the programs and policies being carried out by the government and other specified groups. NASC utilizes mass mailings to bring attention to their cause.

NASC represents the views of its constituency before Congress and state legislatures. NASC has worked to eliminate earning limits on Social Security and to eliminate benefits for children from Social Security and has advocated for the death penalty for crimes against the elderly. In 1989, NASC pushed for the repeal of the 1988 Medicare Catastrophic Coverage Act.

PUBLICATIONS

NASC's bimonthly newsletter is *Senior Guardian*.

Further Information

Christine L. Day, *What Older Americans Think: Interest Groups and Aging Policy* (Princeton, N.J.: Princeton University Press, 1990).

JOAN ORGAN

NATIONAL ASSOCIATION FOR HISPANIC ELDERLY
See Asociacion Nacional Pro Personas Mayores.

NATIONAL ASSOCIATION FOR HOME CARE (NAHC)
519 C Street, N.E.
Washington, D.C. 20002–5809
(202) 547–7424   FAX (202) 547–3540

The National Association for Home Care (NAHC) is a trade association that represents the nation's home health agencies, hospices, and homemaker–home health aide services. Its membership is composed of corporations, institutions, and individuals who provide health care and supportive services for the elderly and disabled who require care in their own homes.

ORIGIN AND DEVELOPMENT

NAHC was established in Washington, D.C., in 1982 as the result of a merger between the National Association of Home Health Agencies (NAHHA) and the Council of Home Health Agencies. The Council of Home Health Agencies was an informal working group of the Community Health Services division of the National League for Nursing.

NAHC was founded to promote the development of the home care industry. Its major goals are to unify the home care industry; provide higher standards of service for home care patients; lobby, educate, and consult with legislative, governmental, and private sector bodies affecting policy and financing in home care; and collect and disseminate information and statistics about the home care market.

NAHC sponsors an annual conference with exhibitions about the home health care industry. The association provides the following services for its members: educational opportunities, legal and accounting consultation, insurance discounts, legislation and regulatory assistance, and an information service.

ORGANIZATION AND FUNDING

The NAHC is governed by a twenty-three-member Board of Directors elected at the annual meeting. The board is structured to represent both geographic and organizational differences among home care providers. Nine sections of home care (voluntary, corporate, institution sponsored, official, private not-for-profit, state association, proprietary, hospice, and homemaker–home health aide) and ten federal regions are represented on the board. The President manages the organization and the sixty-person staff.

In 1991, NAHC had 5,500 members. There are five membership categories:

1. Provider members: Organizations whose primary purpose is to deliver health and social services directly to the sick and disabled in their own homes. There are two types of provider members: free-standing (individually owned and operated) and corporate/subcorporate (agencies with multiple branches)

2. Affiliate members: State and home care associations, which also constitute the NAHC Forum of State Associations

3. Associate members: Commercial suppliers and vendors to the home care industry

4. Allied members: Health groups with an interest in home care, such as consumer health organizations, schools of nursing, medical libraries, and universities

5. Individual members: People employed by or associated with NAHC, provider member agencies, or individual consultants and students

With an annual operating budget of $5 million, NAHC is funded primarily by membership fees, meeting revenues, proceeds from exhibitions, and the annual meeting. Additional revenue is earned from the sale of publications and advertising in its magazine.

POLICY CONCERNS AND TACTICS

NAHC represents home health care agencies and hospices in Washington, D.C. Its major concerns are to affect and support legislation regarding home care and to increase the visibility of home care services. NAHC establishes its priorities for the year by surveying its membership and developing a Blueprint for Action. This agenda is distributed at an annual legislative conference held by NAHC each spring. During the conference, NAHC invites all home care agencies to come to Washington and lobby for home care initiatives. NAHC numbers among its successes reinstitution of the hospital wage index, extension of the waiver of liability presumption for hospices through 1995, and assistance in creating the draft of the standards on home health care for the Joint Commission on Accreditation of Healthcare Organizations. The association also maintains close relationships with its affiliates, the Center for Health Care Law, the National Association for Physicians in Home Care, the Homemaker–Health Aide Association of America, and the Hospice Association of America.

ELECTORAL ACTIVITY

NAHC operates a political action committee registered as the National Association for Home Care Congressional Action Committee (NAHC-CAC). The committee contributes to congressional elections. In 1990, the NAHC-CAC contributed $24,750 to thirty-one Democratic candidates and $3,400 to five Republican candidates, with contributions ranging from $250 to $2,000. Two

Democratic candidates for the House of Representatives from California, Henry A. Waxman and Fortney Stark, received the largest amounts.

PUBLICATIONS

NAHC issues the following publications: *Caring* (monthly magazine), *NAHC Report* (weekly update), *Home Care News* (monthly newspaper), and the *National Home Care and Hospice Directory* (annual).

KIMBERLY S. LENAHAN
QIUSHA MA

NATIONAL ASSOCIATION FOR HOME HEALTH AGENCIES
See Foundation for Hospice and Homecare.

NATIONAL ASSOCIATION FOR SENIOR LIVING INDUSTRIES (NASLI)
184 Duke of Gloucester Street
Annapolis, Maryland 21401–2523
(301) 263–0991   FAX (301) 263–1262

The National Association for Senior Living Industries (NASLI) "serves as an umbrella organization for groups seeking to serve the mature market." NASLI is the international network of businesses, associations, governments, and professionals devoted to improving the quality of life for senior citizens by promoting multiple-industry approaches and opportunities in the marketplace. Formed to help businesses and service organizations worldwide consider ways to meet the shelter, health service, and consumer product needs of the older population, NASLI seeks a planned, consumer-sensitive, and interdisciplinary approach to new opportunities and challenges in the growing market to older persons.

ORIGIN AND DEVELOPMENT

NASLI was founded on July 15, 1985. Forty-five individuals from across the United States were present at the association's organizational meeting in Washington, D.C. Among the prominent NASLI founders were David B. Wolfe (NASLI's first President) and representatives from some of America's leading senior-related organizations and corporations, including the American Association of Retired Persons[*], the Marriott Corporation, Oxford Development, the Institute for Technology Development, Arthur Schuster, the University of Maryland at Baltimore, and Procter & Gamble. The late Rep. Claude Pepper (D, Florida) also played an integral role in the early activities of NASLI.

It pursues four broad goals: to support efforts to redefine the meaning of aging in society, to provide high-quality products and services responsive to the total needs of older persons, to improve and enhance industry skills in order to ensure the continuing satisfaction of older consumers' requirements, and to promote the skills and experience of older adults as a valuable resource.

ORGANIZATION AND FUNDING

Members range from Fortune 500 corporations to nonprofit associations and reflect every professional discipline related to the senior market. NASLI's membership has grown to over 700 corporations and organizations. Members span the globe, from all fifty states in the United States to an international delegation with representation from companies in Japan, Great Britain, Sweden, Australia, Spain, France, Africa, and Canada.

NASLI is organized into ten district professional councils: Aging Organizations; Consumer Products and Services; Developers, Owners and Operators; Education and Research; Financial; Health Care; Legal and Professional Services; Management and Contract Services; Marketing and Advertising; and Planning and Design.

NASLI has a staff of ten persons headed by an Executive Director. In 1991, Darryl R. Callahan held this position. The annual operating budget ranges between $1.5 million and $2 million. Funding is generated from members' dues and conference fees.

POLICY CONCERNS AND TACTICS

NASLI sponsors and co-sponsors the leading educational and networking events in the senior market. Each year the NASLI EXPO attracts the world's business leaders for three days of educational programs, networking, and the largest trade show in the senior-living industry. The association also hosts an annual winter conference for marketing professionals in health care, housing, and consumer products and services. In addition to NASLI's two major national conferences, the association runs regional programs throughout the year, providing members with educational and networking opportunities close to their business headquarters.

PUBLICATIONS

NASLI members benefit from a wide range of publications, audio cassettes, and resource guides. *The NASLI Membership Directory and Buyer's Guide*, updated annually, is used by business leaders in the senior market as a valuable industry guide. NASLI members also receive *NASLI News*, a monthly newsletter dedicated exclusively to member news items and senior market issues. *Spectrum* magazine (monthly) offers feature articles on the wide variety of topics of interest to professionals serving seniors.

To provide NASLI members with the most comprehensive business tools available, NASLI also makes a complete catalog of resources available. Among these many NASLI resources are *The Dictionary of Terms for Senior Citizens and the Industries That Serve Them* (1989) and *Life Satisfaction: The Missing Focus in Marketing to Seniors* (1987).

All of NASLI's major educational programs are professionally recorded as another way to keep members current on the latest innovations and business techniques. The NASLI catalog of audiotapes includes leading mature-market experts speaking on a wide variety of topics.

JOAN ORGAN

NATIONAL ASSOCIATION OF AREA AGENCIES ON AGING
1112 16th Street, N.W., Suite 100
Washington, D.C. 20036
(202) 296-8130   FAX (202) 296-8134

The National Association of Area Agencies on Aging (NAAAA) is a private, nonprofit national advocacy and public interest organization. Its purpose is to represent the interests and concerns of the more than 600 Area Agencies on Aging (AAAs), also known as "the triple As," which were established under the provisions of the 1973 amendments to the Older Americans Act (OAA). The NAAAA seeks to promote ongoing communication within the national governmental network on aging, which consists of the AAAs, the State Units on Aging (SUAs), and the national Administration on Aging (AoA).

ORIGIN AND DEVELOPMENT

The NAAAA was incorporated in 1975 in conjunction with the mandates of the Older Americans Act. It provides legislative information, technical assistance, and training related to the management of the AAAs and programs for persons aged 60 years and older. Through those activities, the organization assists the AAAs in their development of case management systems as the major component of comprehensive, community-based, long-term-care services to help older persons remain independent for as long as possible in their homes and communities. While the organization has always been located in Washington, D.C., NAAAA recently moved to a more central location in the nation's capital, to better serve its broad constituency of the AAAs, the SUAs, local service providers, AAA Advisory Council members, and academic institutions.

Since its inception, the goals of NAAAA have been to advocate for older persons at the national level, to advance new approaches to serving the elderly, to promote and achieve a reasonable and realistic national policy on aging, and to disseminate information to the federal government, the private sector, and the general public.

ORGANIZATION AND FUNDING

The NAAAA is managed by a twenty-two-member Board of Directors and a professional staff of nine, headed by the Executive Director (in 1990, Jonathan Linkous). Local affiliates consist of the more than 500 AAAs that are designated as corporate members of the organization. NAAAA policy is established by a vote of the board and, on major issues, by a vote of the membership. Of the two standing committees, Public Policy and Annual Conference, the former often makes recommendations to the board concerning the organization's policies.

Major funding sources are members' dues, conference revenues, and corporate foundations. Of its annual budget, which ranges from $500,000 to $1 million, ''99% is devoted to elderly issues and concerns.'' The NAAAA holds an annual summer conference, usually in July (scheduled for Salt Lake City, Utah, in 1992). NAAAA's annual Training Institute and workshop sessions are designed largely to develop improved management techniques and practices for AAAs and service providers. Occasionally NAAAA provides special training seminars for new AAA directors.

POLICY CONCERNS AND TACTICS

The primary policy concerns of NAAAA are Older Americans Act programs, followed by transportation, home health care and long-term care, nursing home reform, Medicare and Medicaid programs and funding, and public housing for the elderly. Other major policy issues for the organization are the equitable distribution of resources between health and supportive services for those elderly in need; employment for the elderly; elder abuse; intergenerational issues, broadly defined; and increased housing for low-income elderly.

The NAAAA seeks to influence public policy in several ways: testimony before Congress, provision of information to national legislators and staff, and encouragement of grass-roots activities targeted at individual representatives and specific congressional committees. The organization also conducts and publishes research on specific issues; however, its most important and successful policy tactics are providing information to Congress and encouraging members to contact their national legislators.

The organization has testified before several congressional committees, including House Appropriations, the House and Senate committees on aging, and the two chambers' respective committees on Education and Labor and Labor and Human Resources. NAAAA testimony has focused primarily on OAA funding and reauthorization concerns, but other activities have emphasized the nursing home provisions of the Omnibus Reconciliation Act of 1987 and the Job Training Partnership Act. NAAAA coordinates its actions with the American Association of Retired Persons*, the National Council on the Aging,* and the National Association of State Units on Aging*.

ELECTORAL ACTIVITY

Although the association acts as a lobby, it is a nonpartisan organization and does not contribute to political campaigns. It is possible, however, that some electoral activities are carried on at the local level by NAAAA members.

PUBLICATIONS

The NAAAA publishes a monthly newsletter for its membership, *Network News*, and an annual *Directory of State and Area Agencies on Aging*. Additionally, the organization publishes a number of resource and training guides and manuals such as *Technical Assistance Guide to Program and Management Ac-*

complishments of Area Agencies on Aging (1991) and *Linking Hospitals and the Community—A Guide for Community Agencies* (1988). NAAAA also publishes a brochure series covering basic information useful to family caregivers.

Further Information

"NASUA and NAAAA Change Formal Relationship," *Older American Reports* (May 15, 1987): 8; "NAAAA Gears Up for the Annual Conference." *Aging Network News* 5 (1988): 17–18.

PHOEBE S. LIEBIG

NATIONAL ASSOCIATION OF HOME DELIVERED AND CONGREGATE MEAL PROVIDERS
See National Association of Meal Programs.

NATIONAL ASSOCIATION OF JEWISH HOMES FOR THE AGED
See North American Association of Jewish Homes for the Aged.

NATIONAL ASSOCIATION OF MEAL PROGRAMS (NAMP)
204 E Street, N.E.
Washington, D.C. 20002
(202) 547–6157   FAX (202) 547–6348

The National Association of Meal Programs (NAMP) is the oldest and largest association for professionals providing nutrition services to the elderly and other adults, such as the disabled and persons with AIDS. "NAMP is the voice of senior meals programs."

ORIGIN AND DEVELOPMENT

NAMP was founded in 1973 by a group of senior meal providers who decided to share common concerns and to develop solutions for problems encountered in providing meals either in congregate settings or through home delivery. Initially, NAMP was a loosely organized grass-roots association called the National Association of Home Delivered and Congregate Meal Providers. Its members met once a year, and it was headquartered in Pittsburgh. In 1983, NAMP hired an Executive Director. Two years later, the group's main office moved to Washington, D.C., in recognition of the need to have a full-time staff to carry out its increasing number of activities.

The meals programs operated by NAMP members provide over 140 million meals a year. About 52 percent of its members provide both congregate and home-delivered meals, and the remaining 48 percent are formal Meals-on-Wheels programs. In 1990, there were 550 individual members and 100 corporate members, representing firms involved in food, equipment, services, and products for nutrition programs. NAMP has 10 regional groups, organized according to the standard federal regions, 52 state groups, and 400 local groups representing approximately 4,000 Meals-on-Wheels programs and 15,000 congregate nutrition sites, as well as health and social service agencies. NAMP's major mission is to improve the quality of life and promote independent and community-based living arrangements for the disabled and homebound by delivering nutritionally balanced meals and referring those individuals to additional programs. It seeks to achieve this goal through professional development and training, advocacy, and communications activities.

ORGANIZATION AND FUNDING

The policies of NAMP are guided by a sixteen-member Board of Directors and are carried out by three professional staff members. In 1990, Gail Martin was the Executive Director and Michael Giuffrida the Administrative Director. The organization's policies are established by membership surveys, staff research, and board vote, as well as by canvassing the full membership on particular issues. NAMP national committees provide opportunities for all members to participate in the work of the association. Some of the committees are: Legislative and Advocacy, Nutrition and Technical Assistance, Public Relations, Development, and the National Conference. NAMP has held sixteen annual training conferences and vendor exhibits since 1975. Usually taking place in September, the national conference attracts more than 300 attendees. Regional and state meetings also are held; many are approved for continuing-education credit, as is the annual conference.

Future goals of NAMP focus on the development of public-private partnerships, the elimination of waiting lists for clients, the coordination of new technology and aging, and the revision of menu standards to reflect the updated Recommended Daily Allowances. More immediate goals include the development of a national senior meals directory, a feasibility study on the concept of a seven-day frozen meal system funded through a U.S. Administration on Aging (AoA) grant, and increased funding for other NAMP-sponsored projects.

The major portion of NAMP's annual budget of $200,000 comes from general fund raising (53%) and from individual membership dues (22%). The remainder is derived from corporate memberships, grants from foundations, and other sources.

POLICY CONCERNS AND TACTICS

The premier policy issue for NAMP is nutritional care and its relationship to long-term care, followed by health problems of the elderly, transportation alternatives, public housing, and Social Security benefits. Also of interest to the NAMP membership are legal problems, Medicare and Medicaid programs and funding, elder abuse, and employment opportunities for the elderly.

The organization seeks to influence public policy through testimony before Congress, the provision of information to legislators and congressional staff, and the encouragement of NAMP members to voice their concerns to their representatives and specific congressional committees. To a lesser degree, NAMP also conducts and publishes research on trends in meals programs, which is then used as the basis for stated positions, "thus impacting congressional issues and regulations." In March 1990, NAMP presented testimony before the House Select Committee on Aging concerning the reauthorization of the Older Americans Act. NAMP also testified before the House Agriculture Committee on Commodities in November 1989. NAMP participates in A.S.A.P.* (Advocates Senior Alert Process), a networking project of Families U.S.A. Foundation*, and the Leadership Council of Aging Organizations* and coordinates its actions with the National Council on the Aging*, the National Association of State Units on Aging*, and the National Association of Area Agencies on Aging*.

ELECTORAL ACTIVITY

NAMP does not engage directly in electoral activity. Rather, it focuses on grass-roots public relations activities such as volunteer recognition awards and a speakers' bureau.

PUBLICATIONS

NAMP publishes a bimonthly newsletter, *Between the Lines*, which usually includes a Washington update and information on the activities of others in the field and related areas. The *Annual Membership Directory* lists other professionals in the field and provides information on NAMP corporate members and their products and services.

PHOEBE S. LIEBIG

NATIONAL ASSOCIATION OF NUTRITION AND AGING SERVICES PROGRAMS (NANASP)
2675 44th Street, S.W., Suite 305
Grand Rapids, Michigan 49509
(800) 999–6262   FAX (616) 531–3103

The National Association of Nutrition and Aging Services Programs (NANASP) is a private, nonprofit professional society representing the interests of service providers in the aging network. Dedicated to promoting the growth and improvement of community-based services for older Americans, NANASP seeks to provide avenues for training and communication that are meaningful to service providers working in the field of aging.

ORIGIN AND DEVELOPMENT

NANASP was founded in 1976 and was initially known as the National Association of Title VII Directors, its designation under the 1972 Older Americans Act (OAA) Amendments. The group changed its name in 1978. Its membership includes agencies or organizations that provide direct nutrition and related services. NANASP emphasizes the need for OAA-funded nutrition programs to present a holistic approach to the needs of older persons.

Major emphasis is on community service system development, nutrition, professional education and training, minority elderly, older women, employment, rural elderly, transportation, and voluntarism. NANASP has developed standards for both congregate and home-delivered programs. NANASP's future priorities include the continuing development of community-based care systems, third-party reimbursement for in-home support services, and complementary roles between private industry and nonprofit sector service delivery.

ORGANIZATION AND FUNDING

NANASP's members include over 1,000 directors and staff of congregate and home-delivered nutrition services programs for the elderly. The Executive Director in 1991 was Connie Benton Wolfe.

NANASP receives some funding from the federal government. Support is also generated from members' dues and conference revenues. NANASP maintains an annual budget of approximately $150,000 to $250,000.

POLICY CONCERNS AND TACTICS

NANASP's areas of activity include advocacy, information dissemination, professional education and training, public education and awareness, public policy formulation, applied research, and program development and implementation. NANASP educates federal legislators on the workability of the OAA at the local level, testifies in public hearings and before the House and Senate Financial Oversight committees, and works directly with both the House Select Committee and the Senate Special Committee on Aging. NANASP's membership also works to affect policy at both the regional and the state levels.

NANASP began a collaborative effort in 1991 with the National Association of State Units on Aging* (NASUA) to strengthen the OAA-supported nutrition program. The project addresses some of the program's concerns, such as the difficulty of attracting the younger older person and better serving minority and frail elderly. Noting that older Americans receive about 250 million meals annually under OAA auspices, the NANASP's Executive Director stated that the NASUA-NANASP project will help make the most efficient use of nutrition resources. This educational effort will include sponsoring regional training sessions and the production of a manual.

NANASP is a participant in the Leadership Council of Aging Organizations*.

PUBLICATIONS

NANASP publishes *NANASP News*, a quarterly association newsletter; an annual report, *Monthly Membership Updates*; and the monthly *Special Bulletins*. The organization also issues *The Aging Network's Guide to USDA* (1988).

Further Information. "New Project to Enhance Nutrition Program," *Aging Network News* 7, no. 9 (January 1991): 3.

JOAN ORGAN

NATIONAL ASSOCIATION OF OLDER WORKER EMPLOYMENT SERVICES

See National Council on the Aging Constituent Unit: National Association of Older Worker Employment Services.

NATIONAL ASSOCIATION OF RETIRED CIVIL EMPLOYEES

See National Association of Retired Federal Employees.

NATIONAL ASSOCIATION OF RETIRED FEDERAL EMPLOYEES (NARFE)

1533 New Hampshire Avenue, N.W.
Washington, D.C. 20036
(202) 234–0832   FAX (202) 797–9697

The National Association of Retired Federal Employees (NARFE) is an organization that protects the individual and family interests of civilians who have retired or who will retire from federal service. NARFE supports beneficial legislation and opposes legislation detrimental to its membership.

ORIGIN AND DEVELOPMENT

NARFE came into existence in 1947. It was formerly the National Association of Retired Civil Employees, first organized in 1921.

ORGANIZATION AND FUNDING

In 1991, NARFE had 490,000 members from its 1,700 local chapters. Membership is open to retired civil employees of the U.S. government or its agencies, as well as those receiving workmen's compensation, their spouses, and survivors, and any federal employee of at least five years who is under the civil service or federal employee retirement system.

In 1991, NARFE was under the direction of H. T. Morressey, the President, and had a professional staff of twenty-five. There are fourteen members on the Board of Directors, including four elected resident officers and ten elected field vice-presidents. The board carries out association policy, established by a vote of the elected delegates to biennal national conventions and supplemented by policy decisions of the National Executive Board. NARFE's budget, supported exclusively by membership dues of fifteen dollars per year, is $5 million.

The major objectives of the organization are clear and direct:

1. To sponsor and support legislation that protects the earned benefits and general welfare of its members

2. To oppose legislation that would adversely affect member retirement and health benefit programs

3. To react promptly to biased or unfair commentary in local and national media

4. To keep members informed about issues that affect them

5. To assist members regarding problems with the Office of Personnel Management

6. To kindle public appreciation of federal employees

7. To strengthen the political influence of federal employees

8. To cooperate with other organizations having similar legislative concerns

9. To encourage members to work for the good of their communities

POLICY CONCERNS AND TACTICS

NARFE's primary concern is protecting the civil service retirement system. NARFE contends that there are well-organized groups that believe that government has become inefficient and too expensive. This belief has resulted in cutting benefits from civil service retirees. According to NARFE, the power groups responsible use half-truths and exaggeration to convince the public that the government is out of control. To protect its members, one of the primary objectives of NARFE is to blunt the perceived misinformation by publicizing factual material about the civil service retirement system.

NARFE educates its members through newsletters. The newsletters keep members informed about legislation that might negatively affect the elderly, as well as NARFE's own membership, and encourage members to contact members of Congress and congressional committees when legislation is sponsored that threatens to cut benefits.

NARFE is active in lobbying and frequently testifies before Congress. It has appeared before the following congressional committees, among others: the Ways and Means and Post Office and Civil Service committees of the House and the Finance and Government Affairs committees in the Senate. In the late 1980s, NARFE proposed and pushed the Gorton amendment to the Gramm-Rudman-Hollings law, protecting cost-of-living adjustments (COLAs); in the 1990s, cuts in COLAs are still a concern with the new budget process, called Gramm-Rudman-Hollings III. Utilizing grass-roots pressure and letter campaigns, NARFE successfully countered damaging budget proposals in the late 1980s. Additionally, NARFE works in the courts when members have legal problems concerning their retirement and runs preretirement programs at no cost to the government.

NARFE's future goals are maintaining the purchasing power of retirement income and ensuring adequate, affordable health care services.

ELECTORAL ACTIVITY

As part of NARFE's political activism, the NARFE Political Action Committee (NARFE-PAC) was formed in 1981. In order to receive NARFE-PAC funds, candidates must request them from the PAC.

PUBLICATIONS

NARFE has several publications that educate the membership at large: *Retirement Life*, a monthly magazine sent to dues-paying members; the *Monthly Bulletin*, with general news; the *Service Officer News*, issued quarterly and routed to federation chapter presidents; *PR News and Views*, circulated bimonthly to federation chapter presidents; and the *Washington Letter*, produced semimonthly and mailed to legislative officers and district offices.

DONALD SHAFER

NATIONAL ASSOCIATION OF RSVP DIRECTORS (NARSVPD)
703 Main Street
Paterson, New Jersey 07503
(201) 881–6536   FAX (201) 279–6755

The National Association of RSVP Directors (NARSVPD) supports and provides visibility for the Retired Senior Volunteer Program (RSVP), facilitates communication among RSVP directors, and promotes the physical and mental health of older Americans through its advocacy of volunteerism for older people.

ORIGIN AND DEVELOPMENT

At a meeting of RSVP directors in Chicago in 1976, some of the directors realized that they were striving for similar goals but that they had little opportunity to share information or to offer assistance to each other. To address communication problems and to increase the visibility of RSVP, NARSVPD was founded. Approximately 600 of the 750 directors of the Retired Senior Volunteer Programs across the country belong to NARSVPD.

ORGANIZATION AND FUNDING

The fourteen-member Board of Directors lead the organization. Board membership comprises four nationally elected officers, nine regionally elected representatives, and the immediate Past President of NARSVPD. The board meets twice a year, one of these meetings being held in conjunction with the annual meeting of NARSVPD. The organization employs one staff person in Washington, D.C., on a consulting basis and one part-time clerical assistant, but has no other paid staff.

Membership dues, which are $35 for individuals, provide over half of the organization's annual budget of $35,000–$40,000. The remainder comes from sales of volunteer recognition products to members (pins, trophies, and so forth to recognize volunteer service), occasional grants from private sources for specific projects, and corporate and associate dues (which were $50 and $17.50, respectively, in 1991). Corporations that support the organization's mission are eligible for membership but have no voting privileges and cannot hold office. Staff members of RSVP programs and individuals interested in the organization's goals are eligible for associate membership. Although RSVP receives federal funding, NARSVPD does not. The Board of Directors determines and votes on the policies of the organization.

POLICY CONCERNS AND TACTICS

In general, NARSVPD advocates programs that promote productive aging and volunteerism. It supports legislation that will make it possible for older Americans to enjoy the physical and mental health benefits associated with volunteer service to others.

The organization furthers these goals by encouraging its members and persons sympathetic to RSVP to write to members of Congress, by supplying information to congressional authorization and appropriations committees, and by testifying before Congress. Directors of RSVP also invite their local congressional representatives to visit their projects and to attend award ceremonies for volunteers. The organization does not have a political action committee.

NARSVPD testifies every three years in favor of the reauthorization of the Domestic Volunteer Service Act before House and Senate committees, encourages its members to write to the chairperson of the appropriations committee for the act, and participates in oversight hearings. The organization also has testified before a hearing of the Public Health Service to examine the opportunities and challenges for preventing disease and promoting the health of older Americans. In 1990, the group appeared before the Labor and Human Resources Committee of the Senate to advocate for more volunteer opportunities for older adults in pending national service legislation.

Other concerns of NARSVPD include adequate federal funding for RSVP programs, the support of initiatives that encourage volunteerism among men and among people from lower income levels, the need for another White House Conference on Aging, and the advocacy of increased in-home services for the frail elderly. The organization also supports programs designed to increase the number of senior volunteers in adult literacy programs, respite care, and such intergenerational projects as library programs for children who are alone at home after school.

NARSVPD works in coalition with the National Association of Senior Companion Project Directors[*] and the National Association of Foster Grandparents. It is an active member of the Leadership Council of Aging Organizations[*] and A.S.A.P.[*] (Advocates Senior Alert Process).

PUBLICATIONS

The organization publishes a quarterly newsletter, *NARSVPD News,* to alert members to issues affecting their programs and to the activities of the organization.

Further Information

Frances Butler, and Helen Kershner, "Productive Aging and Senior Volunteerism: Is the U.S. Experience Relevant," *Ageing International* 15 (December

1988): 15; June Divan, "The National Association of RSVP Directors," *Aging Network News* 4 (April 1988): 5.

JEAN R. LINDERMAN

NATIONAL ASSOCIATION OF SENIOR COMPANION PROJECT DIRECTORS (NASCPD)

2001 South State Street, Suite S–1500
Salt Lake City, Utah 84190–2300
(801) 468–2744   FAX (801) 468–3987

The National Association of Senior Companion Project Directors (NASCPD) is a national, nonprofit, professional organization working to address the concerns and needs of senior companion programs (SCPs), which stress low-income elderly working with other frail elderly, primarily in their own homes. Its main missions are to foster communication among project directors, organizations, and agencies serving senior companion programs and ACTION offices and to advocate for the enhancement and expansion of those programs.

ORIGIN AND DEVELOPMENT

The NASCPD was founded in 1978, largely because John Prybl, the first President of NASCPD, saw the need for SCP directors to work more closely with each other and with their colleagues in other programs administered by ACTION, an independent government agency that coordinates volunteer activities. The organization was created to provide opportunities for networking and education for and by SCP directors, similar to the National Association of Retired Senior Volunteer Program Directors[*] (NARSVPD). More than 20,000 elderly are assisted nationally by 5,400 SCP volunteers.

The NASCPD has grown steadily and in 1990 had 130 members. The 1990 President was Dwight Rasmussen. The activities of the association and its members are guided by the Domestic Volunteer Service Act and focus heavily on the exchange of programming ideas in order to prevent duplication and to maximize the quality and level of services benefiting the aging population.

ORGANIZATION AND FUNDING

The NASCPD is governed by an Advisory Council of thirteen members, who volunteer their time. The association employs one part-time professional staff member in Washington, D.C. It convenes an annual conference, usually in October, which is open to all SCP directors. Membership dues account for approximately 90 percent of NASCPD's financial support, with the remainder derived from foundation grants. NASCPD's annual budget is $5,000 and is devoted entirely to elderly concerns and issues.

POLICY CONCERNS AND TACTICS

The NASCPD's national agenda focuses on the following broad policy issues: home health care and long-term care, Medicare and Medicaid programs and funding, respite care, community services system development, elder abuse, informal social supports for the elderly, and issues facing low-income and rural elderly. Its more specific concerns focus on the preservation of government funding for SCP projects, the expansion of existing programs, and policy and programatic issues for SCP projects.

The organization seeks to influence public policy at the national level in several ways. Primary techniques include testifing before Congress and encouraging NASCPD members to write to individual members of the House and Senate as well as specific congressional committees. In November 1989, NASCPD testified on the reauthorization of the Domestic Volunteer Service Act before the Subcommittee on Human Resources of the House Education and Labor Committee. Other policy tactics include supplying information to members and staff of Congress, often through its Washington representative, and, on a far more restricted basis, conducting and publishing research on its major concerns.

The NASCPD coordinates its activities with NARSVPD, the National Association of Foster Grandparent Project Directors, and ACTION offices. It also participates as a member of the Leadership Council of Aging Organizations*.

PUBLICATIONS

Publications are limited to a periodic *NASCPD Newsletter*, which is sent to all members. The newsletter consists of information generated by NASCPD's Washington representative on policy and funding issues.

PHOEBE S. LIEBIG

NATIONAL ASSOCIATION OF STATE UNITS ON AGING (NASUA)
2033 K Street, N.W., Suite 304
Washington, D.C. 20006
(202) 785–0707   FAX (202) 785–1929

The National Association of State Units on Aging (NASUA) is a private, national, public interest organization dedicated to providing general and specialized developmental support to state units on aging. NASUA is the articulating force at the national level through which State Units on Aging promote social policy responsive to the needs of the aging in the United States.

ORIGIN AND DEVELOPMENT

NASUA was founded in 1964, one year preceding the enactment of the Older Americans Act. It was formed as a result of the emerging realization by states that their growing populations of older adults required sharpened recognition and action. The new Older Americans Act required states to designate a unit to receive funds and to develop plans for the aged. Each State Unit on Aging is therefore an agency of the state government, designated by the governor and state legislature to administer the Older Americans Act and to serve as the focal point for all matters relating to older people in the state. Despite relatively modest funding levels, the Older Americans Act gave new impetus to the establishment of state agencies on aging and provided new members for NASUA. The association serves as an organized channel for officially designated state leaders in aging to exchange information, share experiences, and join together in taking action on behalf of the elderly.

ORGANIZATION AND FUNDING

The membership of NASUA consists of fifty-seven state and territorial governmental units charged with advancing the social and economic agendas of older persons in their respective states, generically termed State Units on Aging. In 1984, approximately 1,820 persons, primarily from state units and member agencies, staffed those units. Supported by federal grant-in-aid funds, state units have taken on the task of organizing efficient and effective systems of service delivery so that all funds available for serving older Americans come together in a smooth and planned way at the local level.

NASUA's budget is usually just over $1 million. Around half comes from the federal government. The other half represents a combination of income from dues, publication sales, and consultation fees.

Daniel A. Quirk was Executive Director of NASUA in 1990. The organization employs a staff of thirteen. Divisions include: Development, Elder Rights, Intergovernmental Relations, Long-Term Care, Program Development, Public Relations, and Systems Management. NASUA presents the Louise B. Gerrard Award annually to an individual or a group that has made a major contribution to improving the quality of life for rural older Americans.

POLICY CONCERNS AND TACTICS

NASUA's 1990 policy agenda included the development of a community-based long-term-care system that assists older people to remain in their homes and communities and an elder rights system to protect the benefits available to older people and to expand opportunities for meaningful participation in the social and economic life of the nation. NASUA has developed a variety of programs to fulfill its policy agenda. These programs provide information and expertise to states, agencies, and communities on a variety of issues. Current issues include the training of personnel, management consultation, programs to prevent and combat elder abuse and neglect, and advocacy for residents of long-term-care facilities.

The two techniques utilized most successfully by NASUA to affect public policy are supplying information to congressional representatives, senators, and staff and conducting and publishing research. In addition, NASUA has testified before committees, such as the Education and Labor Committee and the Select

Committee on Aging of the House, the Labor and Human Resources Committee and Special Committee on Aging of the Senate, and the Appropriations Committee in each chamber.

NASUA works closely with the National Association of Area Agencies on Aging.* Together they have sponsored a national training conference, designed to provide the state and area units with a forum for the development of new ideas, effective strategies, and best practices. The two associations work jointly to maintain the National Data Base on Aging, which provides information on services available for older persons and details about state and area agencies on aging. Updated annually, the database also provides information on characteristics of persons served and other statistics related to aging.

PUBLICATIONS

Publications of NASUA include the periodic *Directory of State Units on Aging* (updated in February 1991), as well as "State Action in Aging," a section of *Aging Network News* (published monthly by Hanson and Associates). Other materials include policy briefs, legislative updates, source books, professional development and training manuals, technical assistance documents, and research reports. NASUA also contributes to a taxonomy published by the U.S. Administration on Aging, *Uniform Description of Services for the Aging* (1989). In addition, NASUA maintains Age-Net, an electronic bulletin board.

ELIZABETH MIDLARSKY
GABRIELA HOHN AND ANNETTE ZYGMUNT

NATIONAL ASSOCIATION OF TITLE VII DIRECTORS
See National Association of Nutrition and Aging Services Programs.

NATIONAL BOARD FOR CERTIFICATION IN CONTINUITY OF CARE
See American Association for Continuity of Care.

NATIONAL CAUCUS AND CENTER ON BLACK AGED (NCCBA)
1424 K Street, N.W., Suite 500
Washington, D.C. 20005
(202) 637–8400   FAX (202) 347–0895

The National Caucus and Center on Black Aged (NCCBA) since 1970 has served as a nonprofit, interracial membership organization seeking to improve the quality of life for aging Americans, particularly blacks. The group advocates changes in federal and state legislation, addressing health, economic, housing, and legal concerns of older, low-income Americans. The NCCBA works for improvements in Social Security benefits, Medicare and Medicaid programs, home health care, and employment for older persons and confronts age discrimination.

ORIGIN AND DEVELOPMENT

The NCCBA was formed by the merger of the National Center on Black Aged, founded in 1970 as a research and planning organization, and the National Caucus on the Black Aged, founded in 1971 as a political interest group. By 1983, the organization had about 2,000 members and thirty chapters in twelve states. NCCBA works to rectify the situation reflected in these 1988 statistics: 12 percent of the overall elderly population in the United States live in poverty, and 32 percent of the American black elderly are poor.

ORGANIZATION AND FUNDING

The NCCBA is governed by a twenty-member Board of Directors who set and establish policy through quarterly board meetings in Washington, D.C. The staff numbers twenty-three, with fifteen serving in Washington and eight nationwide. NCCBA's 1991 President, Samuel Simmons, is a former Assistant Secretary of the U.S. Department of Housing and Urban Development and a past director of the National Center for Housing Management.

Ninety-five percent of the NCCBA's $9 million budget comes from government funding, and the remaining monies from foundation grants, individual member dues, and fund raising. In 1991, there were fifty-four chapters, with a total membership of 3,000. The organization is made up of an Executive Office and the divisions of Employment, Housing, Training, and Economic Development and Research. It is further divided into program units, for example, the New Careers Training Program for Older Workers (funded by the Job Training Partnership Act), the Title V Senior Employment Program, and the Environmental Protection Agency (EPA) Senior Environmental Employment (SEE) program. These programs and others, sponsored by the NCCBA, are concerned not only with employment but also with nursing home administration, long-term care, housing management, and commercial property maintenance.

NCCBA-sponsored employment programs involve 1,500 older people in eleven states. The organization also sponsors training and intern programs in gerontology and management and owns rental housing for the elderly. NCCBA grants scholarships and gives other awards, such as the Distinguished Service Award, established in 1986, and the Living Legacy Award, established in 1979.

POLICY CONCERNS AND TACTICS

The primary concerns of the NCCBA have been employment, housing and environment, health care, age discrimination, Social Security and pension policy, and professional education and training. In the 1990s, the organization plans to focus on Social Security, Medicare/Medicaid, and long-term-care and catastrophic health insurance.

To implement its agenda and influence public policy, the group has used a wide range of methods. It has supplied information to members of Congress and their staff and has testified before Congress. NCCBA has supported legislation such as the reauthorization of the Older Americans Act and the Medicare Catastrophic Coverage Act. It has coordinated efforts with the Families U.S.A. Foundation*, American Association of Retired Persons*, and the Commonwealth Fund. NCCBA has testified before the Special Committee on Aging, Committee on Labor and Human Resources, and the Subcommittee on Employment and Productivity in the Senate, and the House Select Committee on Aging, among others. It encourages its members to write to members of Congress and to committees and to work in the courts and on litigation. In addition, the NCCBA conducts research on issues concerning older black Americans and publishes reports on such issues as older women in the workplace and medical services in the southwestern United States.

PUBLICATIONS

The NCCBA's newsletter, distributed to members quarterly, is the *Golden Page*. It presents developments concerning elderly blacks, organizational news, and legislative updates. Published by the organization in 1988 and 1987, respectively, are *Job Placement Systems for Older Workers* (2 vols.) and *The Status of the Black Elderly in the U.S.*, a report for the Select Committee on Aging, U.S. House of Representatives. Bulletins are published irregularly, as are research reports on various topics such as employment and health concerns.

Further Information

George M. Anderson "Old and Poor in the U.S.A.," *America* 163 (November 3, 1990): 328–33.

SUSAN ABRAHAM

NATIONAL CAUCUS ON THE BLACK AGED
See National Caucus and Center on Black Aged.

NATIONAL CENTER ON BLACK AGED
See National Caucus and Center on Black Aged.

NATIONAL CENTER ON RURAL AGING (NCRA)
See National Council on the Aging Constituent Unit: National Center on Rural Aging.

NATIONAL CITIZENS' COALITION FOR NURSING HOME REFORM (NCCNHR)
1224 M Street, N.W., Suite 301
Washington, D.C. 20005–5183
(202) 393–2018   FAX (202) 393–4122

The National Citizens' Coalition for Nursing Home Reform (NCCNHR) is a nonprofit, consumer-based, membership organization concerned with improving the quality of life in nursing homes and of the services provided to residents.

The primary objective of NCCNHR is to advocate for the institutionalized elderly and the disabled on both the national and local levels. NCCNHR has also played a major role as a clearinghouse of information for other organizations serving the elderly.

ORIGIN AND DEVELOPMENT

NCCNHR was established in 1975 by representatives of existing citizen groups who recognized a need to establish improved regulations for nursing home facilities and to advocate for standards for nursing care providers. The first informal meeting of NCCNHR was organized by the Long Term Care Action Project of the National Gray Panthers so that the different member groups could meet each other and develop recommendations to present to an upcoming American Health Care Association* conference. The coalition held its first formal meeting in 1977, when it elected a steering committee, which served as a foundation for the first board of directors. The members also planned one of the coalition's first activities, a national symposium on nursing home reform.

NCCNHR quickly initiated a series of nursing home reform activities. From 1978 to 1982, the group received funding from VISTA to recruit, train, and place volunteers in nursing home projects. NCCNHR was awarded a three-year research grant in 1981 to develop the organization's Clearinghouse, a valuable source of nursing home data for interested groups and individuals.

In 1981, NCCNHR added nursing board and care issues to its agenda of reform. In response to this new focus, the coalition conducted its first national survey on Medicaid discrimination. Recently, the group has concentrated its efforts on curbing abuse of the elderly in nursing homes and promoting community support of local nursing care facilities.

NCCNHR has relied heavily on information and feedback from individual residents and local member groups. On the local and state levels, NCCNHR has organized educational forums for both policymakers and the general public to promote the exchange of ideas among advocates and to identify new policy concerns. Local consumer and professional groups have also coordinated informational seminars with NCCNHR. Since 1977, the coalition has held an annual meeting that involves representatives from state and local organizations throughout the country. The 1990 meeting, Nursing Home Reform: Something Good Is Happening, was attended by over 300 participants, including interested state and federal government officials.

ORGANIZATION AND FUNDING

NCCNHR consists of over 600 individuals and 300 group members. The organization represents members of local consumer groups, state and local long-term-care advocates, national health and professional organizations, and nursing home resident organizations. NCCNHR has seven full-time staff members based in Washington, D.C. A twenty-one-member Board of Directors was led in 1991 by the Director, Elma L. Holder. Ninety percent of NCCNHR's funding is provided by government grants, foundation grants, and funding-raising activities. The remaining monies are obtained from other foundation grants, individual membership dues, and publication proceeds.

POLICY CONCERNS AND TACTICS

NCCNHR has been extremely active in promoting legislative reforms in nursing homes since the organization's inception. In 1982, new regulations were developed by the U.S. Department of Health and Human Services (HHS) that many organizations felt would seriously undermine public inspection of nursing homes. NCCNHR led a campaign against the new legislation by publishing "A Consumer Statement of Principles for the Nursing Home Regulatory System." This spurred a study of nursing home regulations, funded by HHS and conducted by the Institute of Medicine, from 1983 to 1986.

One of the most important programs facilitated by NCCNHR was the Campaign for Quality Care in 1987, involving over fifty national organizations concerned with the well-being of nursing home residents. The campaign resulted in the enactment of the Nursing Home Reform Amendments of the Omnibus Budget Reconciliation Act of 1987 (OBRA), strengthening federal standards and improving the enforcement system for nursing homes. The act included new provisions designating specific training standards for nursing home professionals and protecting the fundamental rights of nursing home residents.

NCCNHR campaigned for the full-scale and immediate implementation of the act. The coalition has continued to inform state advocates, nursing home licensure directors, and others of amendments to the law. NCCNHR has also kept abreast of local consumers' responses to the OBRA regulations. In October 1990, NCCNHR organized a celebration with the Campaign for Quality Care and the Senate Special Committee on Aging to honor congressmen, local politicians, policymakers, and other public officials who were involved with the passage of the OBRA legislation and its amendments.

Providing up-to-date information to policymakers is one of NCCNHR's most important activities. NCCNHR has provided congressmen, senators, and their staff with vital information on nursing home policy and reform. NCCNHR has also filed amicus briefs in litigation involving health care issues of the elderly and encourages members to write letters to their senators and congressional representatives regarding a variety of nursing home concerns. NCCNHR promotes public awareness through national seminars. It has sponsored Nursing Home Residents' Day with the National Coalition of Resident Councils since 1980. The event was expanded to National Nursing Home Residents' Rights Week in 1989 and included a variety of speakers and events on nursing home issues.

PUBLICATIONS

NCCNHR publishes the *Quality Care Advocate*, a bimonthly newsletter, providing information on developments in nursing home reforms, including legislation, regulations, litigation, and consumer groups' advocacy activities. The publication receives support from a grant from the American Association of Retired Persons*.

NCCNHR publishes books, reports, and pamphlets for nursing home consumers and professionals. Its reports have been pivotal in promoting important reforms in the nursing home industry. Past reports have included *The Rights of Nursing Home Residents* (1988) and *A Consumer Perspective on Quality Care: The Residents' Point of View* (1985). In addition, NCCNHR has issued *The Basics* (1990), a guide to the 1987 national reform law.

Further Information

Virginia Fraser, "An Ombudsman Speaks Out on the Consumer's Right to Know," *Provider* (March 1989): 19–20.

EMILY CHERNIACK

NATIONAL COMMITTEE ON AGING
See National Council on the Aging.

NATIONAL COMMITTEE TO PRESERVE SOCIAL SECURITY
See National Committee to Preserve Social Security and Medicare.

NATIONAL COMMITTEE TO PRESERVE SOCIAL SECURITY AND MEDICARE (NCPSSM)
2000 K Street, N.W., Suite 800
Washington, D.C. 20006
(202) 822–9459   FAX (202) 822–9612
The National Committee to Preserve Social Security and Medicare (NCPSSM) is a national, private, nonprofit, individual membership advocacy organization working to protect and strengthen Social Security and Medicare benefits and to defend the insurance basis of those two national programs as the foundations of retirement security for all Americans. The NCPSSM researches and reviews Social Security and Medicare financing and benefits, Medicare regulatory changes, nursing home reform, home health care alternatives, and medical care cost-containment issues and seeks to educate the public on these concerns through forums, speeches, correspondence, telephone communication, and distribution of educational materials.

ORIGIN AND DEVELOPMENT

The NCPSSM was founded in 1982 as the National Committee to Preserve Social Security by James Roosevelt, the late son of former U.S. President Franklin Delano Roosevelt, to serve as a grass-roots political organization. Its initial purpose was to organize senior citizens to act as their own lobbyists, by writing letters and petitions and making personal contacts with members of Congress. A direct-mail fund-raising campaign in 1983, the same year in which the name of the organization was changed to include Medicare, yielded an initial membership of 1 million persons. By 1990, membership had grown to approximately 5 million persons, almost all of whom are Social Security and Medicare beneficiaries.

Roosevelt retired as the National Chairman in June 1990. He was succeeded by Jack Owen, formerly Executive Vice-President of the American Hospital Association*. Since 1989, the President of the NCPSSM has been Martha McSteen who, prior to assuming that position, served in the Social Security Administration in several capacities. McSteen was one of the ten original regional Medicare Administrators and the Acting Commissioner from 1983 to 1986. In 1986, the NPCSSM added a professional lobbying capacity and created a political action committee.

ORGANIZATION AND FUNDING

The NCPSSM is governed by a nine-member Board of Directors, including the President, who set and establish policy. Members of the organization elect board members, who serve staggered three-year terms. Membership surveys are conducted periodically to help define policy priorities. The staff numbers sixty persons, including twenty-six registered lobbyists. NCPSSM is organized into four main components: Legislative Affairs/PAC, Policy and Research, Member Relations, and Communications and Administration.

Individual, non-tax-deductible, yearly membership dues of ten dollars account for 96 percent of the NPCSSM's annual budget of nearly $30 million to $40 million, with the remainder derived from advertising, additional contributions, and investment income. Sixty percent of this budget is spent on legislative advocacy and education, 25 percent on administration, and 15 percent on fund-raising activities. NCPSSM serves as a resource center and advocate for individual member concerns. Nearly all (95%) of the NPCSSM's resources are devoted to issues and concerns of the elderly; the remainder is focused on the disabled.

POLICY CONCERNS AND TACTICS

The NPCSSM's top policy priorities are Social Security benefits and increases, especially the protection of cost-of-living adjustments (COLAs); the preservation of Medicare and Medicaid programs and funding; the development of a national long-term-care financing plan; and nursing home reform. Other issues include

age discrimination, employment for the elderly, and the maintenance and guarantee of private pensions.

The organization seeks to influence public policy at the national level in several
ways. Techniques that have proved most successful are encouraging NCPSSM
members to write to individual members of the House and Senate, as well as
specific congressional committees, contributing to political campaigns, lobbying
members of Congress and staff, and testifying before Congress. On average, the
NCPSSM presents testimony about twenty-five times per session. In recent years,
it has testified on long-term-care protection, family and medical leave, Medicare
beneficiary protection, Medigap insurance reform (standardizing policies that
claim to fill the gaps in medicare coverage), and repeal of the 1988 Medicare
Catastrophic Care Act.

Other tactics include supplying information to members of Congress and their
staff, direct grass-roots action and organized activities such as circulating petitions and holding rallies, litigation, and conducting and publishing research. The
NCPSSM coordinates its legislative program by participating in coalitions of
groups on issues of mutual interest. Such issues include the Family and Medical
Leave Act, pension concerns, and benefits for women and children.

ELECTORAL ACTIVITY

The NCPSSM is heavily engaged in electoral activity through its political
action committee, the National Committee to Preserve Social Security and Medicare Political Action Campaign (NCPSSM/PAC). In 1989–90, the NCPSSM/
PAC contributed $939,802 to 280 congressional candidates. Most contributions
ranged from $1,000 to $5,000 and favored Democrats and incumbents. The
largest amount ($15,000) was given to Democratic Senator Harvey Gantt of
North Carolina.

In addition, the NCPSSM/PAC made independent expenditures of $372,130
on behalf of 31 Democratic candidates in 1989–90 and $30,536 on behalf of
two Republican candidates. The largest amount, $40,179, was expended on
behalf of Senator Harvey Gantt.

PUBLICATIONS

NCPSSM's major publication is a newspaper, *Saving Social Security*, disseminated to members eight times a year and primarily focused on political and
policy issues related to Social Security, Medicare, and long-term-care financing.
The NCPSSM also distributes a column, ''Understanding Social Security,'' to
newspapers nationwide. Occasional research reports and public information pamphlets, such as *Strengthening the Foundation—An Agenda for the 102nd Congress* (1991) and *Buying Your Medigap Policy* (1991), are generated as well.

Further Information

Crocker Coulson, ''Geezer Sleaze: FDR's Son and the Ultimate Interest
Group,'' *New Republic* 196 (20 April 1987): 21–23; Bard Lindeman, ''A Famous

Son, an Old Game," *50 Plus* 28, no. 6 (June 1988): 4–5; Don McLeod, "Roosevelt Committee Polishes Its Image," *AARP Bulletin* (November 1990): 4–5.

PHOEBE S. LIEBIG

NATIONAL COUNCIL OF SENIOR CITIZENS (NCSC)

1313 F Street, N.W.
Washington, D.C. 20004–1171
(202) 347–8800   FAX (202) 624–9595

The National Council of Senior Citizens (NCSC) is one of America's largest membership organizations for the elderly. Through service, advocacy, and influence on Capital Hill, the NCSC promotes the interests of its members and the elderly in general, emphasizing affordable health care.

ORIGIN AND DEVELOPMENT

The NCSC was the first senior citizen organization founded solely to pursue public policy objectives, specifically the passage of Medicare. With roots in the 1960 group Senior Citizens for Kennedy, the NCSC was formally founded in 1961. At the 1961 White House Conference on Aging, Congressman Aime J. Forand, a Rhode Island Democrat, proposed to several union leaders the idea of organizing older Americans to work for the passage of Medicare.

Despite opposition from other labor leaders, Charles Odell of the United Auto Workers* and James Cuff O'Brien of the United Steel Workers decided to go ahead with the project. Both men ran programs for AFL-CIO (American Federation of Labor and Congress of Industrial Organizations) retirees, and together they had led Senior Citizens for Kennedy. With Forand as Chairman, the fledgling organization began a national campaign to sign local and state senior citizen clubs as affiliates.

Originally called the National Council of Senior Citizens for Health Care Through Social Security, the group's sole purpose was the passage of Medicare. Opposing such powerful groups as the American Medical Association (AMA), the American Dental Association, and the American Health Insurance Association, the NCSC concentrated on lobbying and convincing legislators of the need for Medicare. In addition, the NCSC mobilized grass-roots support for the measure, organizing fifty rallies across the nation. President John F. Kennedy spoke at the largest such gathering, of 17,000 senior citizens, in New York City in May 1962. Busloads of NCSC senior citizens personally visited their legislators in Washington, D.C. The bill's passage in 1965 was due in large part to the NCSC's efforts.

Immediately preceding the 1971 White House Conference on Aging, the NCSC joined with other organizations, including the American Association of Retired Persons* (AARP), the National Council on the Aging*, and the National Caucus on the Black Aged (now the National Caucus and Center on Black Aged*), arguing for greater direct representation of the elderly in planning and conducting the conference. In testimony before joint hearings of committees on aging in the

Senate and House in March 1971, representatives of the NCSC and eleven other organizations advocating for the elderly expressed their dissatisfaction, not only with conference preparations but also with the six-year-old U.S. Administration on Aging (AoA). When the White House Conference on Aging convened in 1971, one-third of the delegates belonged to at least one organization representing the aging.

The NCSC quickly expanded from a single-objective group to an organization with wide-ranging interests. By 1972, the group was backing such varied pursuits as the Peace Corps and the nuclear test ban treaty. However, the NCSC's major efforts remained firmly embedded in policies affecting senior citizens. A main concern in 1991 was still affordable medical care; to this end, the NCSC supported proposals for national health insurance.

The NCSC has retained its initial political purpose. As the only advocacy organization for the aged established before 1980 to place its national headquarters in Washington, D.C., originally, the NCSC was more political than most other groups from the beginning. In 1982, NCSC created a political action committee, one of the few groups for the elderly to do so.

The NCSC also developed a wide range of services for its members. These include a direct prescription drug service, supplementary Medicare insurance, noncancellable life insurance, a low-cost travel service, and legal assistance.

ORGANIZATION AND FUNDING

The National Council of Senior Citizens emphasizes its grass-roots strength: 5,000 affiliated clubs with 5 million members. The senior citizen clubs affiliated with NCSC are often composed of trade union retirees or represent ethnic or religious groups. Many NCSC local clubs, though, are social or primarily recreational.

There is no age requirement to join NCSC but members must be 50 years old or older to receive benefits. Since 1979, new clubs must have at least twenty dues-paying, or "Gold Card," members in order to affiliate with NCSC. Dues in 1991 were $12 per year for an individual or a couple.

The NCSC is grouped into ten regions, parallel to the standard federal regions. The local clubs, Area Councils, and State Councils of NCSC are governed by a large general board, which includes the officers, State Council Presidents, at least thirty-four members elected by regions, and twenty-six members elected at large. Regional representation on the board is determined by the number of Gold Card members within a region. The board is authorized at a biennial constitutional convention. A national staff of nearly 120 coordinates the group's activities.

When the National Council of Senior Citizens was founded, contributions from unions and the Democratic National Committee comprised roughly two-thirds of its funding, with the remaining one-third coming from the $1-a-year-membership dues. The character of NCSC's support base has changed significantly. Dues contributed less than $3 million to the 1989–90 total revenue of over $59 million. More than 90 percent of the total came from the federal government in the forms of restricted grants and contracts from government agencies. All of the restricted monies were spent in the category of community services, with the bulk of the dollars supporting the professional costs of maintaining the Senior AIDES employment effort and other programs. Other expenditure categories included information, membership, legislation, political action, housing, and administration. The most money was spent on community services, the least on political action.

One of the group's main emphases has been to increase membership. Over 600 new clubs were chartered in 1990. NCSC has conducted a direct-mail campaign to prospective members in conjunction with several large unions. In 1991, the organization continued discussions with the AFL-CIO Union Benefits program regarding the possibility of NCSC members sharing some AFL-CIO benefits.

At the twentieth NCSC Constitutional Convention in 1990, the group approved the convening of regional conferences, beginning in 1991 and to be held in alternate years thereafter. Such meetings are expected to strengthen the grassroots network and increase communication between the national and local levels of NCSC.

On behalf of the U.S. Department of Labor, NCSC operates Senior AIDES, a program providing part-time employment for limited-income persons aged 55 and older. Part of the Senior Community Services Employment Program (SCSEP), the project, in existence since 1968, is funded by Title V of the Older Americans Act (OAA). In 1990, the AIDES program employed over 10,000 senior citizens in 150 programs in 17 states. Participants held jobs such as teaching assistant, paralegal, child care worker, and home health aide. Each year, about 20 percent of the Senior AIDES obtain unsubsidized jobs, forging a bridge back into the private working world.

Another NCSC employment effort is the Senior Environment Employment (SEE) Program. The Environmental Protection Agency (EPA) and NCSC jointly conduct the SEE Program, authorized by the Environmental Programs Assistance Act of 1984. Senior citizens enrolled in SEE work in EPA offices and laboratories around the United States.

NCSC operates the NCSC Housing Management Corporation (NCSC HMC). With money from the Department of Housing and Urban Development, the NCSC HMC builds and manages housing for low-income seniors. The group is one of America's largest nonprofit developers of subsidized housing for low-income elderly. In 1990, NCSC HMC managed 3,301 housing units for the elderly and disabled across the United States, and was in the process of completing 388 additional units.

The NCSC maintains the National Senior Citizens Education and Research Center (NSCERC), a nonprofit, tax-exempt organization that develops and implements programs for the elderly. In 1990, NSCERC and the NCSC Housing

Management Corporation explored the possibility of purchasing failed savings and loan properties for senior housing. The educational center also provides services such as information and referral to residents of NCSC properties.

NSCERC focuses on long-term care through its Nursing Home Information Service (NHIS). Founded in 1974, the clearinghouse maintains a database on long-term-care facilities, providing consumer information on finding, evaluating, and selecting a nursing home. NHIS also works with private and public agencies to advocate for nursing home residents and for increased access to home health care services.

POLICY CONCERNS AND TACTICS

In its efforts to influence policy toward the aged, the National Council of Senior Citizens employs a variety of tactics, including lobbying, education, grass-roots networking, and direct action on national, state, and local issues. Its fight for the 1972 Mills-Church amendments to Social Security, which raised Social Security by 20 percent, illustrates this diversity. The NCSC, primary supporter for income maintenance, began a grass-roots letter-writing campaign to congressional representatives and used its monthly publication, *Senior Citizens News*, to promote the plan. On Capitol Hill, the NCSC concentrated on convincing undecided, key congressional leaders, such as Senator Russell Long of Louisiana, and effected a snowballing of support. The amendments passed, as H.R. 15390, by an overwhelming majority in both houses.

In the 1980s, the NCSC worked to maintain Social Security benefits while many other social programs were cut. The NCSC expended a great deal of energy in a successful fight to include coverage of prescription drugs in the 1988 Catastrophic Coverage legislation. In addition, the NCSC has objected to Federal Drug Administration rule changes that would make it easier to market drugs not yet proven effective.

True to its origins, NCSC holds as a top priority the preservation of the integrity of Medicare. In 1990, NCSC successfully worked against a federal budget compromise that would have reduced the Medicare program by $60 billion. NCSC members contacted congressional representatives and senators by letter, telephone call, and/or personal visit, and the organization publicly proclaimed its stance in news conferences protesting the cuts. Pressure from the NCSC and organized labor also resulted in separating the surplus of the Social Security trust funds from the deficit calculation of the federal budget, giving a more realistic picture of the deficit amount.

The NCSC was active in the drive to regulate Medigap insurance policies, which cover costs not included in Medicare coverage. In 1990, legislation was enacted requiring state or federal government approval before any such policy can be sold. The legislation also provided for counseling assistance to purchasers of Medigap insurance and prohibited the selling of such insurance to persons already covered.

In the 1990s, the NCSC was allied with the AFL-CIO and a wide coalition of interest groups in the continuing legislative struggles for passage of the Family and Medical Leave Act and the Civil Rights Act. The former passed both houses of Congress in 1990 but was vetoed by President George Bush. The Civil Rights Act became law in 1991.

Foremost among NCSC's future activities is the ongoing effort to secure national health care. At the NCSC national convention in July 1990, over 1,000 NCSC activists demonstrated in front of the American Medical Association, protesting its opposition to national health care. The organization also initiated a health care pledge campaign, soliciting pledges of support for national health care from physicians, public officials, and employers. NCSC intends to present the pledges on Capitol Hill when "an NCSC-backed national health care bill" is introduced.

As a member of the Leadership Council of Aging Organizations*, the NCSC coordinates its efforts with other like-minded groups. NCSC has often worked in concert with the National Council on the Aging* and the American Association of Retired Persons*.

ELECTORAL ACTIVITY

Since 1982, NCSC has maintained the National Council of Senior Citizens Political Action Committee (NCSC-PAC). In 1985–86, the NCSC-PAC contributed $216,750 to 126 congressional candidates, 125 of whom were Democrats. The average contribution was approximately $2,000. In 1989–90, NCSC-PAC contributed $67,250 to the campaigns of 42 Democrats, with $1,000 the average amount contributed. The largest contribution, $10,000, supported the reelection of Senator Thomas Harkin of Iowa.

The NCSC Department of Legislation annually publishes the *NCSC Congressional Voting Record*, rating congressional representatives' responses to elderly issues. Periodic *Legislative Updates*, "Seniorgrams," and the Legislative Hotline telephone service keep grass-roots advocates aware of upcoming legislation.

In preparation for the 1988 election, the NCSC produced a video, *A View of the 1988 Presidential Candidates*. The video included interviews with the seven Democratic candidates and one Republican candidate, probing their positions on senior issues.

The NCSC Political Education Department handles other electoral activity on the state and national levels. In the 1988 presidential election and in subsequent midterm races, the department held voter registration drives, maintained telephone banks to acquaint members with important issues for the elderly, held press conferences for candidates supporting issues important to the elderly, and provided training for voting in caucuses. One state victory claimed by the NCSC was the gubernatorial election of Lawton Chiles in Florida in 1990.

PUBLICATIONS

NCSC publishes the *Retirement Newsletter* (monthly), a four-page newsletter supplied in bulk to pension funds and international unions, informing retirees about federal and state programs for older people. For a fee, the providing subscriber's name can appear on the front of the *Retirement Newsletter*. *Senior Citizen News*, published eleven times a year, provides organizational and legislative information, as well as profiles of members and officers and news of local groups. All NCSC members receive *Senior Citizen News*. In April 1991, the tabloid newspaper format changed to a magazine format, and the publication began to accept advertising. NCSC's Nursing Home Information Service publishes the newsletter *News and Notes from NHIS* six times a year. Additionally, NCSC offers a variety of other publications, such as *Mandatory Medical Assignment: Towards Affordable Health Care* (1987).

Further Information

Adrienne Cook and Tony Capaccio, "What's So Great about the Great Gray Lobby?" *50 Plus* 23 (October 1983): 20–25; Richard Harris, *A Sacred Trust* (New York: New American Library, 1966); Lisa Krieger, "FDA Data Show Improper Drug Testing on Nursing Home Residents, Group Says." *American Medical News* 28 (June 14, 1985): 2–4; Henry J. Pratt, *The Gray Lobby* (Chicago: University of Chicago Press, 1976).

JIMMY E. W. MEYER
RENEE ROMANO

NATIONAL COUNCIL OF SENIOR CITIZENS FOR HEALTH CARE THROUGH SOCIAL SECURITY

See National Council of Senior Citizens.

NATIONAL COUNCIL OF SENIOR CITIZENS POLITICAL ACTION COMMITTEE

See National Council of Senior Citizens.

NATIONAL COUNCIL ON THE AGING (NCOA)

409 Third Street, S.W.
Washington, D.C. 20024
(202) 479–1200   FAX (202) 479–0735

The National Council on the Aging (NCOA) is a national, nonprofit, membership organization composed of senior citizens, voluntary agencies, associations, business organizations, labor unions, and other organizations and individuals united by a commitment to the principle that older Americans are entitled to dignity, security, physical, mental, and social well-being, and full participation in society. It seeks to make society more caring and understanding of older persons so that their rights are protected and their needs met in a humane, effective, and efficient manner. NCOA cooperates with other organizations to promote the welfare of older persons through research and planning in the field of aging and to serve as a resource for organizations and individuals with responsibilities for providing programs and services for older Americans. NCOA provides professional education and training, conducts a number of programs benefiting the elderly, and engages in applied research, advocacy, and information dissemination.

ORIGIN AND DEVELOPMENT

NCOA is one of the oldest advocacy organizations for the aging, having been founded in 1950 by the National Social Welfare Assembly, spearheaded by the efforts of Ollie Randall and Geneva Mathiasen. To commemorate its two founders, NCOA sponsors the Ollie Randall Award, given annually to an individual for outstanding contributions on behalf of older people, and the Geneva Mathiasen National Award, given annually to an individual for major contributions to the organization and its programs. Its earliest projects were funded by several foundations, including the Ford Foundation, to focus on issues of retirement and standards of institutional care.

Originally called the National Committee on Aging, its present name was adopted in 1960. Its major purpose, however, has remained constant: to make American society aware of and promote dialogue about the needs of the elderly— a purpose that has been promoted by its past leaders, Jack Ossofsky and Don Reilly, and by its 1991 President, Daniel Thursz. Through the establishment of its National Institute of Senior Centers in 1970, NCOA served as a particular focal point for senior center activity. More recently, NCOA's social policy agenda has expanded to include intergenerational concerns, as exemplified by the Family Friends Program, which recruits and trains older volunteers to work with chronically ill or disabled children. Also reflecting this broadened agenda was the inauguration of awards in 1989 for outstanding achievement by those who have worked to improve the lives of all citizens, not just accomplishments directly related to aging.

ORGANIZATION AND FUNDING

NCOA is governed by an elected board of approximately forty members, including 7 officers, and an executive committee. Several other directors serve in an honorary capacity. Board members represent geographic and occupational diversity and are drawn from business and industry, academia, religion, labor, state, and local government, and agencies providing services to the elderly across the nation. The board sets organizational policy. NCOA professional staff numbers 110 persons, ninety of whom are based in Washington, D.C.; the others are located nationwide. The staff is distributed among several divisions: Senior Community Service Employment Program, Corporate and Educational Services,

Programs, Constituent Units, Membership, and Development and Public Information.

NCOA supports ten constituent units: NCOA Health Promotion Institute* (HPI); NCOA National Association of Older Worker Employment Services* (NAOWES); NCOA National Center on Rural Aging* (NCRA); NCOA National Institute of Senior Centers* (NISC); NCOA National Institute on Adult Daycare* (NIAD); NCOA National Institute on Community-Based Long-Term Care* (NICLC); NCOA National Institute of Senior Housing* (NISH); NCOA National Interfaith Coalition on Aging* (NICA); NCOA National Voluntary Organizations for Independent Living for the Aging* (NVOILA); and the newest unit, created in May 1991, NCOA National Institute on Financial Issues and Services for Elders (NIFSE). The units are designed to exchange information, establish professional standards, and influence social trends. Each constituent unit is staffed by a program manager at the NCOA. Every NCOA member is entitled to membership in one constituent unit; additional dues are required for membership in more than one. Reduced dues are available to student members. A Delegate Council, an elected body that meets twice a year, advises each constituent unit, subject to NCOA approval. Regional delegates, delegates at large, and the unit officers compose the Delegate Councils.

Particular program areas focus on specific issues such as retirement planning, minorities, humanities, and middle-aged and older women. NCOA holds member status with the United Nations Committee on Non-Governmental Organizations.

NCOA's annual budget ranges from $10 million to $50 million, reflecting the fact that 75 percent of its budget is derived from government funding, usually for specific programs. Annual membership dues of $75 account for less than 10 percent of the organization's budget. Corporate contributions and foundation grants and additional fund raising comprise 5 percent and 10 percent, respectively, of the budget. Nearly all (90%) of NCOA's resources are devoted to the elderly, and most are expended on employment, work, and retirement programs. The remainder is designated for intergenerational programs and activities, such as Generations United*, an umbrella association of senior citizen and child advocacy groups, co-chaired by NCOA. Constituent units do not have separate budgets.

In 1991, NCOA was one of the largest mass membership organizations among the groups advocating for the aging. Of its 6,400 members, 1,800 are organizational members. For the benefit of its members and others, NCOA maintains a library of 14,000 volumes on aging, with emphasis on the psychological, economic, and social aspects of gerontology. NCOA also holds an annual conference, usually in the spring, which includes special exhibits and a series of workshops and presentations to educate its members and others in the field of aging. Constituent units participate in the annual conference. In addition, NCOA holds a series of one-day training programs in cities nationwide on topics such as adult day care standards, senior center programming, and housing management.

NCOA's largest program focus is the Senior Community Service Employment Program (SCSEP), sponsored by the U.S. Department of Labor. NCOA has received SCSEP funds for most of the program's existence—more than a quarter of a century.

POLICY CONCERNS AND TACTICS

Although NCOA's original articles of incorporation prohibited official lobbying, from the beginning NCOA helped to shape the national public policy agenda on a number of issues, especially home health and long-term care, employment for the elderly, Social Security benefits, Medicare and Medicaid programs and funding, and public housing for the elderly. Other issues include age discrimination, nursing home reform, legal problems, transportation, literacy, and private pensions. Current long-range policy goals include the development of a national long-term-care policy and national health insurance based on social insurance principles. NCOA's Public Policy Committee plays an important role in shaping the organization's policy positions.

NCOA seeks to influence public policy at the national level in several ways. The techniques that have proved most successful have been delivering testimony before Congress on a continuing basis, supplying information to members of Congress and their staff, and conducting and publishing research on issues affecting the elderly. NCOA has commissioned public opinion polls, pursued litigation, and encouraged NCOA members to write to individual members of the House and Senate, as well as specific congressional committees. In recent years, NCOA has testified on Social Security appeal procedures, the Older Americans Act, improvement in senior employment programs, and the Medicare Catastrophic Coverage Act. It has supported the Americans with Disabilities Act by providing information, one of the few aging-network groups to do so.

NCOA also seeks to influence the policy agenda through advocacy by drawing attention to issues not being met through legislative means. Its advocacy and policy activities are often carried out with a variety of other organizations, inside and outside the aging network. NCOA shares the rotating chairmanship of the Leadership Council of Aging Organizations* with the American Association of Retired Persons* and the National Council of Senior Citizens*.

ELECTORAL ACTIVITY

NCOA does not engage in electoral activity. It does not contribute to political campaigns or endorse candidates.

PUBLICATIONS

NCOA has carried out an extensive publications program for many years, including the now-defunct quarterly, *Aging and Work*. A newsletter, *NCOA Networks*, is disseminated to members six times a year. Each constituent unit has a regular section in *NCOA Networks*, highlighting programs related to that unit and featuring pertinent resources. Each member also receives the bimonthly magazine *Perspective on Aging*, an annual report, and *Abstracts in Social Gerontology* (formerly *Current Literature on Aging*), a quarterly annotated bibliography indexed annually (also available by subscription). Specialized research reports are generated three times a year; manuals for specific program implementation are disseminated on a timely basis. Recent publications include *Planning a Family Friends Project: A Working Guide* (1988), *Eldercare in the Workplace* (1989), and *Respite Resource Guide* (1990). NCOA also helped produce and disseminates a videotape on long-term care, *Coming of Age in America* (1990).

Further Information

Adrienne Cook, "What's So Great about the Great Gray Lobby?" *50 Plus* (October 1983): 21a–22, 24, 61; Christine Day, *What Older Americans Think: Interest Groups and Aging Policy* (Princeton, N.J.: Princeton University Press, 1990); Carolyn Reece, "Older Volunteers and Youth with Disabilities Team Up to Find Jobs," *Children Today* (January–February 1988): 14.

PHOEBE S. LIEBIG

NATIONAL COUNCIL ON THE AGING (NCOA) CONSTITUENT UNIT: HEALTH PROMOTION INSTITUTE (HPI)

c/o National Council on the Aging
409 Third Street, S.W.
Washington, D.C. 20024
(202) 479–1200 or (202) 479–6677

ORIGIN AND DEVELOPMENT

The NCOA Health Promotion Unit (HPI) was created by its parent organization in 1989 to:

1. Provide information, technical assistance, and networking opportunities to health promotion professionals working with older adults

2. Reach out to professionals who serve older adults but have not had contact with an organization devoted to aging

3. Serve as an advocate for national health promotion policy, to provide older Americans with informational materials

4. Increase awareness among all health promotion professionals concerning the needs of older persons.

ORGANIZATION AND FUNDING

HPI had more than 600 individual and organizational members in 1991. Membership is open to NCOA individual or organizational members interested in or working on the continuing wellness of older persons, including care providers, pharmacists, educators, health policymakers, and medical care professionals. A twenty-member Delegate Council leads the unit, with NCOA approval.

POLICY CONCERNS AND TACTICS

Utilizing education and research, HPI works to bring the issue of maintaining wellness in later life before policymakers and the general public. In its first year, HPI sponsored a one-day seminar at the 1990 annual NCOA conference and, with the support of the American Pharmaceutical Manufacturers Association, prepared an educational program on medication management. Working with the U.S. Public Health Service, HPI is also developing health objectives for the year 2000.

JIMMY E. W. MEYER

NATIONAL COUNCIL ON THE AGING (NCOA) CONSTITUENT UNIT: NATIONAL ASSOCIATION OF OLDER WORKER EMPLOYMENT SERVICES (NAOWES)

c/o National Council on the Aging
409 Third Street, S.W.
Washington, D.C. 20024
(202) 479–1200 or (202) 479–6641

ORIGIN AND DEVELOPMENT

The National Association Of Older Worker Employment Services (NAOWES) was established as an NCOA constituent unit in 1981 to give guidance and leadership to existing and evolving older worker employment services. NAOWES helps employers modify training programs to utilize older workers effectively, designs skills assessments for second-career clients, and keeps in close contact with the job market.

ORGANIZATION AND FUNDING

NAOWES had more than 400 members in 1991, representing both private and public employment agencies, on the local and state levels. An eighteen-member Delegate Council leads the unit, subject to NCOA approval.

POLICY CONCERNS AND TACTICS

NAOWES emphasizes the need for a fair share of federal and other public funding for programs for middle-aged and older workers. It advocates on public policy issues such as job sharing, flextime, and retirement reform. NAOWES works closely with the NCOA Senior Community Service Employment Program, sponsored by the U.S. Department of Labor. NAOWES also monitors enforcement of the Age Discrimination in Employment Act to ensure that older workers have retraining opportunities in today's technologically changing work world.

JIMMY E. W. MEYER

NATIONAL COUNCIL ON THE AGING (NCOA) CONSTITUENT UNIT: NATIONAL CENTER ON RURAL AGING (NCRA)

c/o National Council on Aging
409 Third Street, S.W.
Washington, D.C. 20004
(202) 479–1200 or (202) 479–6683

The National Center on Rural Aging (NCRA) is one of the ten constituent units of the National Council on the Aging* (NCOA). NCRA focuses attention on the special needs of the rural elderly and seeks to increase and improve services to meet those needs through the development of public policy and coordination of assistance to the rural elderly.

ORIGIN AND DEVELOPMENT

Founded in 1978 as a result of a grass-roots effort, NCRA provides information and technical assistance related to issues affecting older adults in rural areas, works with government agencies at all levels, and supports appropriate legislation.

ORGANIZATION AND FUNDING

In 1990, NCRA's membership numbered approximately 500. Membership in the NCRA is acquired through membership in the NCOA. Members include service providers, academicians, and others interested in issues related to the rural aged. Roughly two-thirds of NCRA's members are individuals, with organizations comprising the remaining third. A nineteen-member Delegate Council governs the NCRA. NCRA and NCOA have co-sponsored the National Conference on Rural Elderly.

POLICY CONCERNS AND TACTICS

NCRA asserts that rural areas lack adequate local resources to handle the challenges they face due to the lack of government support and investment in community and economic development. NCRA is most concerned with equity in funding for older adults in rural areas, improved rural transportation services, access to health services, and improved living circumstances for older farmworkers.

NCRA supports several policy changes associated with the reauthorization of the Older Americans Act (OAA) to increase funds and services provided to the rural elderly. Citing fiscal policies that result in lower federal per capita spending in rural areas, despite the high cost of providing services in these areas, NCRA advocates funding formulas that increase the amount of funds provided to rural states and to rural areas in all states. NCRA supports OAA funding of home care services and preventive health services to compensate for medical under-service and transportation inadequacies. NCRA advocates the use of geographic isolation in the determination of social need. The group suggests that 30 percent of OAA research and demonstration funding be earmarked for rural aging issues.

Other NCRA policy positions include stabilization of intercommunity public and private transit service through federal legislation, increased funding from the Urban Mass Transit Administration, and implementation of the transportation provisions of the 1990 Americans with Disabilities Act. NCRA also supports a "Rural Homeless" initiative within the McKinney Homeless Assistance Act to finance temporary housing for migrant farmworkers and other rural homeless.

CLEVE REDMOND

NATIONAL COUNCIL ON THE AGING (NCOA) CONSTITUENT UNIT: NATIONAL INSTITUTE OF SENIOR CENTERS (NISC)

c/o National Council on the Aging
409 Third Street, S.W.
Washington, D.C. 20024
(202) 479–1200 or (202) 479–6683

ORIGIN AND DEVELOPMENT

National Institute of Senior Centers (NISC) was founded in 1970 as a constituent unit of National Council on the Aging* (NCOA) to assist senior citizen centers in maintaining and expanding their operations and to encourage organizations or communities to develop new facilities. Federal funding for senior centers, mandated by Title V of the Older Americans Act (OAA), was forthcoming in the 1970s. By developing standards, publishing operating manuals, holding workshops for center volunteers and practitioners, and advocating for senior centers and their participants, the NISC has helped to shape and expand the field of community-based service and recreation centers for older persons. In 1990, as many as 10 million to 15 million older persons utilized the services of an estimated 12,000 senior centers across the United States.

ORGANIZATION AND FUNDING

The NISC had nearly 1,700 members in 1991, representing centers in every state and the District of Columbia. A sixty-eight-member Delegate Council, which includes state delegates, advises the unit, with NCOA approval.

POLICY CONCERNS AND TACTICS

NISC emphasizes a holistic view of older persons, recognizing their varying needs, interests, and talents. The unit stresses the importance of community linkages—the coordination of services with other community agencies. Through research and publication, training, and advocacy for policies affecting senior centers, the NISC educates policymakers and the public in general about the need for and the needs of senior centers and their participants. For example, in 1990–91 the NISC led a nationwide advocacy effort to increase funding for OAA health promotion programs. In 1990, NISC completed a revision of its 1978 guidelines, releasing a new edition of *Senior Center Standards and Self-Assessment Workbook*. The fourteen-month effort, which involved field-testing of the suggested guidelines, was funded in part by the U.S. Administration on Aging. NISC has recently undertaken surveys designed to illuminate varieties of service and methods of service delivery. One such survey, funded by Families U.S.A. Foundation* in 1989, found widespread interest in the expansion of public affairs activities at senior centers.

PUBLICATIONS

The NCOA-published *Senior Center Standards and Self-Assessment Workbook* (1991) addresses the complexities of beginning and operating a senior center.

JIMMY E. W. MEYER

NATIONAL COUNCIL ON THE AGING (NCOA) CONSTITUENT UNIT: NATIONAL INSTITUTE OF SENIOR HOUSING (NISH)
c/o National Council on the Aging
409 Third Street, S.W.
Washington, D.C. 20024
(202) 479–1200 or (202) 479–6677

ORIGIN AND DEVELOPMENT

The National Institute of Senior Housing (NISH) was created in 1981 as a constituent unit of the National Council on the Aging* (NCOA) to facilitate information exchange and to advocate on behalf of maintaining and expanding affordable, high-quality housing for older persons.

ORGANIZATION AND FUNDING

Membership of NISH, numbering 700 in 1991, is broad-based, including professionals from the fields of architecture, housing management, housing development, and social service. An eighteen-member Delegate Council leads the group, with NCOA approval.

POLICY CONCERNS AND TACTICS

NISH recognizes that the housing needs of future generations of older persons will differ from those of earlier generations, due in part to increased and healthier longevity. To this end, NISH provided information for and closely monitored the progress of the Cranston-Gonzalez National Affordable Housing Act of 1990. In 1989, NISH submitted modifications for federal legislation to continue a direct loan program for subsidized senior citizen housing, especially critical to nonprofit sponsors.

JIMMY E. W. MEYER

NATIONAL COUNCIL ON THE AGING (NCOA) CONSTITUENT UNIT: NATIONAL INSTITUTE ON ADULT DAYCARE (NIAD)
c/o National Council on the Aging
409 Third Street, S.W.
Washington, D.C. 20024
(202) 479–1200 or (202) 479–6680

ORIGIN AND DEVELOPMENT

The National Institute on Adult Daycare (NIAD) was founded in 1979 as a constituent unit of the National Council on the Aging* (NCOA) to address the complex issues involved in providing day care for adults who are frail and/or functionally impaired. In 1984, NIAD formulated and published the first national standards for adult day care, revised and reissued in 1990 as *Standards and Guidelines for Adult Day Care.*

ORGANIZATION AND FUNDING

NIAD had over 1,400 members in 1991, representing more than 1,200 adult day care centers nationwide. An eighteen-member Delegate Council, responsible to NCOA, leads the unit.

POLICY CONCERNS AND TACTICS

NIAD utilizes research and education to accomplish its goals of standardizing and improving adult day care programs and helping day care participants achieve maximum independence. The 1990 revision of the national standards involved more than simple rewriting. Sponsored by a grant from the Vira I. Heinz Endowment of Pittsburgh, Pennsylvania, one component of the project was the preparation of profiles of progams serving special populations or serving in unusual environments, as models for future efforts. Another research example was a 1989–90 national survey of adult day care services—their scope, availability, characteristics, licensure, costs, and financing. This survey was mandated by federal legislation (the Medicare Catastrophic Coverage Act) and funded in part by the American Association of Retired Persons* and the federal Health Care Financing Administration. NIAD also strongly promotes Medicare coverage of adult day care. Future plans include the completion and publication of a manual for training adult day care workers and an accompanying instructors' book.

PUBLICATIONS

NIAD offers occasional position papers, such as "Adult Day Care: A Treatment Program for Persons with Functional Impairment" (1990).

JIMMY E. W. MEYER

NATIONAL COUNCIL ON THE AGING (NCOA) CONSTITUENT UNIT: NATIONAL INSTITUTE ON COMMUNITY-BASED LONG-TERM CARE (NICLC)

c/o National Council on the Aging
409 Third Street, S.W.
Washington, D.C. 20024
(202) 479–1200 or (202) 479–6689

ORIGIN AND DEVELOPMENT

National Institute on Community-based Long-term Care (NICLC) was established in 1983 as a constituent unit of the National Council on the Aging* (NCOA) to advocate for the development of a comprehensive and coordinated long-term-care system and to promote quality assurance efforts. NICLC educates the general public and policymakers about the variety of choices on the long-term-care continuum, particularly home- and community-based care.

ORGANIZATION AND FUNDING

In 1991 NICLC had 1,500 members, representing the fields of public health, health planning, and social service, as well as health care providers. An eighteen-member Delegate Council advises the unit, responsible to NCOA.

POLICY CONCERNS AND TACTICS

NICLC maintains that long-term care must be integral to national comprehensive health care coverage. To this end, in the late 1980s, the group helped to shape NCOA testimony on long-term-care needs before the Pepper Commission, a congressional commission established to study long-term care and headed by Representative Claude Pepper (D, Florida). NICLC supports legislation at the federal level to ensure employee long-term-care coverage by employers. As a part of its educational activities, NICLC sponsors a consumer information program, Long-Term Care CHOICES. Held in a variety of communities across the country, such as Chicago and Buffalo, the program involves sponsors, such as county agencies, and the local media in an effort to publicize area long-term-care resources.

PUBLICATIONS

NCOA publications pertinent to this unit include *Long-Term Care CHOICES*

(1988), a manual for planning and conducting a community forum; *Care Management Standards* (1988) and *CHOICES: Slide Presentation* (1988).

JIMMY E. W. MEYER

NATIONAL COUNCIL ON THE AGING (NCOA) CONSTITUENT UNIT: NATIONAL INTERFAITH COALITION ON AGING (NICA)

c/o National Council on the Aging
409 Third Street, S.W.
Washington, D.C. 20024
(202) 479–1200 or (202) 479–6689

The National Interfaith Coalition on Aging (NICA) is a nondenominational, nonprofit organization created to be a communication and educational resource for religious workers and groups who work with older Americans. A constituent unit of the National Council on the Aging* (NCOA) since 1991, NICA includes as members people and groups of the Jewish, Catholic, Protestant, and Orthodox faiths, as well as secular individuals and organizations.

ORIGIN AND DEVELOPMENT

The National Interfaith Coalition on Aging was organized at the National Interfaith Conference on Aging held in Athens, Georgia, in March 1972, in response to the recommendation of the 1971 White House Conference on Aging. It was organized with four main objectives: to create a databank for the collection and dissemination of information and successful programs of religious institutions; to assist and develop the role of church and synagogue in improving the quality of life for the aged; to stimulate and coordinate interdenominational and ecumenical programs and efforts on behalf of the elderly; and to support and encourage the continued involvement of older persons in society. Early activities included GIST-Gerontology in Seminary Training, which sponsored workshops, symposia, and curriculum plans to create an awareness of gerontology for Christian and Jewish clergy; the Survey of Aging Programs under Religious Auspices (1972–76), which identified and analyzed religious services for the elderly; and sponsorship of the National Intra-decade Conference on Spiritual Well-Being held in 1977 in Atlanta. The coalition also co-sponsored many educational conferences and training workshops for gerontological workers, created a library–information center, and developed a newsletter to improve communication and advocacy for the elderly.

NICA developed the following priorities for the 1980s in preparation for the 1981 White House Conference on Aging: expansion of communication among religious organizations, expansion of membership in the coalition and the creation of a national interfaith policy on aging, increased legislative activism, and development of theology for and positive images of aging. The goals of the 1970s and 1980s reflected the concern with establishing the existence and national role of NICA, whereas the goals for the 1990s focus on NICA's developing opportunities for the elderly in the local community. NICA's established "Priorities for the '90's" are the expansion of religious programs for the elderly, increased continuing education for religious workers who serve the elderly, and strengthening community-wide response to needs of the elderly. In January 1991, NICA became one of the ten constituent units of the NCOA.

ORGANIZATION AND FUNDING

As an NCOA unit, NICA is governed by the board of the parent organization, with the advice of the NICA Delegate Council, a thirty- to thirty-five-member body composed of representatives of major national religious groups. Delegate Council members are appointed by the groups they represent. In 1991, NICA had more than 500 affiliate members.

POLICY CONCERNS AND TACTICS

The primary purpose of NICA is to promote cooperation and communication among organizations and individuals concerned with the physical needs, such as housing and health care, and the spiritual welfare of the elderly. To meet this purpose, NICA organizes training and continuing-education programs for clergy and lay individuals, conducts regional conferences and forums, provides resources for those developing programs and providing ongoing ministry to the elderly, and promotes advocacy and policy formulation.

PUBLICATIONS

Prior to 1991, NICA published *NICA Inform*, a quarterly newsletter, and the *Journal of Religious Gerontology*, also quarterly. Since its 1991 affiliation with NCOA, NICA news appears in a section in the bimonthly NCOA newsletter, *Networks*.

Further Information

Thomas Cook, Jr., *The Religious Sector Explores Its Mission in Aging* (Athens, Ga.: National Interfaith Coalition on Aging, 1976).

KIMBERLY S. LENAHAN

NATIONAL COUNCIL ON THE AGING (NCOA) CONSTITUENT UNIT: NATIONAL VOLUNTARY ORGANIZATIONS FOR INDEPENDENT LIVING FOR THE AGING (NVOILA)

c/o National Council on the Aging
409 Third Street, S.W.
Washington, D.C. 20024
(202) 479–1200 or (202) 479–6682

ORIGIN AND DEVELOPMENT

The National Voluntary Organizations for Independent Living for the Aging (NVOILA) was founded in 1971 and became a constituent unit of the National Council on the Aging* (NCOA) in 1973. NVOILA unites diverse voluntary organizations around the common interest of maintaining self-sufficiency for frail and chronically ill older persons through services and support systems.

ORGANIZATION AND FUNDING

NVOILA's members number more than 100 national groups from a variety of fields who are committed to the welfare of older Americans. A seventeen-member Delegate Council governs the organization, with the approval of NCOA. NVOILA presents the annual Voluntarism in Action for Aging award; recent national winners have been the American Podiatric Medicine Association and the American Foundation for the Blind.

POLICY CONCERNS AND TACTICS

NVOILA pays close attention to legislation related to disability, as well as to actions in the public or private sectors that widen intergenerational or senior citizen volunteer opportunities. In 1991, seventeen NVOILA member organizations participated in a project funded by the U.S. Administration on Aging to increase awareness and knowledge of population changes and their social and economic implications.

JIMMY E. W. MEYER

NATIONAL DISPLACED HOMEMAKERS NETWORK
1625 K Street, N.W., Suite 300
Washington, D.C. 20006
(202) 467–NDHN   FAX (202) 467–5366
The National Displaced Homemakers Network works to meet the special needs of older women who have provided unpaid service to their families and have depended on their spouses for income but who have lost that income through death, divorce, separation, desertion, or disability and who lack the means to support themselves.

ORIGIN AND DEVELOPMENT

Tish Sommers, a displaced homemaker through divorce, conceived the idea of establishing multiservice centers to provide peer counseling and job training adapted to the special concerns of women in similar situations. Sommers, founder of the Older Women's League* with Laurie Shields, coined the term *displaced homemaker*. The term was first used in a bill submitted in April 1975 to fund a center in California. The Alliance for Displaced Homemakers was organized to build grass-roots support for the measure, concentrating its work in the districts of those committee members considering the bill. The alliance effort, coordinated by Laurie Shields, was instrumental in securing state approval of a two-year, $200,000 pilot project for a Displaced Homemakers' Center. The center opened on the campus of Mills College in Oakland, California, in the spring of 1976. Another center for displaced homemakers, New Directions for Women, opened in Baltimore, in October 1976 through the efforts of state representative Helen Koss, who persuaded the Maryland legislature to fund a three-year, $570,000 project.

The California Alliance for Displaced Homemakers broadened its activities to other states. With funding from the board of the National Organization for Women (NOW) and the women's divisions of major Protestant denominations, alliances were organized to lobby for state funding of more centers and the passage of federal legislation. By August 1977, thirteen states had been persuaded to establish displaced homemaker programs.

Federal legislation to fund programs was considered in 1977, through the efforts of Congresswoman Yvonne Burke (D, California) and Senator Birch Bayh (D, Indiana). In testimony before House and Senate committees, Sommers and Shields described the difficulties of older women seeking employment and the lack of existing programs geared to their needs. They pointed out that many of these women were too young for Social Security and, unless disabled or caring for young children, were not eligible for federal welfare assistance programs. The displaced homemaker bills became part of the 1978 amendment to Title III of the Comprehensive Employment and Training Act (CETA). Under Title III, services were open to anyone regardless of age, but planners were directed to give special consideration to the needs of women aged 40 years and older. The U.S. Department of Labor made $5 million available for the programs in 1979–80, with state and local governments acting as prime sponsors for the CETA-funded centers.

With federal funds available, the organizing work of the Alliance for Displaced Homemakers was phased out, and in its place the Displaced Homemakers Network was established in 1978. Based in Washington, D.C., it acted as a national clearinghouse to collect data, to exchange program information with state and local units, and to ensure the continuity of federal assistance. The network achieved federal recognition in 1980 when it was awarded a sole-source contract by the U.S. Department of Labor to provide technical assistance for CETA-funded displaced homemakers programs. In 1991, the Displaced Homemakers Network was renamed the National Displaced Homemakers Network.

ORGANIZATION AND FUNDING

In 1991, the National Displaced Homemakers Network had 3,000 members and a staff of ten, maintaining contact with more than 1,000 programs serving approximately 300,000 women a year. Jill Miller was the Executive Director. The network publishes resource materials; maintains a library of program data; distributes manuals, press kits, and other materials; compiles statistics for research; publishes reports; sponsors workshops; and holds national conferences. Ten regional networks hold conferences and facilitate the exchange of information between state and local organizations in their region and the national network. Displaced Homemakers programs received federal assistance from the 1982 Job Training Partnership Act and the 1984 Carl D. Perkins Vocational Act, which makes available approximately $80 million annually for vocational and educational services to women and girls. In 1990, the Displaced Homemakers Self-sufficiency Assistance Act became law, which, when funded, will provide funds to states to support local services.

Federal money for the programs is disbursed through the states; state and local funding is also provided. The state sets up guidelines for program operation, including management, accounting, and reporting procedures, to ensure coordination between local units and the state social welfare, health, and employment agencies.

Local program sponsors include state and regional universities, community colleges, boards of education, community-based organizations, community action agencies, and area-wide development districts. The programs vary in content and emphasis and range in size from comprehensive centers offering support services and employment assistance, with budgets of $100,000 or more, to programs of $26,000 offering brief courses on self-awareness and job search skills. Some directors define job training as their major mission, while others view counseling and confidence building as more vital. Outside advisory boards are frequently set up to facilitate working relationships with other community groups and to help obtain employment for displaced homemakers.

POLICY CONCERNS AND TACTICS

The policy of the National Displaced Homemakers Network is to promote nationwide awareness of the economic difficulties faced by displaced homemakers and to demonstrate that older women are competent, employable, and valuable members of society. To maintain a stable source of federal funding, the network tries to establish displaced homemakers' eligibility for funding under various vocational and employment assistance laws. In 1990, the network advocated for the successful passage of the Displaced Homemakers Self-sufficiency Assistance Act. To ensure that its programs are financed, it monitors the progress of other relevant bills in Congress and the activities of the departments implementing the legislation. The network also works on health, civil rights, education, and housing issues that affect displaced homemakers.

The network utilizes the media to publicize its activities and to document the need for expanded programs. A Status Report of Displaced Homemakers and Single Parents in the United States (1987) noted that 40 percent of all displaced homemakers over the age of 20 lived below the federal poverty level at the time. Another report, The More Things Change (1990), showed that from 1980 to 1989, the displaced homemaker population increased nationally by 12 percent.

The policies and methods of the National Displaced Homemakers Network are continued on the state and local level through a multilevel organizational structure.

PUBLICATIONS

The National Displaced Homemakers Network publishes a quarterly *Network Newsletter* and a yearly *Displaced Homemaker Program Directory*, as well as guides to pertinent legislation, such as the *Guide to the Displaced Homemakers Self-sufficiency Assistance Act* (1990). In conjunction with the American Association of Retired Persons*, the network has produced a video, *Partners in Change* (1989), which profiles four displaced homemakers and employers of midlife and older women.

Further Information

Laurie Shields, *Displaced Homemakers: Organizing for a New Life*. (New York: McGraw-Hill, 1981).

MARY B. STAVISH

NATIONAL GRAY PANTHERS
See Gray Panthers Project Fund.

NATIONAL HISPANIC COUNCIL ON AGING (NHCoA)
2713 Ontario Road, N.W., Suite 200
Washington, D.C. 20009
(202) 265–1288   FAX (202) 745–2522

The National Hispanic Council on Aging (NCHoA) is a national, nonprofit, membership-based advocacy organization that works to promote the physical, emotional, and spiritual well-being of older Hispanics and to highlight their many unmet needs. The NHCoA promotes self- and mutual help as primary approaches for the development of interventions on behalf of the elderly, their families, and supportive networks. Its programs are conceptualized within the frameworks of empowerment and the intergenerational family. The NHCoA plays a key role in developing demonstration projects for the Hispanic elderly and participates in public policy debates by compiling research data on the Hispanic elderly, conducting community forums and training and demonstration projects, evaluating legislation and governmental policy as it affects the Hispanic elderly, and developing educational and informational resources.

ORIGIN AND DEVELOPMENT

The NHCoA was established in 1980 by a group of Hispanic professionals active in the field of aging who saw the need for a national advocacy group for the Hispanic elderly. By 1990, membership had grown to more than 3,000 individuals who work in administration, planning, direct services, research, or education for the benefit of Hispanic older persons. Over half of its membership consists of individuals 55 years of age and older. Many members and staff are professional gerontologists. In 1991, Marta Sotomayor was the President and Executive Director.

ORGANIZATION AND FUNDING

The NHCoA is governed by a twelve-member Board of Directors, drawn primarily from academia, foundations, and the public policy arena. The board, elected by the outgoing board, develops policies that guide program development and supports and counsels the organization in its various activities. The board meets regularly in different parts of the country, with particular efforts to meet in conjunction with the annual meetings of the Gerontological Society of America[*] and the American Society on Aging[*]. Board membership represents various geographical areas of the United States and Puerto Rico. NHCoA has chapters and affiliates in practically every state and in Puerto Rico. NHCoA has three full-time and four part-time paid staff in Washington, augmented by 150 volunteer staff members across the nation.

Major funding sources include corporations and businesses, foundations, federal, state, and local governments, members' dues, and publication sales. Most of the organization's funds are contracts and grants earmarked for training, demonstration projects, and publications. All of NHCoA's resources are devoted to Hispanic elderly issues and concerns.

In 1987, NHCoA initiated its Management Intern Program to expand professional employment opportunities for Hispanics working in health and human services by improving their credentials and adding to their administrative experience. The program is supported in part by the U.S. Administration on Aging (AoA). The organization also sponsors training conferences and workshops with other groups, both Hispanic and non-Hispanic, to strengthen local leadership.

POLICY CONCERNS AND TACTICS

The NHCoA's policy agenda priorities for Hispanic elders are health care, intergenerational relations, age discrimination, and employment, as well as the education and training of current and future professionals in the field of aging who are or will be delivering more culturally appropriate services. "The advocacy function of the NHCoA is carried out through research and program evaluation, leadership development, institution and capacity building, and developing educational materials." The organization works with the Leadership Council of Aging Organizations[*] and other coalitions on such issues as Medicare benefits improvement and the Social Security rollback proposal. In addition, staff and volunteers have met with the U.S. Commissioner on Aging regarding the AoA's priorities for its discretionary funds. On occasion, the NHCoA presents testimony to Congress on such issues as the reauthorization of the Older Americans Act and provides information to members of Congress and their staff concerning the unmet needs of Hispanic elders. NHCoA also sponsors a Summer Policy Internship program, placing Hispanics on congressional committees and in national agencies.

Program focus for the 1990s includes augmenting the pool of Hispanic gerontologists, developing leadership, working with the aging-network coalitions, and researching, creating, and evaluating educational materials and programs.

PUBLICATIONS

The NCHoA publicizes NHCoA's activities and legislative news in three newsletters issued four times a year: *Noticias*, *Noticias en Espanol*, and *Alcance*, for Hispanic-American families. Other publications, some of them available in Spanish, include *The Hispanic Older Woman* (1985), *The Hispanic Elderly: A Cultural Signature*, (1988) and *My Friend, My Enemy* (1990), an intergenerational approach to dealing with and preventing drug abuse. The organization has created a video, *Nosostros Los Viejos* (Your Challenges, Our Rewards, 1987) about the Hispanic elderly and professionals, and NHCoA's programs.

Further Information

Fernando Torres-Gil, "Ethnic Associations," in *The Encyclopedia of Aging*, ed. George Maddox (New York: Springer, 1987).

PHOEBE S. LIEBIG

NATIONAL HISPANIC MEDIA CENTER
See Asociacion Nacional Pro Personas Mayores.

NATIONAL HISPANIC RESEARCH CENTER
See Asociacion Nacional Pro Personas Mayores.

NATIONAL HOMECARING COUNCIL
See Foundation for Hospice and Homecare.

NATIONAL HOSPICE ORGANIZATION (NHO)
1901 North Moore Street, Suite 901
Arlington, Virginia 22209
(703) 243–5900   FAX (703) 525–5762

The mission of the National Hospice Organization (NHO) is to "integrate hospice care into the United States' health care system." The nonprofit, membership organization represents hospices, nurses, physicians, allied health care workers, and volunteers involved in the care of terminally ill patients.

ORIGIN AND DEVELOPMENT

The National Hospice Organization was established in 1978 and grew out of the movement to provide care and support services for the terminally ill and their families. The modern hospice movement, based on a concept of caring for patients and families as a unit of care, began in England under the leadership of Cicley Saunders. Hospice services can be provided in either the home or a hospital setting. NHO has established standards of care for hospices, provides both lay and professional information, and conducts legislative advocacy to expand reimbursement for hospice care, primarily within the structure of the Medicare benefit program.

ORGANIZATION AND FUNDING

The National Hospice Organization has approximately 5,000 members (1991), composed of institutions (e.g., hospices, hospitals, and home health agencies), professionals involved in the delivery of hospice care, and volunteers. There is a twenty-person Board of Directors composed of six appointed advisory members, ten regional delegates elected by the membership of their regions, and four at-large delegates, elected by NHO membership. The full-time staff includes fourteen people. John J. Mahoney was President of the National Hospice Organization in 1991. Policy is established by the voting membership and the Board of Directors.

Funding for the organization is derived from individual, institutional, and organizational membership dues, as well as income from educational seminars. The annual budget ranges between $1 million and $5 million. The organization holds an annual convention, usually during November, National Hospice Month.

POLICY CONCERNS AND TACTICS

Major areas of advocacy on behalf of the elderly include home health care and long-term care, health concerns of the elderly, and managed care (i.e., implications for people with chronic illnesses and disabilities). The National Hospice Organization's policy goals are to promote the well-being and optimal functioning of older adults, to increase the knowledge, skills, and productivity of hospice caregivers, and to contribute to the knowledge base in gerontology and long-term care. In the 1980s, the National Hospice Organization worked successfully to have hospice care provided as a permanent benefit under Medicare; the Omnibus Budget Reconciliation Act of 1990 included an expansion of the Medicare hospice benefit.

The National Hospice Organization testifies before Congress, supplies information to members of Congress and their staffs, conducts and publishes research on issues related to hospice care, and encourages its members to write to members of Congress in support of legislation affecting hospice care and benefits.

PUBLICATIONS

A resource guide, various informational pamphlets, and technical assistance materials are published by the NHO, as well as an annual *Guide to the Nation's Hospices*. Other publications include an annual report, the *Hospice Journal* (quarterly), the *Hospice Bulletin*, a periodic legislative update, the *NHO Newsline* (bimonthly) and *Hospice Magazine* (quarterly).

Further Information

Barbara Coleman, *A Consumers Guide to Hospice Care* (Washington, D.C.: National Consumers League, 1990); Paul R. Torrens, ed., *Hospice Programs and Public Policy* (Chicago: American Hospital Publishers, 1985).

NANCY C. ERDEY

NATIONAL INDIAN COUNCIL ON AGING (NICOA)
6400 Uptown Boulevard, N.E.
City Centre, Suite 510-W
Albuquerque, New Mexico 87110
(505) 888–3302   FAX (505) 888–3276

Created to be the national focal point for advocacy on behalf of American Indian and Alaskan native elderly, the National Indian Council on Aging (NICOA), a nonprofit organization funded by the U.S. Administration on Aging (AoA) and the U.S. Department of Labor, works to ensure that older American Indians and Alaskans have equal access to improved comprehensive services and that Indian and Alaskan native elders have access to a caring environment— one that contributes to an independent and dignified quality of life. NICOA disseminates information, presents testimony before Congress, and communicates with service providers and advocacy groups.

ORIGIN AND DEVELOPMENT

The first National Indian Conference on Aging was held in Phoenix, Arizona, June 15–17, 1976, with funding from the AoA. Over 1,500 members of 171 native American tribes and communities identified unmet needs and recommended remedial action in five workshop groups: income, physical well-being, physical environment, legal problems, and legislation. One recommendation, implemented immediately, was to establish the National Indian Task Force on Aging, designed to pursue the objectives established and to bring about the actions recommended. The thirty-five task force members elected at the conference set about the task of incorporating themselves as the National Indian Council on Aging (NICOA) and submitted an application for funding of the task force to the AoA. NICOA thus began its advocacy efforts on behalf of American Indian and Alaskan elders.

Major functions of the organization include advocacy, information dissemination, basic research, and technical assistance to tribal programs. NICOA offers such special services and resources as bulletins and legislative alerts to the advocacy network for the American Indian and Alaskan elderly regarding pertinent developments and suggesting speakers for conferences and congressional testimony. NICOA sponsors a biennial conference.

Since its creation, the NICOA has assisted in increasing the awareness of the general public, specifically service providers, to the needs of older American Indians and Alaskan natives. In addition, Indian and Alaskan native elderly have become increasingly aware and informed of the programs designed to meet their needs. They have created their own organizations and have begun to affect policies and legislation that have an impact on their lives.

ORGANIZATION AND FUNDING

NICOA consists of over 240 American Indian and Alaskan native persons aged 55 years and over and other associate members, who are young and/or of a different ethnic background. The voting membership of NICOA, however, is open only to American Indian and Alaskan native elders (aged 55 years and over). NICOA's Board of Directors is composed of thirteen members—one from each of twelve regions and one representative from the National Title VI Grantees Association. NICOA consists of ten staff members, headed by Dave Baldridge in 1991.

Individual members support a two-way flow of information between NICOA and local American Indian and Alaskan native communities and bring the specific concerns of their constituencies to the national level. Additionally, members serve on committees of NICOA established to address specific concerns.

The national headquarters is located in Albuquerque, New Mexico, and is the base of operations for all NICOA advocacy and research efforts. NICOA is also affiliated with autonomous State Indian Councils on Aging in Washington, Oregon, Idaho, California, Nevada, Arizona, New Mexico, Oklahoma, and Minnesota. Through these contacts, NICOA addresses issues at every level (national, state, and local).

The annual operating budget ranges from $150,000 to $250,000. Major sources of funds are federal grants and membership dues.

POLICY CONCERNS AND TACTICS

Health care, community-based long-term care, housing and environment, income supports, community service system development, and employment are major concerns of the organization. NICOA's priorities for the 1990s and beyond involve the completion and distribution of an agenda for the American Indian and Alaskan native aging population, including the provision of comprehensive in-home care for native American elders, legislative reform, including funding for improved services, and improved housing with supportive community-based services.

NICOA pursues its objectives through national advocacy, training, technical assistance, research, and information dissemination. The organization works cooperatively with government agencies and groups within the aging network. NICOA has testified before Congress on such matters as the rural elderly, the impact of the Older Americans Act on minority elderly, and age discrimination.

Further Information

NICOA issues *Elder Voices* periodically and "NICOA Update." The group offers such publications as *Let Us Continue in Unity* (1984), and *Access: A Demonstration Project* (1982). NICOA also makes available proceedings of the biennial conferences.

JOAN ORGAN

NATIONAL INSTITUTE OF SENIOR CENTERS
See National Council on the Aging Constituent Unit: National Institute of Senior Centers.

NATIONAL INSTITUTE OF SENIOR HOUSING
See National Council on the Aging Constituent Unit: National Institute of Senior Housing (NISH).

NATIONAL INSTITUTE ON ADULT DAYCARE
See National Council on the Aging Constituent Unit: National Institute on Adult Daycare.

NATIONAL INSTITUTE ON COMMUNITY-BASED LONG-TERM CARE
See National Council on the Aging Constituent Unit: National Institute on Community-Based Long-Term Care.

NATIONAL INTERFAITH COALITION ON AGING
See National Council on the Aging Constituent Unit: National Interfaith Coalition on Aging.

NATIONAL PACIFIC/ASIAN RESOURCE CENTER ON AGING (NP/ARCA)
Melbourne Tower, Suite 914
1511 Third Avenue
Seattle, Washington 98101
(206) 624–1221   FAX (206) 624–1023
The National Pacific/Asian Resource Center on Aging (NP/ARCA) is a national, nonprofit, nonmembership organization working to ensure and improve the delivery of health care and social services to older members of the highly diverse Pacific Islander/Asian community in America.

ORIGIN AND DEVELOPMENT

The NP/ARCA was founded in 1979, the newest organization among the key ethnic elderly associations (the National Caucus and Center on the Black Aged*, the Asociacion Nacional Pro Personas Mayores*, the National Indian Council on Aging*, and the National Hispanic Council on Aging*). Like these other associations, its creation was stimulated by the 1971 White House Conference on Aging. In addition, an eighteenth-month grant was funded by the federal Administration on Aging (AoA) in 1976. The purpose of that grant, the Pacific/Asian Elderly Research Project, was to compile and analyze data on the delivery and utilization of social and health services by that community. One of the outcomes was a dissemination conference in May 1978 at which several recommendations were generated, including the development of a permanent national center to address the needs of elderly Pacific/Asians. The formation of this proposed center, NP/ARCA, was ensured by subsequent AoA funding in 1979.

The main missions of NP/ARCA are to ensure a meaningful, secure, and dignified existence for Pacific/Asian elderly, historically subjected to racially discriminatory legislation, and to expand the knowledge and technical expertise of service providers about the unique needs of this group of the elderly. NP/ARCA seeks to accomplish these missions by compiling and disseminating statistics and information about the cultural and linguistic diversity among Pacific/Asians and the implications for effective and sensitive service delivery systems, providing technical assistance to local Pacific/Asian community groups to improve their ability to meet the needs of older individuals, and developing training programs for health care and social service providers and organizations.

ORGANIZATION AND FUNDING

In 1990, the Executive Director of NP/ARCA was Louise Kamikawa, the organization's founder. She works with a staff of eight full-time employees, seven of them in the Seattle office. The other staff member works as a project director in Los Angeles and oversees the operation of a Senior Community Service Employment Program (SCSEP) there. NP/ARCA also conducts a SCSEP in Seattle, as well as a Senior Environmental Employment (SEE) Program. These programs are designed to provide part-time employment for low-income Pacific/Asians aged 55 years and over. The professional staff of NP/ARCA is augmented by two consultants, one in Los Angeles and one in Washington, D.C.

NP/ARCA is funded by an AoA grant and has received additional funding from the AoA, the Environmental Protection Agency, and the Department of Labor for the two employment programs since 1989. NP/ARCA's annual budget is approximately $400,000, of which about 10 percent comes from donations.

POLICY CONCERNS AND TACTICS

The major policy concerns of NP/ARCA revolve around the facilitation of access to services by Pacific/Asian elders, with a specific focus on community services system development. Its major activities include generating information for use by Congress, through its consultant in the nation's capital, and collaborating with other associations for the ethnic elderly and with the A.S.A.P. (Advocates Senior Alert Process). NP/ARCA also provides resources materials to service groups and state units and area agencies on aging and advocates for inclusion of minority persons in an advisory capacity at state and local levels. NP/ARCA successfully ensured the collection of information about Pacific/Asians for the 1990 census. In November 1988, the center's Executive Director presented testimony before the Federal Council on Aging relevant to a 1991 White House Conference on Aging.

ELECTORAL ACTIVITY

NP/ARCA is restricted from engaging in electoral activity by its federal funding and its nonprofit status.

PUBLICATIONS

In keeping with its major function as a resource center, NP/ARCA has an extensive publication program and a resource library of more than 500 volumes. Bimonthly NP/ARCA publishes *Update*, which includes descriptions of model programs operating in Pacific/Asian communities, analysis of policy issues, pending legislation, and rules and regulations important to its constituency. Biennially, the center produces the *National Community Service Directory: Asian/Pacific Elderly* and the *National Consultation Resource Roster*. It has also published and disseminated *Pacific/Asian Elderly: Bibliography* (1990); *The Wisdom of Age* (1981), the proceedings of a conference on Pacific/Asians; *Guide to the Utilization of Family and Community Support Systems* (1983); and a medical handbook.

Further Information

D. Watanabe, "An Action Oriented Study: Pacific Asian Elderly Research Project," *Generations* (Summer, 1977): 8–9.

PHOEBE S. LIEBIG

NATIONAL PENSION ASSISTANCE PROJECT
See Pension Rights Center.

NATIONAL RETIRED TEACHER'S ASSOCIATION
See American Association of Retired Persons.

NATIONAL SENIOR CITIZENS EDUCATION AND RESEARCH CENTER

See National Council of Senior Citizens.

NATIONAL SENIOR CITIZENS LAW CENTER (NSCLC)

1815 H Street, N.W., Suite 700
Washington, D.C. 20006
(202) 887–5280   FAX (202) 785–6792

The National Senior Citizens Law Center (NSCLC) is a national legal services support center specializing in legal services to the elderly. The NSCLC does not accept individual clients but does provide a significant amount of assistance to lawyers, advocates, and legislators on legal issues concerning the elderly. The NSCLC also serves as a clearinghouse of legal information for the elderly, addressing Social Security concerns, age discrimination, and problems with pension plans, Medicare and Medicaid, nursing homes, and consumer products.

ORIGIN AND DEVELOPMENT

The NSCLC was founded in 1972 by the Legal Services Corporation. In 1976, the center established a clearinghouse for legal problems, which was funded by the U.S. Administration on Aging (AoA).

ORGANIZATION AND FUNDING

NSCLC has eighteen staff members who handle approximately 4,000 requests for aid and information each year. Approximately $600,000 of NSCLC's annual $1 million budget is funded by the federal government through the Legal Services Corporation. The balance comes from private foundations, charitable contributions, AoA grants, and fees. NSCLC maintains two offices, one in Washington, D.C., and the other in Los Angeles.

POLICY CONCERNS AND TACTICS

Besides providing technical assistance to attorneys and advocates for the elderly, NSCLC litigates in conjunction with other legal service organizations and programs funded by the Older Americans Act (OAA). The cases in which it has participated deal with important retirement and pension issues. The center also files amicus curiae briefs with the U.S. Supreme Court, often in conjunction with advocacy groups such as the Gray Panthers Project Fund*. NSCLC has testified before Congress on such matters as the oversight of the Age Discrimination in Employment Act and the extension and reauthorization of the OAA and on legislation such as the Older Workers Benefit Protection Act.

PUBLICATIONS

NSCLC's major publication is a newsletter to Legal Aid offices nationwide, *NSCLC Washington Weekly*. The center also publishes the monthly *Nursing Home Law Letter*. In addition, NSCLC has produced professional books, such as *Age Discrimination* (1987), *Evaluating Legal Services* (1986), and *Representing Older Persons* (1985).

Further Information

Frank Greve, "Legal Eagles," *50 Plus* (December 1987): 16–19; R. M. Lukoff, "Representing the Elderly," *Trial* 21 (March 1985): 74–75.

T. DEAN HANDY

NATIONAL SOCIAL WELFARE ASSEMBLY
See National Council on the Aging.

NATIONAL VOLUNTARY ORGANIZATIONS FOR INDEPENDENT LIVING FOR THE AGING
See National Council on the Aging, Constituent Unit: National Voluntary Organizations for Independent Living for the Aging (NVOILA).

NEW DIRECTIONS FOR WOMEN
See National Displaced Homemakers Network.

NEW YORK ASSOCIATION FOR THE BLIND
See Lighthouse National Center for Vision and Aging.

NORTH AMERICAN ASSOCIATION OF JEWISH HOMES AND HOUSING FOR THE AGING (NAJHHA)
10830 North Central Expressway, Suite 150
Dallas, Texas 75231
(214) 696–9838   FAX (214) 360–0753

The North American Association of Jewish Homes and Housing for the Aging (NAJHHA) is a private, nonprofit organization that represents homes and housing for the Jewish elderly in the United States and Canada. Focusing on issues of high-quality care, NAJHHA serves as an important conduit for communication between religious and nonreligious sectors, provides educational opportunities for people serving the elderly, and encourages advocacy for the aging.

ORIGIN AND DEVELOPMENT

The NAJHHA was founded in 1960 because administrators of Jewish nursing homes needed to share information and to provide professional training for those involved in the care of the elderly. The founders also believed that by combining their concerns into a single voice, they could better serve as advocates for the elderly. The original group of founders included Jacob Gold, Solomon Geld, Mitchell Waife, and the 1990 Executive Vice-President of the organization, Herbert Shore.

The original name of the organization was the National Association of Jewish Homes for the Aged. In 1982, the name was changed to reflect a broadening constituency of members who were concerned with the welfare of the Jewish elderly.

ORGANIZATION AND FUNDING

In 1990, NAJHHA was under the executive direction of Herbert Shore and staffed by two employees. Organizational decisions are made by a fifteen-member Board of Directors consisting of administrators of homes and housing for the elderly. In addition, NAJHHA is governed by nine officers, including the President, the President-elect, and three Vice-Presidents. The board and officers are elected by the members.

The NAJHHA annual budget is in excess of $200,000 and is derived from conference revenues and membership dues. Funds are used for administrative expenses, educational workshops and professional institutes, and publications. The 1990 membership consisted of 105 Jewish nursing homes and just under 100 housing units.

The NAJHHA serves elderly people, nonphysician health care providers, and diverse volunteer associations. NAJHHA is organized into the following committees: Public Policy and Legislation, Quality Assurance, Alzheimer's Task Force, Recruitment, Professional Practice, and Position Papers. The organization is affiliated with the American Association of Homes for the Aging*, the Council of Jewish Federations, and the Conference of Jewish Communal Service.

NAJHHA usually holds an annual conference in February. Administrators, trustees of homes for the elderly, and other leaders attend the event. A professional institute is held in the summer and attracts nursing home directors and social service workers from within the Jewish service community.

POLICY CONCERNS AND TACTICS

The organization consistently focuses on ensuring high-quality care for the elderly. The NAJHHA is interested in a variety of policy areas concerning the Jewish elderly in the United States and Canada, including long-term care, volunteer activity, health care, pension and Social Security policy, and social service delivery. It provides professional education to health care workers in the form of annual conferences and professional institutes and influences public policy on the aging by taking political action and being involved in lobbying. NAJHHA also prepares position papers as advocates for the elderly. The organization's recruiting initiative encourages professionals to enter the field of long-term care. It also supports planning for creative services such as outreach to communities and college campuses. Current priorities in 1991 included addressing the ongoing shortage of nursing personnel, monitoring regulatory processes, and reimbursement.

PUBLICATIONS

Publications include *Perspectives*, a quarterly newsletter, annual conference proceedings, and a biennial membership directory.

ELIZABETH MIDLARSKY
SUSAN ALEXANDER

NURSING HOME ADVISORY AND RESEARCH COUNCIL (NHARC)
P.O. Box 18820
Cleveland Heights, Ohio 44118
(216) 321–0403

The Nursing Home Advisory and Research Council (NHARC) is a nonprofit, nonmembership association focused on improving conditions in nursing homes through its advocacy arm, Concerned Relatives of Nursing Home Patients. Concerned Relatives, a membership organization of relatives, friends, and guardians of nursing home residents, provides education and works for legislative change.

ORIGIN AND DEVELOPMENT

NHARC was incorporated in 1975 to fund Concerned Relatives. NHARC's 1990 Executive Director, Mary Adelaide Mendelson, created NHARC and its subsidiary following research into nursing home conditions, in preparation for testimony given before the House Ways and Means Committee. This research led to Mendelson's book, *Tender Loving Greed* (1974). Through Concerned Relatives, NHARC has consistently sought to improve the quality of life for nursing home residents.

ORGANIZATION AND FUNDING

NHARC is governed by a Board of Directors with ten members and an Executive Director. Two staff members manage NHARC and Concerned Relatives. A newsletter committee helps fulfill NHARC's mission of affecting public policy by informing the consumer public. NHARC conducts research on pertinent issues, while Concerned Relatives provides education and advocacy. In 1990, Concerned Relatives of Nursing Home Patients had 1,200 members. Although the membership extends across the United States, northeast Ohio represents the largest geographic concentration.

NHARC receives funding solely through private contributions. The total annual budget of around $50,000 is used to support the work of the organization.

POLICY CONCERNS AND TACTICS

The primary concerns of NHARC and its subsidiary are nursing home reform and Medicare and Medicaid. Concerned Relatives has occasionally provided testimony before the U.S. Congress and the Ohio Assembly and has supplied information to legislators. Concerned Relatives also informs families and social service workers on nursing home placement, Medicare and Medicaid reimbursement, and selection of a nursing home.

PUBLICATIONS

NHARC publishes a newsletter, *Insight*. Free to members of Concerned Relatives, the subscription cost for others is $15 for six issues. *Insight* includes an update on legislative issues, Medicare and Medicaid, legal topics, and medical information. The group also publishes brochures, such as *Selecting a Nursing Home*.

Further Information

Mary Adelaid Mendelson, *Tender Loving Greed: How the Incredibly Lucrative Nursing Home Industry Is Exploiting America's Old People and Defrauding Us All* (New York: A. A. Knopf, 1974).

TAMARA ZURAKOWSKI

NURSING HOME INFORMATION SERVICE
See National Council of Senior Citizens.

O
/

OASIS (OLDER ADULT SERVICE AND INFORMATION SERVICE)
See American Association for International Ageing.

OFFICE ON AGING AND LONG-TERM CARE
See American Hospital Association Section for Aging and Long-term Care.

OLDER AMERICANS CONSUMER COOPERATIVE
See United Seniors Health Cooperative.

OLDER WOMEN'S EDUCATIONAL FUND
See Older Women's League.

OLDER WOMEN'S LEAGUE (OWL)
730 11th Street, N.W., Suite 300
Washington, D.C. 20001
(202) 783–6686   FAX (202) 638–2356
   The Older Women's League (OWL) is a national, nonprofit, advocacy organization committed to improving the lives of midlife and older women. OWL is the first national membership organization devoted solely to the policy concerns and personal needs of aging women and the first to highlight women's role as caregivers of the elderly.

ORIGIN AND DEVELOPMENT

   Tish Sommers and Laurie Shields, organizers of Alliance for Displaced Homemakers (now National Displaced Homemakers Network*) in 1975, founded the Older Women's League at the close of the first White House Mini-Conference on Older Women held in 1980. About 300 charter members comprised the new national organization. The founders had laid the groundwork two years previously with the Older Women's Educational Fund, a research and education entity. OWL organized in response to the overwhelming predominance of women among the aged poor and among caregivers of the elderly. OWL was founded to publicize and rectify the situation of millions of older American women who lack pension resources and health insurance. Its motto is "Don't Agonize—Organize!"

OWL grew quickly, expanding from the original 300 members to 3,000 by 1982. In 1990 there were over 20,000 OWL members and more than 130 local chapters throughout thirty-seven states. Originally located in Oakland, California, the headquarters moved to Washington, D.C., in 1982.

"OWL works forcefully to provide mutual support for its members, to achieve economic and social equity, and to improve the image and status of older women." Programs launched by OWL include national campaigns to educate the public, as well as policymakers at all levels, about the needs of older women; grass-roots leadership development to train OWL organizers to build strong local chapters and facilitate effective actions; and actions and studies exposing employment discrimination against midlife and older women.

ORGANIZATION AND FUNDING

The Older Women's League is managed by a fifteen-member Board of Directors, including seven regional members. The sixteen-member staff consists of professionals, clerical staff, and volunteers. OWL holds a triennial convention, in addition to regional conferences and other special gatherings. Membership dues and individual contributions comprise approximately 40 percent of the $800,000 annual budget, and foundation grants equal about 40 percent. Additional fund raising provides the other 20 percent of the group's financial support.

POLICY CONCERNS AND TACTICS

OWL's national agenda, as adopted in 1990, focuses on the following six concerns:

1. A national universal health care system
2. A more equitable and adequate Social Security system and a more adequate Supplemental Security Income (SSI)
3. Increased access to housing and housing alternatives
4. Combating discrimination in the workplace and improving the image of midlife and older women
5. Staying in control to the end of life
6. Expanded employer-sponsored pension coverage

In its first decade of existence, OWL testified before a wide variety of congressional committees within a broad subject range. In May 1990, OWL endorsed more equitable retirement policies for women before the Sub-committee on Retirement and Employment of the House Select Committee on Aging and in

April of the same year, called for Social Security reform before the House Ways and Means Committee. In February 1989, OWL presented information on age discrimination to the Senate Labor Committee; in March 1988, the group discussed fraud and long-term care before the Federal Trade Commission. The Older Women's League advocated for family and medical leave before the House Education and Labor Committee in February 1988.

OWL claims a prominent role in the enacting of recent legislation. As a result of the organization's efforts, the 1986 Tax Reform Act and the 1988 Budget Act included improvements in pension equity for women, such as mandatory pension coverage for a larger pool of low-paid workers. OWL co-sponsored, with other feminist groups, the Retirement Equity Act of 1984, which extended survivor benefits and options.

Education remains a central focus of OWL's mission. Annual reports, issued since 1987 in celebration of Mother's Day, provide one example of the group's national information campaign. The "issue-specific research documents" are released to the media at a news conference, to Congress, and to local OWL chapters. In 1990, the twelve-page Mothers' Day Report focused on financial matters: *Heading for Hardship: Retirement Income for American Women in the Next Century*. *Failing America's Caregivers: A Status Report on Women Who Care* was the title of the 1989 Mother's Day report. The day that report was issued, OWL held a roundtable "to address the issues raised in the report and to explore possible policy initiatives."

At the state level, OWL develops model state legislation in critical areas such as respite for caregivers. OWL also trains members for direct and effective citizen advocacy. Local chapters present workshops to educate aging women regarding their special needs and to provide a springboard for action on these issues. Topics include employment of older women, housing options, health concerns, and legal questions.

The OWL Powerline is another educational and advocacy activity. Saturdays and Sundays during congressional sessions, telephone calls to (202) 783–6689 access a three-minute recorded summary of pertinent congressional activity, Supreme Court rulings, agency reports, and press conference results. The message is updated weekly. Because of low weekend telephone rates, OWL claims that the average cost of a call to the Powerline is less than a dollar.

The Older Women's League conducted an advertising campaign in the early 1980s to bring its concerns to the public. One advertisement, showing a tear on the face of the Statue of Liberty, says, "When it comes to the treatment of older women, America takes a lot of liberties."

ELECTORAL ACTIVITY

Midway through 1988, the Older Women's League sent a Vote in '88 Campaign action kit to its chapters. "The intent was to stimulate thought and questions for members to pose to candidates at all levels of government." In addition, OWL worked with the National Women's Political Caucus in 1988 to offer women's issue forums and receptions at both the Democratic and Republican national conventions. OWL does not have a political action committee.

PUBLICATIONS

Educational materials developed by the organization include information packets, research reports, a leader training curriculum, and a video. OWL also offers a book by Sommers and Shields, *Women Take Care: Consequences of Caregiving in Today's Society* (1987). The materials uniquely analyze their subjects "from the viewpoint of older women, a constituency which has been invisible too long." The bimonthly *OWL Observer* newsletter keeps members informed of relevant news, policy concerns, and activities. Occasional Gray Paper publications address topics such as pensions, divorce, and health care in retirement. Testimony statements by the organization on a variety of central issues, from long-term care to equal rights, are also available.

Further Information

Patricia Huckle, *Tish Sommers, Activist, and the Founding of the Older Women's League* (1991); Elaine Somerville, "A Champion of America's Older Women," *Modern Maturity* (October 1983): 112–114.

JIMMY E. W. MEYER

OPPORTUNITIES FOR OLDER AMERICANS FUND
1511 K Street, N.W., Suite 443
Washington, D.C. 20005
(202) 638–1007   FAX (202) 638–5917

The Opportunities for Older Americans Fund encourages community leaders to recognize and utilize the resources of older Americans. The public, nonprofit fund uses networks to increase volunteer, employment, and training opportunities for the elderly.

ORIGIN AND DEVELOPMENT

The Opportunities for Older Americans Fund began in 1986. The group's founding philosophy is: "It is in the national interest to encourage policymakers, educators, and public and private sector leaders to recognize the potential contribution of older persons towards meeting community needs." Stephanie deSibour has been President since the Opportunities Fund's inception.

ORGANIZATION AND FUNDING

A twelve-member Executive Board establishes policy, and an Advisory Board of thirty professionals in aging and related areas assists the board in program development. The Advisory Board consists of leaders of agencies based in the Washington, D.C., area whose prime interest is service for and/or by the elderly. Thus, the Advisory Board supplies a vital link to the fund's constituency.

The Opportunities for Older Americans Fund has an annual budget of approximately $90,000 and maintains two professional staff. Approximately 65 percent of its budget is derived from foundation grants, 30 percent from corporate contributions, and 5 percent from individual donors.

POLICY CONCERNS AND TACTICS

The Opportunities for Older Americans Fund facilitates programs that focus on aging issues. It does not lobby. The only overt influence exerted on public policy results from the programs brought to the public's attention by the fund's brokerage and educational activities.

The Opportunities Fund helps nonprofit organizations on aging identify resources for productive options for older people. Encouraging community support throughout the metropolitan area of the District of Columbia, the fund supports programs and services that allow older people to live with dignity and independence. A recent program on intergenerational mentoring, Linking Lifetimes, was funded by the Mott Foundation on the recommendation of the Opportunities for Older Americans Fund.

The Opportunities Fund also provides technical assistance for program development to other groups. Through the fund's institutional structure, individuals can participate in the philanthropic process. In an effort to strengthen community initiatives, the fund supplies issue analysis, research assistance, planning, and information exchange as part of its goal to develop positive interorganizational responses to the needs of the older adult. From time to time, the fund coordinates activities with such national organizations as the National Council on the Aging*, the American Association of Retired Persons*, and local senior service organizations.

All of the fund's resources are focused on issues of productive aging. As part of its public education and program development agenda, it sponsors activities in senior employment, literacy, senior housing, intergenerational programs, community service, and the arts.

The focus of the Opportunities for Older Americans Fund in the 1990s is to expand opportunities for older people as employees, volunteers, teachers, and caregivers, emphasizing volunteerism, employment, intergenerational relations, and professional education and training. The group's future priorities include expanding options for intergenerational activity, expanding employment options including training for older adults, and promoting senior volunteer initiatives.

PUBLICATIONS

Opportunities for Older Americans Fund has contributed to *A Directory of Housing Programs for Seniors* (1990) and has assisted in the publication, *Growing Older in Greater Washington* (1989).

JAMES BANKS

P

PACIFIC/ASIAN ELDERLY RESEARCH PROJECT
See National Pacific/Asian Resource Center on Aging.

PEABODY HOME
See Aging in America.

PELHAM HOUSE
See Aging in America.

PENSIONER'S EMPOWERMENT PROJECT
See Pension Rights Center.

PENSION RIGHTS CENTER
918 16th Street, N.W., Suite 704
Washington, D.C. 20006
(202) 296–3776

The Pension Rights Center is a nonprofit, public interest group committed to protecting and promoting the pension interests of workers and retirees. The center's goal is a retirement income system that is fair, adequate, and responsive to the needs of individuals and the economy.

ORIGIN AND DEVELOPMENT

The Pension Rights Center was founded in 1976 by Karen W. Ferguson to represent the interests of people who looked to private pensions for a secure retirement. Initially the organization focused on ensuring that government regulations implementing the Employee Retirement Income Security Act (ERISA) of 1974 reflected congressional intent and on making employees aware of their rights under that law. ERISA imposed new federal standards on private pension plans, increasing the number of people earning pensions and the security of their benefits.

ORGANIZATION AND FUNDING

The center, under Ferguson's direction, has grown to include a professional staff of ten and a twelve-member Board of Directors. Its policies are determined by the center's Executive Committee based on recommendations by the board.

The organization receives 39 percent of its income from foundation grants, 20 percent from government funding, 28 percent from contracts and donations from individuals and organizations, and 13 percent from other sources.

Major 1991 projects of the Pension Rights Center included the Women's Pension Project, which seeks to prevent poverty among older women by working for fairer pension policies, and the National Pension Assistance Project, which is committed to increasing the availability of legal assistance to individuals with pension problems.

POLICY CONCERNS AND TACTICS

The principal issues of concern to the Pension Rights Center relate to fairer pension policies. The group targets inequities in pension policies and recommends workable reform measures. Center staff are frequently invited to testify before House and Senate committees considering pension legislation. In recent testimony, they have supported measures designed to increase the number of workers receiving pensions, deter mismanagement of pension money, improve the pension rights of divorced women, and eliminate barriers to the enforcement of legal rights.

The Pension Rights Center serves as a media resource center, and staff regularly appear on radio and television to explain complex pension concepts, provide analyses of pension policy issues, and offer advice on how workers can monitor the investment of company pension money by their employers. When resources permit, the center works with pensioner groups seeking cost-of-living adjustments and helps individuals gain the pensions to which they are entitled. The Pension Rights Center also operates a lawyer referral service for individuals seeking legal assistance.

PUBLICATIONS

The Pension Rights Center's publications include *Protecting Your Pension Money* 1990, a basic handbook explaining how to tell if the people investing pension money are following federal rules; *Can You Count on Getting a Pension?* (1990) a summary of vesting rules for company and union pension plans; *Your Pension Rights at Divorce: What Women Need to Know* (1991), an easy-to-understand explanation of the many different rules applicable to the division of pensions at divorce; and *SEPs: The Pension Plan [Almost] Nobody Knows About* (1989), a description of low-cost pension plans. It also publishes the *National Pension Assistance Project Newsletter* and *News from the Pension Rights Center* annually.

MARY B. STAVISH

P.R.I.D.E. FOUNDATION (PROMOTE REAL INDEPENDENCE FOR THE DISABLED AND ELDERLY)
71 Plaza Court
Groton, Connecticut 06340
(203) 445–1448

The P.R.I.D.E. Foundation (Promote Real Independence for the Disabled and Elderly) is a nonprofit agency that encourages independent living and improvement of the quality of life for the disabled and elderly by improving and promoting clothing accessibility and the importance of comfortable, good-looking apparel. P.R.I.D.E. promotes public awareness through educational programs and consulting services.

ORIGIN AND DEVELOPMENT

P.R.I.D.E. is a small organization that focuses on a single issue: clothing rights. The group's 1990 Executive Director, Evelyn S. Kennedy, founded P.R.I.D.E. in 1978. P.R.I.D.E. designs and develops prototype garments and devices that help maximize individual autonomy in home management and personal grooming. The organization provides practical information to individuals and institutions regarding construction or alteration of clothing to meet special needs.

P.R.I.D.E. conducts workshops and programs for such groups as disabled veterans and stroke victims, as well as for healthcare providers, volunteer organizations, and other interest groups such as the National Council on the Aging[*]. P.R.I.D.E. has sponsored seminars on clothing concerns and rights throughout the United States and abroad.

Utilizing P.R.I.D.E.'s Traveling Trunk Show, health care agencies and institutions promote staff awareness and involvement in clothing rights. P.R.I.D.E. has also developed a successful training program for the disabled with entry-level occupational skills in sewing.

ORGANIZATION AND FUNDING

P.R.I.D.E. Foundation has a staff of two and a budget of less than $25,000. It is an independent organization with no institutional affiliation or membership constituency. During the early 1980s, volunteers and student interns helped design and construct sample garments and participated in training classes and workshops. A professional staff member now offers private consultation and is available for seminars and lectures. The organization developed a workbook,

Dressing with Pride (1981), funded in part by a seed grant from Sears, Roebuck and Company. It instructs the user about modifying and altering ready-to-wear garments to suit special needs.

Additional funding for the organization has come from other foundations, private donations, and federal Title X funds. All honoraria are returned to the foundation to support its goals and objectives. In the early 1980s, P.R.I.D.E. received grants from the Connecticut Department of Health and the U.S. Department of Labor.

POLICY CONCERNS AND TACTICS

The P.R.I.D.E. Foundation affects public awareness and policy change in the context of the right of an individual to well-fitting, comfortable, and appropriate clothing. The goal of P.R.I.D.E. is to promote independent and autonomous dressing for the disabled and elderly. This focus on the right to wear clothing that meets the special needs of the individual includes the right to comfortable and fashionable clothing. In an institutional setting, well-being can be enhanced by clothes that maximize dignity and privacy. P.R.I.D.E. encourages care providers to ensure that personal articles of clothing are appropriate and secure.

P.R.I.D.E. occasionally presents its arguments to government bodies. In 1984, Kennedy testified before a committee of the state legislature of Connecticut on the issue of clothing rights for the mentally retarded in state institutions. Kennedy has participated in a consumer action panel that acted as a mediator for consumer problems, making suggestions to manufacturers about solutions to the special clothing needs of the elderly. The issue of good-looking, comfortable apparel, appropriately sized to meet the changing needs of the older body, is only beginning to be addressed. Through advocacy and education, P.R.I.D.E. Foundation works to increase public awareness and encourage institutional and commercial policy changes to accommodate people with special clothing needs.

PUBLICATIONS

In addition to the workbook, *Dressing With Pride* (1981), P.R.I.D.E. has published *Clothing Accessibility: an Aide to the Disabled* (1983).

Further Information

"P.R.I.D.E. Responds to Esthetic Clothing Needs of Older Persons," *Perspective on Aging* 13, no. 4 (July–August, 1984): 18–21.

                                                    BETH DINATALE JOHNSON

PROJECT AYUDA
See Asociacion Nacional Pro Personas Mayores.

PROJECT RESPETO
See Asociacion Nacional Pro Personas Mayores.

PROMOTE REAL INDEPENDENCE FOR THE DISABLED AND ELDERLY
See P.R.I.D.E (Promote Real Independence for the Disabled and Elderly).

R

/

RAINBOW COMMUNICATIONS
See Asociacion Nacional Pro Personas Mayores.

RETIRED AND OLDER WORKERS DEPARTMENT, UNITED AUTO WORKERS
See United Auto Workers Retired and Older Workers Department.

THE RETIRED OFFICERS ASSOCIATION (TROA)
201 North Washington Street
Alexandria, Virginia 22314–2529
(703) 549–2311   FAX (703) 838–8173

The Retired Officers Association (TROA) is an independent nonprofit organization, operated exclusively to benefit uniformed services personnel and their families and survivors. TROA's motto is "Service to Country and Our Members."

ORIGIN AND DEVELOPMENT

TROA was founded in Los Angeles, on February 23, 1929, with the understanding that retired officers, their families and survivors, would benefit by joining together in an association to counsel and offer assistance to all officers on retirement concerns. In the 1940s, TROA's managers realized that due to the demands and pressures of World War II and its aftermath, reorganization and expansion was critical. On April 12, 1944, with a membership of 2,600, TROA relocated to Washington, D.C. TROA is concerned with the entire uniformed services community—officer and enlisted, active duty and reserve. In 1991, TROA's membership numbered 375,000, the largest military officers' association in the country.

The major goals and services of TROA are to publish *The Retired Officer Magazine* and to obtain fair and equitable treatment on Capitol Hill for active and reserve uniformed services personnel, retirees, their families, and survivors. In addition, TROA's professional staff provides individual counsel in the following areas: employment assistance, personal affairs, dependent scholarship loans and grants, survivor assistance, retirement information, advice, and assistance related to negotiated favorable rates (e.g., extended car warranty program, mail order prescription drug program, health testing, group health and life insurance plans, financial services, and a travel program).

ORGANIZATION AND FUNDING

TROA is governed by a Board of Directors consisting of thirty-six retired officers from the seven uniformed services—Army, Navy, Air Force, Marine Corps, Coast Guard, Public Health Service, and National Oceanic and Atmospheric Administration—representing both the regular and reserve forces. Four of the association's national officers—the Chairperson of the board and three Vice-Chairpersons—are elected by the Board of Directors from among its members. Also elected as association officers by the Board of Directors (from outside its membership) are the President, Comptroller, and Secretary, all of whom serve on TROA's professional, salaried staff. President in 1991 was Vice-Admiral Thomas J. Kilcline, USN-Ret.

TROA maintains 408 local/state–affiliated branches and has a staff of seventy-nine. Membership is open to all women and men who are or who were commissioned or warrant officers in any component of the seven uniformed services. Persons can elect to become life members of TROA or to renew their membership annually. Members who are not yet retired from the uniformed services enjoy all privileges of membership, including voting, but are not eligible to serve on TROA's Board of Directors.

Auxiliary membership is available to widowers and widows of deceased members, as well as surviving spouses of individuals who would have been eligible for membership. Auxiliary members enjoy all privileges of membership except voting and serving on the Board of Directors. Surviving spouses of life members are automatically enrolled as life members without further charges.

The operating budget is over $8 million. Dues were $20 a year in 1991. Major sources of funds are membership dues (75%) and investments, magazine advertisements, and royalties (25%).

POLICY CONCERNS AND TACTICS

With four registered professional lobbyists, TROA represents the military community on Capitol Hill, including active duty, reserve, retired, their families, and survivors. TROA has significantly contributed to such legislation as the original Military Survivor Benefit Plan and the Civilian Health and Medical Program for the Uniformed Services.

In addition, TROA spearheaded a major effort to have Congress repeal the Medicare Catastrophic Coverage Act (1989), blocked annual attempts to eliminate, cap, or delay cost-of-living adjustments (COLAs) to military retired pay, prevented the imposition of a user fee for each outpatient visit to a military medical facility, and played a major role in increasing Servicemen's Group Life Insurance and Veterans' Group Life Insurance (SGLI/VGLI) VA coverage for active duty and reserve personnel.

PUBLICATIONS

TROA issues *The Retired Officer Magazine*, a monthly publication that contains reports on Congress and the uniformed services, advice on service benefits and entitlements, and diverse feature articles, and publishes resource and educational materials, such as the *SBP Made Easy: The Survivor Benefit Plan* (1988). TROA also offers a variety of informational brochures such as *A Tradition of Service* (1990).

JOAN ORGAN

RETIRED PROFESSIONAL ACTION GROUP
See Gray Panthers Project Fund.

RETIRED SENIOR VOLUNTEER PROGRAM
See National Association of Retired Senior Volunteer Program Directors.

S
/

SAGE
See Senior Action in a Gay Environment.

SAINT LUKE'S HOME FOR INDIGENT CHILDREN
See Aging in America.

SAVE OUR SECURITY (SOS)
1331 F Street, N.W.
Washington, D.C. 20004
(202) 624–9557   FAX (202) 624–9595

Save Our Security (SOS), also known as the Coalition to Protect Social Security, is a coalition of organizations that have Social Security beneficiaries and contributors as members. SOS aims to improve and protect the existing Social Security and health care system in the United States, using the media to promote public awareness, as well as engaging in congressional lobbying and presenting testimony.

ORIGIN AND DEVELOPMENT

SOS was founded in 1979 by Wilbur Cohen, who had been Secretary of Health, Education and Welfare under President Lyndon Johnson and was the first employee of the Social Security Administration. The coalition was created to counteract proposed cutbacks in Social Security benefits and to strengthen the Social Security and health-care systems.

ORGANIZATION AND FUNDING

A Board of Directors of about twenty members governs SOS. Monthly policy meetings are held; the general membership votes to set organization policy. In

1991, Arthur S. Flemming, former Secretary of Health, Education and Welfare under President Dwight D. Eisenhower, was chair of SOS. There were two professional staff persons in 1991: Roberta Feinstein Havel, Executive Director, and Carol Forester, Administrative Assistant. Committees of SOS include: Independent Agency and Administration, Health Care, Supplemental Security Income, and Women's Issues.

Over 100 national, state, and local organizations are SOS members, as well as some individuals. Contributions from members comprise the major portion of the group's approximately $100,000 budget.

POLICY CONCERNS AND TACTICS

SOS presents its arguments for a strong and expanded Social Security system through speaking engagements, congressional testimony, and the media, while also lobbying for pertinent legislation. SOS utilizes the media to communicate with the public and Congress and to mobilize grass-roots supporters. For instance, on Friday, November 13, 1987, Congress was seriously discussing limiting increases in Social Security cost-of-living adjustments (COLAs). Arthur Flemming contacted Claude Pepper (D, Florida), then chair of the House Rules Committee. Pepper cut a three-minute videotape from his home in which he stated that he would block all future budget proposals that proposed to freeze COLAs. SOS sent the tape to the networks and contacted lobbyists of other advocacy groups to oppose the limits.

SOS regularly testifies before congressional committees on issues of Social Security benefits, health care, Supplemental Security Income (SSI), and benefits for persons with disabilities. Since 1979, the group has appeared before the following committees: Ways and Means, Rules, Appropriations and Select Committee on Aging in the House and Finance, Appropriations, Government Operations, and Special Committee on Aging committees in the Senate. SOS also provides information to members of Congress, and litigates. The group encourages its members to contact members of Congress on critical issues.

PUBLICATIONS

SOS publishes several issue briefs on Social Security, such as *Social Security: The Compromise and Beyond* (1983), and *Social Security in the U.S.: A Discussion Guide on Social Insurance with Lesson Plans* (1989).

MARIS J. DENEKE

SECTION FOR AGING AND LONG-TERM CARE SERVICES

See American Hospital Association Section For Aging and Long-term Care Services.

SENIOR ACTION IN A GAY ENVIRONMENT (SAGE)
208 West Thirteenth Street, Second Floor
New York, New York 10011
(212) 741–2247   FAX (212) 366–1947

Senior Action in a Gay Environment (SAGE) is a nonprofit organization dedicated to meeting the needs of older gays and lesbians. It has three primary goals: to serve as a social and education center with a program of activities, to provide services for older lesbians and gay men who are homebound or confined to nursing homes or hospitals, and to sponsor educational programs for social service providers, gay people of all ages, and the general public to sensitize them to the special needs of the older gay population.

ORIGIN AND DEVELOPMENT

SAGE was founded in New York city in 1977 by a group of volunteers and was incorporated in April the following year. It targeted its services specifically toward older gay men and lesbians, many of whom are isolated from the larger elderly and gay communities and the social and health services available to them. In 1980, SAGE acquired its first staff members and a home at St. Luke-in-the-Fields Church.

SAGE acts as a multi-service senior center providing socialization and social services to help establish supportive connections for its members. The professional staff and volunteers provide case assessment, friendly visiting, counseling, information and referral, social group activities, and advocacy. They also supervise social work interns from local universities to supplement their staff. SAGE operates a 1 P.M. to 5 P.M. Daily Drop-In. Its educational work includes in-service training for volunteers, social service providers, and institutions serving older gays, as well as extensive programs to increase public awareness of the vital issues concerning lesbian and gay aging.

ORGANIZATION AND FUNDING

SAGE has a staff of nine headed by the Executive Director, Arlene Kochman. It has a membership of about 4,000 and an annual budget of $520,000, the bulk of which comes from member fund raising (40%) and membership dues (30%). About 22 percent of the budget derives from foundation and government grants and less than 8 percent from revenue generated by SAGE activities. Committees functioning within the organization are Assessors, Friendly Visiting, Group Activities, Oral History Project, Office Volunteers, Third World Outreach, Woman's Task Force, Brunch Committee, and Drop-In. An eighteen-member Board of Directors elected by the membership, together with the Executive Director, determine the policies of the organization. Approximately 500 volunteers served over 1,000 men and women each month in 1990. Although centered in New York City, SAGE provides technical assistance to volunteers, professionals, and service organizations in San Francisco, Chicago, Philadelphia, New Jersey, and other communities.

POLICY CONCERNS AND TACTICS

The major policy issues concerning SAGE are entitlements for the elderly, specifically home health care and long-term care, legal problems, improved public housing, maintenance and guarantees of private pensions, Social Security benefits, and transportation alternatives. One of the organization's future goals is to participate in the formation of a gay and lesbian elderly retirement community. In addition to involvement in policy issues directed toward its elderly clientele, SAGE is also concerned with lesbian and gay rights, health issues, domestic partner benefits, and wills and estates.

SAGE attempts to influence public policy by encouraging its members to write to members of congressional committees dealing with pertinent matters. The organization also communicates its policy positions through its educational programs and the media.

PUBLICATIONS

SAGE publishes the monthly *SAGE Bulletin* directed to its members, as well as a semiannual free journal for the public entitled *Sage News*, with an estimated circulation of 12,000.

MARY B. STAVISH

SENIOR AIDES
See National Council of Senior Citizens.

SENIOR CITIZEN SCHOOL VOLUNTEER PROGRAM
See Generations Together.

SENIOR CITIZENS FOR KENNEDY
See National Council of Senior Citizens.

SENIOR ENVIRONMENTAL EMPLOYMENT PROGRAM
See National Council of Senior Citizens.

SKILLS EXCHANGE PROGRAMME
See International Federation on Ageing.

SOCIETY OF PROFESSIONAL BENEFIT ADMINISTRATORS (SPBA)
2 Wisconsin Circle, Suite 670
Chevy Chase, Maryland 20815–7002
(301) 718–7722   FAX (301) 718–9440
The Society of Professional Benefit Administrators (SPBA), a national, non-profit management organization, represents third-party administration firms of

self-funded benefit plans. The SPBA frequently provides information to government agencies that create and regulate insurance policy in the United States.

ORIGIN AND DEVELOPMENT

The Society of Professional Benefit Administrators was organized following the passage of the Employment Retirement Income Security Act (ERISA, 1974) protecting employee pensions. Charles Jackson, James Dawson, Robert Kelly, Steven Sherman, and William Batte of the International Foundation of Employee Benefit Plans saw the need for an organization representing third-party administrators to monitor policy.

The organization was founded and incorporated in 1975 as the American Society of Professional Administrators, a name that changed in 1977. Originally expecting no more than 60 firms to join, in 1990 SPBA had 430 member firms and is growing at a rate of 50 to 60 new firms each year. Clients of these firms represent organizations that provide insurance and benefits for one-third of all workers in the United States, such as labor unions, church groups, and state government.

ORGANIZATION AND FUNDING

The SPBA is managed by a nine-person Board of Directors (Chair, Vice-Chair, Secretary-Treasurer, Immediate Past Chair, and five other board members). The current Board of Directors elects the succeeding members. The organization employs an Executive Director and four staff.

Membership dues and fees from meetings supply the $950,000 annual budget. The annual dues range from $475 to $2,500 and are assessed in a range of ten categories, based on the total gross income of the member firm. In order to qualify for membership, 50 percent of a firm's income must derive from third-party administration fees.

POLICY CONCERNS AND TACTICS

The society's primary concern is to promote the free choice of employee benefits. Its charter lists as its first tenet, "to encourage and preserve the right and free choice of labor and management of the form of employee benefits most appropriate to their particular circumstances." To that end, SPBA opposes mandated benefits, national health insurance, the taxing of health benefits, and any other policies that circumscribe employee choice. Its role, however, is advisory rather than directly legislative. SPBA emphasizes the dissemination of information to its members and to government agencies. It works to keep its members informed of proposed legislation, regulations, and interpretations affecting employee benefit plans. It focuses on such issues as ERISA, health insurance, and taxes. The professional staff provides current regulatory information and makes referrals to government employees for clarification. The goal is to make it feasible for third-party administrators to ensure regulatory compliance for their clients.

SPBA informs legislators and their staff on pertinent issues and occasionally testifies before congressional committees.

SPBA advocates for increased access to health care through the establishment and consistent regulation of METs/MEWAs (Multiple Employer Trusts/Multiple Employer Welfare Arrangements). Trade associations or entrepreneurs sponsor these insurance plans, developed in the 1970s and 1980s. SPBA claims that confusion over the legal status of METs/MEWAs has resulted in inconsistent underutilization of the plans. In congressional testimony, SPBA has encouraged the deregulation and/or the setting of universal standards for METs/MEWAs to improve access to health care and health insurance.

Future concerns for the society include promoting fair and realistic ways to fund services for older persons and cost controls for those services, especially medical.

PUBLICATIONS

SPBA provides current information to its members through the *SPBA Update*, a periodic, informal memo that reviews the most current information and trends in regulatory policy. This involves tracking more than 1,500 new laws, regulations, and major court cases each year. SPBA also publishes the *SPBA Roster*, a membership directory, and the annual *Directory of Third-Party Administration Firms*. The *Directory* lists all third-party administration firms that are members of SPBA and includes information about plans and benefits offered, services provided, locations of service provision, and names of contact people. It contains extensive background information regarding third-party administration and self-funded benefit plans.

ELIZABETH MIDLARSKY
GLEN MILSTEIN

U /

UNITED AUTO WORKERS (UAW)
RETIRED AND OLDER WORKERS DEPARTMENT
8731 East Jefferson Avenue
Detroit, Michigan 48214
(313) 926–5557   FAX (313) 824–5750

The Retired and Older Workers Department of the United Auto Workers (UAW) Union is one of the oldest union-based organizations dealing with concerns of the older and retired worker. In 1990, the organization had a membership of 425,000 workers in the United States and Canada.

ORIGIN AND DEVELOPMENT

The UAW's commitment to older and retired workers began as a result of the economic and labor relations climate of post–World War II America. In the late 1940s the membership of the UAW was growing older. As the large automakers began to speed up the assembly lines, many older workers were transferred to lower-paying jobs, and many found themselves without pension plans.

In 1949, delegates to the UAW Convention recommended that the union extend the collective bargaining process to include retirement and pension benefits and job security for members. Therefore, the issue of pension benefits and job security for older workers became major parts of the first UAW contract negotiations with the three largest automakers.

The first company with which the UAW negotiated was Ford Motor Company. The 1949 proposed contract included the first company-based pension system in the automobile industry. After a threatened strike, Ford decided to include the pension plan in the contract. The plan's provisions included a $100 per month pension to the retired worker, in addition to Social Security benefits.

The Ford contract established three principles to guide the UAW's future negotiations: (1) the auto company and the union would jointly administer the pension program and establish major policies, including eligibility and credited service for retired workers; (2) the company would fund the entire program; and (3) the company would ensure that sufficient funds existed to provide an agreed pension for the entire lifetime of the worker.

In the early 1950s, the UAW began negotiations with the two other largest automakers, General Motors and Chrysler. After a 104-day strike, Chrysler finally agreed to include a pension plan in the contract similar to the pension plan established at Ford. The negotiations with General Motors required a change in policy.

In the early 1950s, Congress had increased the basic Social Security benefit for retired workers. Since the increase of Social Security benefits decreased the cost to General Motors of a pension plan, the UAW proposed that General Motors pass on the savings to the workers. Thus, the UAW had separated the company pension plan from Social Security. This allowed the UAW to write pension benefit increases into future contracts. With this change in policy, the UAW created a system whereby issues that were of interest to older and retired workers could be negotiated into contracts.

ORGANIZATION AND FUNDING

The structure of the Older and Retired Workers Department was established at the twentieth UAW convention in 1966. Article 53 of the UAW constitution was added to provide for the establishment of Retired Workers Chapters in any UAW local with twenty-five or more retirees. The retirees establish policy and administer their own programs. The local chapter elects a retiree to sit on the local's Executive Board and a delegate to a Regional Workers Council. The Regional Council then elects one of its number to the International Retired Worker's Advisory Council. These members are automatic delegates to the United Auto Workers International Convention. The Retired and Older Worker Department was also created under Article 53 to establish Older Worker Councils in areas where a UAW local did not exist. The department acts as a clearinghouse of information and discussion.

The 1966 convention established a system to fund the organization of retirees. Voluntary dues of $1, increased to $2 in 1986, were established to pay the cost of the program. In a few years, the department and its programs were self-supporting. Forty percent of each dollar paid in dues helps fund the International Retired Workers Department. Thirty-five percent of each dollar stays in the local chapter, and 25 percent of each dollar funds regional programs.

POLICY CONCERNS AND TACTICS

Since its establishment, the Retired and Older Workers Department has been guided in its policy and programs from a local and regional level. Early in its existence, the International Retired and Older Workers Department established a number of Drop-in Centers in the Detroit area. Since the 1970s, every major local has established such centers funded by the local chapter. These provide recreational programs along with assistance in informing retired workers about retirement programs, insurance, and medical benefits.

The Retired and Older Workers Department testifies before Congress in conjunction with the UAW. Retired and Older Workers have presented testimony for Supplemental Security Income (SSI) and for increased benefits under Medicare and Social Security.

The Regional Council's purpose is to alert the local chapters within its region to changes in retiree benefits, to pertinent legislation on the local, state, and national levels that affects older and retired workers, and to mobilize retired and older workers within the region for public hearings and demonstrations. Much of the Regional Council's policy reflects the interests and concerns of local chapters within the region.

The International Retired and Older Workers Department organizes retiree programs on national and international levels, updates materials as issues change, and produces guides to assist newly elected chapter and council officers and their committees. It prepares special materials on issues requiring immediate support. The department also has an ongoing relationship with offices of other organizations that represent the older or retired worker, such as the American Association of Retired Persons[*]. The department provides information to such organizations for the purpose of mobilizing retired and older workers on specific issues.

PUBLICATIONS

"News of the Retired and Older Workers Department" appears in a column of UAW's monthly *Solidarity*. The department also offers booklets on medical conditions.

DAVID BERNATOWICZ

UNITED SENIORS HEALTH COOPERATIVE (USHC)
1331 H Street, N.W., Suite 500
Washington, D.C. 20005
(202) 393–6222   FAX (202) 783–0588

The United Seniors Health Cooperative (USHC) is a nonprofit membership organization working to improve the quality and reduce the cost of health and social services for elderly residents in the Washington, D.C., metropolitan area. USHC influences national policy for the elderly by testifying before Congress, conducting and publishing research, and creating computer software and consumer publications.

ORIGIN AND DEVELOPMENT

USHC was founded in 1984 as the Older Americans Consumer Cooperative. The name was changed in 1986. At the end of that year, USHC enrolled 1,100 members from the Washington, D.C., area. In 1991 there were 11,000 members.

ORGANIZATION AND FUNDING

USHC is governed by a sixteen-member Board of Directors, both elected and appointed. Policies are set and established jointly by the members and the board. There are thirteen staff members, headed by the President and Chief Executive Director. James Firman has held this position since USHC's inception.

The annual budget is over $900,000. Approximately one-third is provided by the individual membership dues of $10, another third by corporate dues, and one-third by additional fundraising activities.

As a cooperative, members are both the owners of the organization and the beneficiaries of the services. Membership is open to anyone in the Washington, D.C., area. Active member involvement has helped to shape the services provided. Members regularly assist staff with research and counseling, as well as with computer data entry. Individual members serve on active committees and task forces and participate in consumer panels, user test groups, and surveys. USHC also has corporate members, including Hospital Senior Clubs. The cooperative offers a number of programs and services to its members, including a Medicare and Medigap insurance counseling service (on policies designed to fill gaps in Medicare coverage) and group rates on health care services.

POLICY CONCERNS AND TACTICS

The policy concerns of the USHC center on improving the quality of and lowering the cost of health care for the elderly. USHC has supported the Catastrophic Coverage Act (1988), changes in Medicaid, Medicare, and Social Security, and long-term-care insurance. USHC testifies before Congress and publishes research on these issues. USHC also supplies information to members of Congress and encourages its constituency to contact legislators on pertinent issues.

PUBLICATIONS

USHC issues a member newsletter, *Health Report*, presenting the group's activities and informing members on health care and financial topics. The cooperative also publishes a variety of consumer books, such as *Long-term Care: A Dollar and Sense Guide* (1991) and *Managing Your Healthcare Finances: Getting the Most Out of Medicare and Medigap Insurance* (1991). USHC also offers computer software to help organizations and municipalities determine benefits eligibility and for insurance counseling. Other applications for the software are being developed.

Further Information

James P. Firman, ''A Health Care Cooperative Looks at Ways to Pay for Health and Long-term Care,'' *Aging* (Spring 1988): 20–21, 44–45.

T. DEAN HANDY

UNIVERSITY CENTER FOR SOCIAL AND URBAN RESEARCH
See Generations Together.

V
---/---

VETERANS OF FOREIGN WARS OF THE UNITED STATES (VFW)
406 West 34th Street
Kansas City, Missouri 64111
(816) 756–3390   FAX (816) 968–1169

The Veterans of Foreign Wars of the United States (VFW) is a national fraternal and educational organization dedicated to assisting American veterans and their dependents. VFW accomplishes its goals through service, education, and advocacy.

ORIGIN AND DEVELOPMENT

The VFW traces its origins to 1899 when the American Veterans of Foreign Service (AVFS) was founded in Columbus, Ohio, by James Romanis, James C. Putnam, and other veterans of the Spanish-American War to promote benefits for ex-servicemen. In 1914, the AVFS merged with the National Society of the Army of the Philippines, also founded in 1899, to form the Veterans of Foreign Wars.

In 1936, the VFW was chartered by Congress as an organization devoted to the following goals: ''to assist worthy comrades,'' to perpetuate their memory and assist their widows and orphans, to maintain allegiance to the U.S. government, to maintain and extend the institutions of freedom, and to defend the United States of America. Over time, the organizational goals of the VFW have expanded to include advocating for veterans' rights, in addition to promoting nationalism, fraternalism, and special member benefits.

ORGANIZATION AND FUNDING

VFW's membership totals over 2 million, thus making it the second-largest veterans' organization (next to the American Legion). The appointed head of the organization in 1991 was Howard E. Vander Clute, Jr., Adjutant General; James L. Kimey served as Commander-in-Chief in 1990–91. The VFW has 10,600 posts in fifty-five departments across the nation. It is headed by a forty-member Council of Administration, most of whom are elected. The organization employs some fifteen staff in Washington, D.C., and thirty in its national headquarters in Kansas City, Missouri. Delegates from the membership vote at state and national conventions to set organization policy, often voting on resolutions introduced at the post level.

The VFW offers various programs and services: Americanism, Buddy Poppy, Civil Service and Employment, Community Activities, National Legislative Service, National Security and Foreign Affairs, Political Action Committee, Safety, National Veterans Service, Voice of Democracy, and Youth Activities. An affiliate of the VFW is the Ladies Auxiliary, established in 1914.

Virtually all of VFW's annual budget, an estimated $20 million, is obtained from individual membership dues. As an ongoing fund-raising project, the VFW sells "buddy poppies," red crepe-paper flowers, to support the VFW's National Veterans Service and fund its National Home in Eaton Rapids, Michigan.

POLICY CONCERNS AND TACTICS

The old-age veteran population will increase substantially in the next decades. In the early 1990s, there were approximately 7 million aged veterans—25 percent of the veteran population. By the year 2000, the number of veterans over the age of 65 is expected to reach 9 million. VFW recognizes the need to focus attention on the needs of this burgeoning group.

The legislative agenda of VFW is broad, covering such diverse aspects as protecting the American flag, maintaining funding for the Department of Veterans Affairs, ensuring one open national cemetery per state, and preferential employment for veterans. Veteran's benefits cover health care, compensation and pensions, education, housing, and life insurance. Veterans' legislation has long been developed in what has been described as a closed system. Congressional committees operate together with the VFW and other veterans' lobby groups and the Department of Veterans Affairs to work on such legislation. Some have called this strong lobby the "iron triangle."

Through its National Legislative Service, which employs a staff of lobbyists in Washington, D.C., the VFW has been instrumental in securing benefits for veterans relative to rehabilitation, education, and vocational training. The VFW worked for veterans' rights after World War I, World War II, and the Korean and Vietnam wars. It lobbied for passage of the GI Bill of Rights, for federal assistance to disabled veterans, and for benefits for all who have served in the armed forces. In March 1991, the VFW Commander-in-Chief testified before the Joint Hearing of the House and Senate Veterans' Affairs committees on an entire range of veterans' issues, including long-term health care and maintenance of veterans' pensions. The VFW also utilizes a variety of other tactics to influence policy, such as encouraging its constituency to contact members of Congress, conducting and publishing research, and representing veterans before federal agencies. In the 1990s, the VFW's top priority is adequate funding for the Department of Veterans Affairs health care budget.

ELECTORAL ACTIVITY

The VFW maintains a political action committee, the Veterans of Foreign Wars Political Action Committee (VFW-PAC), which in 1990 endorsed over 200 congressional candidates for reelection from across the United States. To receive a VFW-PAC endorsement, the senator or congressional representative must have received a roll call vote rating of 70 percent or better on legislation important to the organization, based on an average for one six-year term. Not all of these endorsed candidates received funds from VFW-PAC, however. VFW-PAC contributed $35,750 to the campaigns of fifty-five Democratic candidates and $48,500 to the campaigns of eighty-one Republican candidates.

PUBLICATIONS

The VFW publishes *National Headquarters Communicator* (nine times a year) and *Washington Action Reporter* (monthly). The *VFW Magazine* (eleven times a year) contains member news, benefit updates, and legislative reports, along with a half-dozen feature articles in each issue.

Further Information

Martha Baum and Bennett M. Rich, *The Aging: A Guide to Public Policy* (Pittsburgh: University of Pittsburgh Press, 1984); William Bottoms, *The VFW: An Illustrated History of the Veterans of Foreign Wars of the U.S.* (Rockville, Md.: Woodbine House, 1991); Elaine Fox and George E. Arquitt, ''The VFW— A Case Study in the 'Iron Law of Oligarchy' and Goal Displacement,'' *Qualitative Sociology* 4, (Fall 1981): 198–216; Edward L. and Frederick H. Schapsmeier, *Political Parties and Civic Action Groups* (Westport, Conn.: Greenwood Press, 1981).

JULIEANNE PHILLIPS

VFW
See Veterans of Foreign Wars of the United States.

VFW-PAC
See Veterans of Foreign Wars of the United States.

VILLERS ADVOCACY ASSOCIATES
See Families U.S.A. Foundation.

VILLERS FOUNDATION
See Families U.S.A. Foundation.

W

WESTERN GERONTOLOGICAL SOCIETY
See American Society on Aging.

WOMEN'S PENSION PROJECT
See Pension Rights Center.

Y

YOUTH IN SERVICE TO ELDERS (YISTE)
See Generations Together.

Z
———————— / ————————

ZONTA INTERNATIONAL
557 West Randolph Street
Chicago, Illinois 60601–2206
(312) 930–5848   FAX (312) 930–0951

Zonta International is a private, nonprofit, international service organization of business executives and professionals. It aims to improve the legal, political, economic, and professional status of women and to advance understanding, goodwill, and peace through a world fellowship of executives united in the Zonta ideal of service. From its inception, Zonta has sought to address the concerns of women, including women and aging, through advocacy, information, public policy formulation, public awareness, and professional education and training.

ORIGIN AND DEVELOPMENT

On November 8, 1919, in Buffalo, New York, a small group of executive women met to consider the formation of an organization similar to the men's service clubs of the Rotary and Kiwanis. World War I had afforded an opportunity to women to demonstrate their abilities in responsible executive positions, in civic and social welfare, in commercial and industrial development of their communities, and in service projects of local and national importance. The idea of a service club for professional and executive women was appealing. Within a short time, a group of nearly 100 women organized in the city of Buffalo, to form the Confederation of Zonta Clubs. The Sioux Indian name *Zonta* was chosen because it means "trustworthy" and "honest."

In November 1927, Zonta incorporated in Illinois, and the name changed to Zonta International after the acceptance of the Toronto, Ontario, Club. The group established permanent headquarters in Chicago in January 1928; Zonta then numbered approximately fifty clubs with a membership of over 1,900 women.

By 1933, Zonta International numbered 115 clubs with a membership of over 3,000; in 1954, there were 300 clubs with a total membership of 10,500. In 1990, Zonta was represented in fifty-five countries with 1,050 clubs and 35,000 members worldwide.

ORGANIZATION AND FUNDING

Zonta International is managed by a twelve-member Board of Directors and a staff of fifteen. On the Board of Directors are the four officers who comprise Zonta's International Executive Committee: President, Vice-President, Second Vice-President, and Treasurer. These international officers are elected by the membership at the biennial convention for a two-year term. At this convention, the President and her administration announce the international directives of Zonta for the next two years. These directives correspond to the agenda of Zonta's six program committees: Status of Women, Service, United Nations, International Relations, Membership and Classification, Organization and Extension, and ZClub. After the biennial convention, each of Zonta's twenty-six districts holds a fall conference where the District Governors are elected to two-year terms and the national initiatives are discussed. Each district is divided into areas of local clubs, which decide how to implement the international directives on the local level.

Membership dues and charitable contributions comprise the bulk of the group's financial support. Zonta's annual budget ranges between $2.5 million and $5 million.

POLICY CONCERNS AND TACTICS

Zonta's major policy concern in the field of aging is quality of life for older women. One of the 1988–90 goals of the Status of Women Committee was to encourage local clubs to develop community projects specifically for aging women and to emphasize the collective ''will to age well.'' Zonta stresses the female character of the aging society: by the year 2031, there will be 1 million more women than men in the world over the age of 65. Zonta affects public policy through service and education.

Various local clubs have participated in a number of programs and services for aging women, including furnishing and equipping hospitals, nursing homes, and homes for the aged and donating funds for their construction and for research. In some communities, Zonta offers casework and employment counseling, financial aid, and legal guidance. Members participate in finding foster homes and in providing custodial care for the aged. One affiliate is building an apartment house of rental units, with health, education, and religious services for retired men and women with low to middle incomes. Other clubs sponsor surveys and studies and conduct forums dealing with the challenges of aging, employment opportunities, and retirement concerns. Zonta attempts to ensure that social policies and programs address the needs of older women, the majority of the elderly, and works toward making a future where older women are valued.

PUBLICATIONS

Zonta's publications include *Zontian*, a quarterly magazine that features articles about the organization's programs and activities; *Zontian Program Issue*, published biennially, which focuses on the international directives for the next two years; and *Headquarters Newsletter*, issued twice a year, which informs clubs about the work of their executive officers.

Zonta has published two monographs: *Zonta Amelia Earhart Manual* (1984) and *Zonta United Nations Manual* (1983).

JULIEANNE PHILLIPS

APPENDIX A: SELECTED ADDITIONAL ORGANIZATIONS

———————————— / ————————————

Aging Network Services
4400 East-West Highway
Suite 907
Bethesda, Maryland 20814
(301) 657–4329

Alexander Graham Bell Association for the Deaf
3417 Volta Place, N.W.
Washington, D.C. 20007–2778
(202) 337–5220

Alliance for Aging Research
2021 K Street, N.W., Suite 305
Washington, D.C. 20006
(202) 293–2856

American Academy of Family Physicians
8880 Ward Parkway
Kansas City, Missouri 64114–2797
(816) 333–9700

American Association for Adult and Continuing Education
1112 16th Street, N.W., Suite 420
Washington, D.C. 20036
(202) 463–6333

American Association for Geriatric Psychiatry
P.O. Box 376 A
Greenbelt, Maryland 20768
(301) 220–0952

American Association of Preferred Provider Organizations
401 North Michigan Avenue
Chicago, Illinois 60611
(312) 245–1555

American Council of Life Insurance
1001 Pennsylvania Avenue, N.W.
Washington, D.C. 20004–2599
(202) 624–2000

American Dental Association
211 East Chicago Avenue
Chicago, Illinois 60611
(312) 440–2860

American Dietetic Association
216 West Jackson Boulevard, Suite 800
Chicago, Illinois 60606–6995
(312) 899–0040

American Federation for Aging Research
725 Park Avenue
New York, New York 10021
(212) 570–2090

American Foundation for Aging Research
Biochemistry Department, Box 7622
North Carolina State University
Raleigh, North Carolina 27695
(919) 737–5679

American Foundation for the Blind
15 West 16th Street
New York, New York 10011
(212) 620–2067

American Health Planning Association
c/o Suzanne W. Nichols
P.O. Box 770097
Oklahoma City, Oklahoma 73177
(405) 271–6868

American Home Economics Association
1555 King Street
Alexandria, Virginia 22314
(703) 706–4600

American Humanist Association
P.O. Box 146
Amherst, New York 14226–0146
(716) 839–5080

American Longevity Association
1000 West Carson Street
Torrance, California 90509
(213) 544–7057

American Medical Association
515 North State Street
Chicago, Illinois 60610
(312) 464–5000

American Nurses Association
2420 Pershing Road
Kansas City, Missouri 64108
(816) 474–5720

American Occupational Therapy Association
1383 Piccard Drive
P.O. Box 1725
Rockville, Maryland 20850–4375
(301) 948–9626

American Pharmaceutical Association
2215 Constitution Avenue, N.W.
Washington, D.C. 20037
(202) 628–4410

American Protestant Health Association
1701 East Woodfield Road, Suite 311
Schaumburg, Illinois 60173
(708) 240–1010

American Psychiatric Association
1400 K Street, N.W., Suite 1050
Washington, D.C. 20005
(202) 682–6000

American Psychological Association
1200 Seventeenth Street, N.W.
Washington, D.C. 20036
(202) 955–7600

American Public Health Association
1015 15th Street, N.W.
Washington, D.C. 20005
(202) 789–5600

American Public Welfare Association
810 First Street, N.E., Suite 500
Washington, D.C. 20002–4267
(202) 682–0100

American Senior Citizens Association
P.O. Box 41
Fayetteville, North Carolina 28302
(919) 323–3641

American Society for Geriatric Dentistry
Parker Jewish Geriatric Institute
271–11 76th Avenue
New Hyde Park, New York 11042
(718) 343–2100

Association for Anthropology and Gerontology
c/o Philip B. Stafford
P.O. Box 1149
Bloomington, Indiana 47402
(812) 336–9300

Association for Death Education and Counseling
638 Prospect Avenue
Hartford, Connecticut 06105
(203) 232–4825

Association for Gerontology and Human Development in Historically Black Colleges and
Universities
c/o Willamae Kilkenny, Director, Urban Gerontology-Geriatric Program
Morgan State University
Box 670
Baltimore, Maryland 21239
(301) 444–3581, (301) 828–4294

Association of High Medicare Hospitals
1015 18th Street, N.W., Suite 900
Washington, D.C. 20036
(202) 785–9670

Association of Junior Leagues International
660 First Avenue
New York, New York 10016
(212) 683–1515

Association of Retired Americans
206 East College
Grapevine, Texas 76051
(800) 622–8040

Betterment for United Seniors
96 Harry S. Truman Drive
Largo, Maryland 20772
(301) 499–8707

B'nai B'rith International
Senior Citizens Housing Committee
1640 Rhode Island Avenue, N.W.
Washington, D.C. 20036
(202) 857–6580

Brookdale Center on Aging of Hunter College
425 East 25th Street
New York, New York 10010
(212) 481–4426

Catholic Charities U.S.A.
1731 King Street, Suite 200
Alexandria, Virginia 22314
(703) 549–1390

Catholic Golden Age
400 Lackawanna Avenue
Scranton, Pennsylvania 18503
(717) 342–3294

Catholic Health Association of the United States
4455 Woodson Road
St. Louis, Missouri 63134
(314) 427–2500

Center for the Study of Aging
706 Madison Avenue
Albany, New York 12208
(518) 465–6927

Center for Understanding Aging
Framingham State College
Framingham, Massachusetts 07101
(508) 626–4979

Center for Women Policy Studies
2000 P Street, N.W., Suite 508
Washington, D.C. 20036
(202) 872–1770

Commonwealth Fund Commission on Elderly People Living Alone
c/o Johns Hopkins University
School of Hygiene and Public Health
624 North Broadway, Room 453
Baltimore, Maryland 21205
(301) 955–3775

Daughters of the Elderly Bridging the Unknown Together (DEBUT)
Area 10 Agency on Aging
2129 Yost Avenue
Bloomington, Indiana 47401

Ebenezer Society
2722 Park Avenue
Minneapolis, Minnesota 55407
(612) 879–1467

Educational Organization for United Latin Americans
1842 Calvert Street, N.W.
Washington, D.C. 20009
(202) 483–5800

Education Network for Older Adults
350 Arballo Drive, Unit 12 H
San Francisco, California 94132
(415) 586–2019

Elder Craftsmen
135 East 65th Street
New York, New York 10021
(212) 861–5260

Elderhostel
75 Federal Street, Third Floor
Boston, Massachusetts 02110
(617) 426–7788

Eldermed America
20500 Nordhoff Street
Chatsworth, California 91311
(800) 227–3463

Ethel Percy Andrus Gerontology Center
University of Southern California
University Park—MC 0191
Los Angeles, California 90098–0191
(213) 740–6060

Family Survival Project Clearinghouse
425 Bush Street, Suite 500
San Francisco, California 94108
(415) 434–3388

Fifty-Plus Runners Association
730 Welch Road, Suite B
Palo Alto, California 94304
(415) 723–9790

Foundation Aiding the Elderly
P.O. Box 254849
Sacramento, California 95865–4849
(916) 481–8558

Grandparents Anonymous
1924 Beverly
Sylvan Lake, Michigan 48320
(313) 682–8384

Grandparents'/Children's Rights
5728 Bayonne Avenue
Haslett, Michigan 48840
(517) 339–8663

Group Health Association of America
1129 20th Street, N.W., Suite 600
Washington, D.C. 20036
(202) 778–3200

Health Insurance Association of America
1025 Connecticut Avenue, N.W., Suite 1200
Washington, D.C. 20036
(202) 223–7780

Healthcare Forum
830 Market Street, Eighth Floor
San Francisco, California 94102
(415) 421–8810

Hospice Education Institute
Five Essex Square, Suite 3-B
P.O. Box 713
Essex, Connecticut 06426
(203) 767–1620

Institute for Retired Professionals
New School for Social Research
66 West 12th Street
New York, New York 10011
(212) 741–5682

Institute for the Puerto Rican/Hispanic Elderly
105 East 22nd Street, Room 615
New York, New York 10010
(212) 677–4181

International Exchange Center on Gerontology
University of South Florida
Box 3208
Tampa, Florida 33620–3208
(813) 974–3468

International Foundation of Employee Benefit Plans
18700 West Bluemond Rd.
P.O. Box 69
Brookfield, Wisconsin 53005
(414) 786–6700

International Psychogeriatric Association
3127 Greenleaf Avenue
Wilmette, Illinois 60091
(708) 866–7227

International Senior Citizens Association
1102 South Crenshaw Boulevard
Los Angeles, California 90019
(213) 857–6434

International Society for Retirement Planning
c/o Malcolm Rodman
11312 Old Club Road
Rockville, Maryland 20853
(301) 881–4113

Kellogg International Program on Health and Aging
University of Michigan
1065 Frieze Building
Ann Arbor, Michigan 48109
(313) 998–7730

Little Brothers—Friends of the Elderly
1658 West Belmont Avenue
Chicago, Illinois 60657
(312) 477–7702

Medical Group Management Association and Center for Research in Ambulatory Health
Care Administration
104 Inverness Terrace East
Englewood, Colorado 80112
(303) 799–1111

National AFL-CIO Cope Retiree Program
815 16th Street, N.W., Room 306
Washington D.C. 20006
(202) 637–5124

National Association for Retired Credit Union People
P.O. Box 391
Madison, Wisconsin 53701
(608) 238–4286

National Association of Activity Professionals
1225 I Street, N.W., Suite 300
Washington, D.C. 20005
(202) 289–0722

National Association of Attorneys General Committee on the Elderly and the Law
444 North Capitol Street, N.W.
Washington, D.C. 20001
(202) 628–0435

National Association of Boards of Examiners for Nursing Home Administrators
808 17th Street, N.W., Suite 200
Washington, D.C. 20006
(202) 223–9750

National Association of Families Caring for Their Elders
1141 Loxford Terrace
Silver Spring, Maryland 20901
(301) 593–1621

National Association of Foster Grandparents Program Directors
7500 Silver Star Road, Building 9
Orlando, Florida 32818
(407) 298–4180

National Association of Home Builders
15th and M Streets, N.W.
Washington, D.C. 20005
(202) 822–0200

National Association of Housing Cooperatives
1614 King Street
Alexandria, Virginia 22314
(703) 549–5201

National Association of Older American Volunteer Program Directors
11481 Bingham Terrace
Reston, Virginia 22091
(703) 860–9570

National Association of Social Workers
7981 Eastern Avenue
Silver Spring, Maryland 20910
(301) 565–0333

National Council of Catholic Women
1275 K Street, N.W., Suite 975
Washington, D.C. 20005
(202) 682–0334

National Council on Family Relations
3989 Central Avenue Northeast, Suite 550
Minneapolis, Minnesota 55421
(612) 781–9331

National Mental Health Association
1021 Prince Street
Alexandria, Virginia 22314
(703) 684–7722

National Organization of Social Security Claimants' Representatives
19 East Central Avenue, Second Floor
Pearl River, New York 10965
(914) 735–8812

National Senior Sports Association
10560 Main Street
Fairfax, Virginia 22030
(703) 385–7540

National Stroke Association
300 East Hampden Avenue, Suite 240
Englewood, Colorado 80110
(303) 762–9922

Oasis (Older Adult Service and Information System)
7710 Carrondelet, Suite 125
St. Louis, Missouri 63105
(314) 862–2933

Office of Older Adult Ministries
General Board of Discipleship
United Methodist Church
10001 19th Avenue, South
Nashville, Tennesee 37202–0840
(615) 340–7134

Over the Hill Gang, International
13791 East Rice Place
Aurora, Colorado 80015
(303) 750–2724

Project Share
129 Jackson Street
Hempstead, New York 11550
(516) 485–4600

Retirement Research Foundation
1300 West Higgins Road, Suite 214
Park Ridge, Illinois 60068
(708) 823–4133

RSVP International
200 Madison Avenue, Twenty-fifth Floor
New York, New York 10016
(212) 686–7788

Salvation Army
United States National Headquarters
799 Bloomfield Avenue
Verona, New Jersey 07044
(201) 239–0606

Second Careers Program
3923 West Sixth Street, Suite 216
Los Angeles, California 90020
(213) 380–3166

Senior Gleaners
3185 Longview Drive
North Highlands, California 95660
(916) 971–1530

Senior Scholars
c/o Kathy Manos
Department of Continuing Education
Case Western Reserve University
Cleveland, Ohio 44106
(216) 368–2090

Shared Housing Resource Center
6344 Greene Street
Philadelphia, Pennsylvania 19144
(215) 848–1220

Third Age Center
Fordham University
113 West Sixtieth Street, Room 704
New York, New York 10023
(212) 636–6000

Urban Institute
2100 M Street, N.W.
Washington, D.C. 20037
(202) 833–7200

Vacation and Senior Centers Association
275 Seventh Avenue
New York, New York 10001
(212) 645–6590

APPENDIX B: ORGANIZATIONAL MEMBERS OF COALITIONS ON AGING, 1991

———————————— / ————————————

A.S.A.P. (ADVOCATES SENIOR ALERT PROCESS) PARTICIPANTS

American Society on Aging

Asociacion Nacional Pro Personas Mayores

Association for Gerontology in Higher Education

Catholic Golden Age

Families U.S.A. Foundation

Gray Panthers Project Fund

National Association of Foster Grandparent Program Directors

National Association of Meal Programs

National Association of Nutrition and Aging Services Programs

National Association of Retired Senior Volunteer Program (RSVP) Directors

National Association of Senior Companion Project Directors

National Caucus and Center on Black Aged

National Council of Senior Citizens

National Council on the Aging

National Pacific/Asian Resource Center on Aging

Older Women's League

GENERATIONS UNITED PARTICIPANTS

American Academy of Child and Adolescent Psychiatry

American Academy of Pediatrics

American Association for International Aging

American Association of Children's Residential Centers

American Association of Homes for the Aging

American Association of Retired Persons

American Association of University Women

American Diabetes Association

American Federation of Teachers

American Foundation for the Blind

American Home Economics Association

American Occupational Therapy Association

American Orthopsychiatric Association

American Public Welfare Association

American Red Cross

American Society on Aging

Asociacion Nacional Pro Personas Mayores

Association for the Care of Children's Health

Association of Junior Leagues

Big Brothers/Big Sisters of America

Boy Scouts of America

B'nai B'rith International

B'nai B'rith Women

Camp Fire

Catholic Charities USA

Center for Law and Social Policy

Center for Population Options

Child Care Action Campaign

Child Welfare League of America

Children's Defense Fund

Children's Foundation

Christian Children's Fund

Congressional Award Foundation

Council of Jewish Federations

Epilepsy Foundation of America

Family Resources Coalition

Family Service America

Foundation for Exceptional Children

Future Homemakers of America

Generations Together

Girl Scouts of the U.S.A.

Girls Clubs of America

Gray Panthers Project Fund

Home and School Institute

Institute for Educational Leadership

International Council on Social Welfare

Joint Action in Community Service

Joseph P. Kennedy, Jr., Foundation

Lutheran Office for Governmental Affairs

National Adoption Center

National Assembly of National Voluntary Health and Social Welfare Organizations

National Association for Home Care

National Association for the Education of Young Children

National Association of Area Agencies on Aging

National Association of Community Action Agencies

National Association of Counties

National Association of Foster Grandparents Program Directors

National Association of Homes for Children

National Association of Meal Programs

National Association of Retired Senior Volunteer Program Directors

National Association of Service and Conservation Corps

National Association of Social Workers

National Association of State Boards of Education

National Association of State Units on Aging

National Benevolent Association of the Christian Church

National Black Child Development Institute

National Caucus and Center on Black Aged

National Center on Aging and Community Education

National Citizens' Coalition for Nursing Home Reform

National Coalition of State Juvenile Justice Advisory Groups

National Commission to Prevent Infant Mortality

National Committee for Adoption

National Committee for Prevention of Child Abuse

National Community Action Foundation

National Community Education Association

National Council of Catholic Women

National Council of Jewish Women

National Council of Senior Citizens

National Council on Child Abuse and Family Violence

National Council on Family Relations

National Council on the Aging

National Crime Prevention Council

National Education Association

National Farmers Union

National Indian Council on Aging

National Mental Health Association

National Network of Runaway and Youth Services

National Perinatal Association

National PTA

National Puerto Rican Forum

National Recreation and Parks Association

National Rural and Small Schools Consortium

National School Volunteer Program

National Urban League

National Women's Political Caucus

New Age

Older Women's League

OMB Watch

Opportunities for Older Americans

Orphan Foundation

Peer-Project on Equal Education Rights

Positive Youth Development Institute

Presbyterian Church USA

Public/Private Ventures

Salvation Army

Save the Children

70001 Training and Employment Institute

Temple University Institute on Aging

Travelers Aid Association of America

Travelers Aid International

Understanding Aging

United Church Board for Homeland Ministries

United Way of America

Waif

Young Men's Christian Association of the U.S.A.

Young Women's Christian Association of the U.S.A.

Youth Service America

LEADERSHIP COUNCIL OF AGING ORGANIZATIONS (LCAO) PARTICIPANTS

AFL-CIO Department of Employment Benefits

American Association for International Aging

American Association of Homes for the Aging

American Association of Retired Persons

American Society on Aging

Asociacion Nacional Pro Personas Mayores

Association for Gerontology in Higher Education

Association for Gerontology and Human Development in Historically Black Colleges and Universities

Association of Federal, State, County and Municipal Employees Retiree Program

Catholic Golden Age

Families U.S.A. Foundation

Gerontological Society of America

Gray Panthers Project Fund

National Association for Families Caring for Their Elders

National Association of Area Agencies on Aging

National Association of Foster Grandparents Program Directors

National Association of Meal Programs

National Association of Nutrition and Aging Services Programs

National Association of Older American Volunteer Program Directors

National Association of Retired Federal Employees

National Association of Retired Senior Volunteer Program Directors

National Association of Senior Companion Project Directors

National Association of State Units on Aging

National Caucus and Center on Black Aged

National Council of Senior Citizens

National Council on the Aging

National Hispanic Council on Aging

National Pacific/Asian Resource Center on Aging

National Senior Citizens Law Center

Older Women's League

United Auto Workers Retired and Older Workers Department

LONG-TERM-CARE CAMPAIGN PARTICIPANTS

Alzheimer's Association

Amalgamated Clothing and Textile Workers Union

American Association for Counseling and Development
American Association for Marriage and Family Therapy
American Association of Retired Persons
American Association of University Women
American Association on Mental Retardation
American Baptist Churches
American College of Health Care Administrators
American Diabetes Association
American Federation of Government Employees
American Federation of Labor–Congress of Industrial Organizations
American Federation of State, County and Municipal Employees
American Federation of Teachers
American Health Planning Association
American Jewish Congress
American Medical Student Association
American Nurses Association
American Occupational Theraphy Association
American Physical Therapy Association
American Public Health Association
American Public Welfare Association
American Society on Aging
American Speech–Language–Hearing Association
Americans for Direct Action
Americans for Indian Opportunity Association
Amyotrophic Lateral Sclerosis Association
Association for Retarded Citizens of the United States
Association of Community Organizations for Reform Now
B'nai B'rith Women
BPW/USA (National Federation of Business and Professional Women)
Cathedral College of the Laity
Catholic Charities USA
Catholic Golden Age
Center for Community Change
Center for Law and Social Policy
Center on Budget and Social Policy Priorities
Central Conference of American Rabbis
Child Welfare League
Christic Institute

Church of the Brethren Washington Office
Church Women United
Citizen Action
Coalition of Labor Union Women
Congress of National Black Churches
Consumer Federation of America
Consumers Union
Council of Jewish Federations
Epilepsy Foundation of America
Family Service America
Family Survival Project
Families U.S.A. Foundation
Federally Employed Women
Gray Panthers Project Fund
International Ladies' Garment Workers' Union
Joseph P. Kennedy, Jr., Foundation
Lupus Foundation of America
National Alliance for the Mentally Ill
National Association for Home Care
National Association for the Advancement of Colored People
National Association for the Hispanic Elderly
National Association of Area Agencies on Aging
National Association of Counties
National Association of Foster Grandparent Program Directors
National Association of Meal Programs
National Association of Neighborhoods
National Association of Nutrition and Aging Services Programs
National Association of Private Geriatric Care Managers
National Association of Protection and Advocacy Systems
National Association of Rehabilitation Professionals in the Private Sector
National Association of Retired Federal Employees
National Association of Retired Senior Volunteer Program Directors
National Association of Senior Companion Project Directors
National Association of Social Workers
National Association of State Units on Aging
National Caucus and Center on Black Aged
National Center for Policy Alternatives
National Citizens' Coalition for Nursing Home Reform

National Community Action Foundation

National Consumers League

National Council of Catholic Women

National Council of Churches

National Council of Jewish Women

National Council of Negro Women

National Council of Senior Citizens

National Council on Independent Living

National Council on the Aging

National Displaced Homemakers Network

National Easter Seal Society

National Education Association

National Farmers Union

National Head Injury Foundation

National Health Council

National Hispanic Council on Aging

National Institute for Women of Color

National Institute on Adult Daycare

National Institute on Community-Based Long-Term Care

National League for Nursing

National Mental Health Association

National Multiple Sclerosis Society

National Organization for Women

National Parkinson Foundation

National PTA

National Rehabilitation Association

National Union of Hospital and Health Care Employees

National Urban League

National Voluntary Organizations for Independent Living for the Aging

National Women's Health Network

National Women's Law Center

National Women's Political Caucus

9 To 5—National Association of Working Women

NOW Legal Defense and Education Fund

Older Women's League

Oley Foundation for Home Parenteral and Enteral Nutrition

Organization of Chinese Americans

Paralyzed Veterans of America

Public Employees Department, AFL-CIO

Rural Coalition

Self Help for Hard of Hearing People

Service Employees International Union

Sick Kids Need Involved People

Tourette Syndrome Association

Union of American Hebrew Congregations

United Auto Workers

United Cerebral Palsy Association

United Food and Commercial Workers Union

United Methodist Church Board of Global Ministries, Health and Welfare Ministries Department and Women's Division

United Seniors Health Cooperative

United States Conference of Local Health Officers

United States Conference of Mayors

United States Student Association

Visiting Nurse Associations of America

Women's League for Conservative Judaism

World Institute on Disability

SAVE OUR SECURITY (SOS) PARTICIPANTS

A. Philip Randolph Institute

Advocates for the Handicapped

Affiliated Leadership League of and for the Blind in America

Amalgamated Clothing and Textile Workers, AFL-CIO

Amalgamated Transit Union, AFL-CIO

American Association of Homes for the Aging

American Association of Retired Persons

American Association of University Professors

American Association of University Women

American Association of Workers for the Blind

American Association on Mental Deficiency

American Coalition for Citizens with Disability

American Council of the Blind

American Ethical Union

American Federation of Government Employees

American Federation of Labor–Congress of Industrial Organizations

American Federation of State, County, and Municipal Employees

American Flint Glass Workers

American Foundation for the Blind

American Jewish Committee

American Society on Aging

American Veterans Committee

Americans for Democratic Action

Associated Actors and Artists of America

Association for Retarded Citizens

Bakers, Confectionery and Tobacco Workers International Union

Center for Community Change

Center for Independent Living

Coalition of Labor Union Women

Communications Workers of America

Council of State Administrators of Vocational Rehabilitation

Disabled American Veterans

Epilepsy Foundation of America

Families U.S.A. Foundation

Food Research and Action Center

Fund to Assure an Independent Retirement

Graphic Communications International Union

Gray Panthers Project Fund

Human Development Studies

International Association of Bridge, Structural and Ornamental Iron Workers

International Association of Machinists and Aerospace Workers

International Brotherhood of Electrical Workers

International Chemical Workers Union

International Ladies' Garment Workers Union

International Longshoremen's Association

International Union of Electronic, Electrical, Technical, Salaried, Machine, and Furniture
    Workers

International Union of Operating Engineers

Joseph P. Kennedy, Jr., Foundation

Laborers International Union of North America

Leadership Conference of Women Religious of the U.S.A.

Legal Research and Services for the Elderly

Longshoremen's and Warehousemen's Union

Mechanics Educational Society

Metal Trades Department, AFL-CIO

National Alliance for the Mentally Ill

National Association for Human Development

National Association for the Advancement of Colored People

National Association of Counties

National Association of Letter Carriers

National Association of Private Residential Facilities for the Mentally Retarded

National Association of Retired Federal Employees

National Association of State Universities and Land Grant Colleges

National Black Lay Catholic Caucus

National Black Lung Association

National Board of the YWCA

National Caucus and Center on Black Aged

National Center for Urban Ethnic Affairs

National Coalition for Older Women's Issues

National Conference of Catholic Charities

National Consumers League

National Council of Catholic Women

National Council of Churches

National Council of Jewish Women

National Council of La Raza

National Council of Negro Women

National Council of Senior Citizens

National Council on the Aging

National Education Association

National Farmers Union

National Indian Council on Aging

National Maritime Union of America, AFL-CIO

National Mental Health Association

National Multiple Sclerosis Society

National Organization of Social Security Claimants' Representatives

National Rural Letter Carriers Association

National Senior Citizens Law Center

National Society for Children and Adults with Autism

National Urban Coalition

National Urban League

National Women's Political Caucus

Oil, Chemical, Atomic Workers Union, AFL-CIO

Older Women's League

Paralyzed Veterans of America

Presbyterian Church U.S.A.

Retail Wholesale and Department Stores

Save our Children's Security

Screen Extras Guild

Secure our Children

Senior Citizens Task Force/Planning Organization

Service Employees International Union

UAW Retired and Older Workers Department

United Association of Journeymen and Apprentices of the Plumbing and Pipe Fitting Industry of the U.S. and Canada

United Automobile, Aerospace and Agricultural Implement Workers of America International Union

United Brotherhood of Carpenters and Joiners

United Cerebral Palsy Associations

United Food and Commercial Workers

United Furniture Workers of America

United States Catholic Conference

United Steelworkers of America

Women's Equity Action League

Workmen's Circle

SELECTED BIBLIOGRAPHY
———————————— / ————————————

Aaron, H. J., B. P. Bosworth, and G. Burtless. *Can America Afford to Grow Old?* Washington, D.C.: Brookings Institution, 1989.

Achenbaum, Andrew. *Shades of Gray: Old Age, American Values, and Federal Policies Since 1920*. Boston: Little, Brown, 1983.

———. *Social Security: Visions and Revisions*. New York: Cambridge University Press, 1986.

Americans for Generational Equity (AGE). *Tomorrow's Elderly: Planning for the Baby Boom Generation's Retirement*. Washington, D. C.: AGE, 1986.

Aronson, Miriam K. *Understanding Alzheimer's Disease—What It Is, How to Cope with It, Future Directions*. New York: Charles Scribner's Sons, 1987.

Association for Gerontology in Higher Education (AGHE). *National Directory of Educational Programs in Gerontology*. 5th ed. Washington, D.C.: AGHE, 1990.

Baum, Martha, and Bennett M. Rich. *The Aging: A Guide to Public Policy*. Pittsburgh: University of Pittsburgh Press, 1984.

Biegel, D. E., and A. Blum, eds. *Aging and Caregiving: Theory, Research and Policy*. Newbury Park, Calif.: Sage Publications, 1990.

Binstock, Robert, ed. *Handbook of Aging and the Social Sciences*. 3d ed. New York: Academic Press, 1990.

Birren, James E., and K. Warner Schaie, eds. *Handbook of the Psychology of Aging*. 3d ed. New York: Academic Press/Harcourt Brace Jovanovich, 1989.

Browne, William, and Laura Katz Olson, eds. *Aging and Public Policy: The Politics of Growing Old in America*. Westport, Conn.: Greenwood Press, 1983.

Burwell, Brian. *Shared Obligations: Public Policy Influences on Family Care for the Elderly*. Baltimore: U.S. Health Care Financing Administration, 1986.

Butler, R. N. *Why Survive? Being Old in America*. New York: Harper & Row, 1975.

Clark, William F., et al. *Old and Poor: A Critical Assessment of the Low-Income Elderly*. Lexington, Mass.: Lexington Books, 1988.

Commonwealth Fund Commission on Elderly People Living Alone. *Old, Alone and Poor: A Plan for Rescuing Poverty Among Elderly People Living Alone*. Baltimore: Commonwealth Fund, 1987.

Cosby, Robert L., and Teri Flynn, eds. *Housing for Older Adults: Options and Answers*. Washington, D.C.: NCOA, 1986.

Coyle, Jean M., ed. *Women and Aging: A Selected, Annotated Bibliography*. Westport, Conn.: Greenwood Press, 1989.

Crystal, Stephen. *America's Old Age Crisis: Public Policy and the Two Worlds of Aging*. New York: Basic Books, 1982.

Davis, Lenwood G., ed *The Black Aged in the United States: A Selectively Annotated Bibliography*. Rev. updated 2d Ed. Westport, Conn.: Greenwood Press, 1989.

Day, Christine L. *What Older Americans Think: Interest Groups and Aging Policy*. Princeton, N. J.: Princeton University Press, 1990.

Derthick, Martha. *Policymaking for Social Security*. Washington, D.C.: Brookings Institution, 1979.

Eekelaar, John, and David Pearl, eds. *An Aging World: Dilemmas and Challenges for Social Policy*. Oxford: Clarendon Press, 1989.

Eisdorfer, C., D. A. Kessler, and A. N. Spector, eds. *Caring for the Elderly: Reshaping Health Policy*. Baltimore: Johns Hopkins University Press, 1989.

Employee Benefit Research Institute (EBRI). *America in Transition: Benefits for the Future*. Washington D.C.: EBRI, 1987.

Estes, Carroll. *The Aging Enterprise*. San Francisco: Jossey-Bass, 1979.

Eustis, Nancy N., Jay N. Greenberg, and Sharon Patten. *Long-term Care for Older Persons: A Policy Perspective*. Monterey, Calif.: Brooks/Cole, 1984.

Gelfand, Donald E. *The Aging Network: Programs and Services*. 3d ed. New York: Springer, 1988.

Glasse, Lou, and Jon Hendricks, eds. "Gender and Aging." *Generations* 14 (Summer 1990): entire issue.

Graebner, William. *A History of Retirement*. New Haven: Conn: Yale University Press, 1981.

Harel, Z., P. Ehrlich, and R. Hubbard. *The Vulnerable Aged: People, Services, and Policies*. New York: Springer, 1990.

Harrington, Charlene, et al. *Long Term Care of the Elderly: Public Policy Issues*. Beverly Hills, Calif.: Sage, 1985.

Health of an Aging America: 1989 Bibliography: A Guide to Reports about Older Americans. Hyattsville, Md.: National Center for Health Statistics, 1989.

Huckle, Patricia. *Tish Sommers, Activist, and the Founding of the Older Women's League*. Knoxville: University of Tennessee Press, 1991.

Hudson, Robert B., ed. *The Aging in Politics*. Springfield, Ill.: Charles C. Thomas, 1981.

Kingson, Eric. *Ties That Bind: The Interdependence of Generations*. Cabin John, Md.: Seven Locks Press, 1986.

Lammers, William. *Public Policy and the Aging*. Washington, D.C.: Congressional Quarterly Press, 1983.

Longman, P. *Born to Pay: The New Politics of Aging in America*. Boston: Houghton Mifflin, 1987.

Losing a Million Minds: Confronting the Tragedy of Alzheimer's Disease and Other Dementias. Washington, D.C.: Office of Technology Assessment, 1987.

Mace, Nancy L., and Peter V. Rabins. *The 36-Hour Day*. Rev. ed. Baltimore: Johns Hopkins University Press, 1991.

Mahlmann, Dianne E., and David M. Weiss, eds. *National Guide to Funding in Aging*. New York: Nassau County Department of Senior Citizens Affairs and the Foundation Center, 1987.

Marmor, T. R., and J. L. Mashaw, eds. *Social Security: Beyond the Rhetoric of Crisis*. Princeton, N.J.: Princeton University Press, 1988.

Minkler, Meredith, and Carroll Estes. *Readings in the Political Economy of Aging*. Farmingdale, N.Y.: Bawood, 1984.

Montgomery, R. J., and E. E. Guice, eds. *Women and Aging: Now and in the Future*. Detroit: Wayne State University Press, 1990.

National Citizens' Coalition for Nursing Home Reform (NCCNHR). *A Consumer's Perspective on Quality Care: The Residents' Point of View*. Washington, D.C.: NCCNHR, 1985.

National Coalition on Older Women's Issues. *Midlife and Older Women: A Resource Directory*. Washington, D.C.: National Coalition on Older Women's Issues, 1986.

National Conference of State Legislatures. *State Legislative Issues Concerning the Elderly 1986–1990: A Survey*. Denver: The Conference, 1987.

National Council on the Aging (NCOA). *Long-term Care CHOICES: A Manual for Organizing a Successful Consumer Education Campaign*. Washington, D.C.: NCOA, 1988.

National Institute on Aging (NIA). *Resource Directory for Older People*. Gaithersburg, Md.: NIA, 1989.

Neugarten, Bernie, ed. *Age or Need? Public Policies for Older People*. Beverly Hills, Calif.: Sage, 1982.

Olson, L. K. *The Political Economy of Age: The State, Private Power, and Social Welfare*. New York: Columbia University Press, 1982.

Oriol, William E., comp. *Federal Public Policy on Aging since 1960: An Annotated Bibliography*. Westport, Conn.: Greenwood Press, 1987.

Pauly, Mark V., and William L. Kissick, eds. *Lessons from the First Twenty Years of Medicare: Research Implications for Public and Private Sector Policy*. Philadelphia: University of Pennsylvania Press, 1988.

Pearman, William A., and Philip Starr. *Medicare: A Handbook on the History and Issues of Health Care Services for the Elderly*. New York: Garland, 1988.

Pierce, Robert M. *Long-term Care for the Elderly: A Legislator's Guide*. Denver: National Conference of State Legislators, 1987.

Pifer, A., and L. Bronte, eds. *Our Aging Society: Paradox and Promise*. New York: W. W. Norton, 1986.

Pratt, Henry J. *The Gray Lobby*. Chicago: University of Chicago Press, 1976.

Rabin, David L., and Patricia Stockton. *Long-term Care for the Elderly: A Factbook*. New York: Oxford University Press, 1987.

Regnier, V., and J. Pynoos. *Housing the Aged: Design Directives and Policy Considerations*. New York: Elsevier Science Publishing Company, 1987.

Rivlin, Alice M. *Caring for the Disabled Elderly: Who Will Pay?* Washington, D.C.: Brookings, 1988.

Rosenwaike, I., and B. Logue. *The Extreme Aged in America: A Portrait of an Expanding Population*. Westport, Conn.: Greenwood Press, 1985.

Shearer, Gail. *Long Term Care: Analysis of Public Policy Options*. Washington, D.C.: Consumers Union, 1989.

Strange, Heather, and Michele Teitelbaum. *Aging and Cultural Diversity: New Directions and Annotated Bibliography*. Amherst, Mass.: Bergin & Garvey Publishers, 1987.

Tedrick, T. *Aging: Issues and Policies for the 1980's*. New York: Praeger Publishers, 1987.

Torres-Gil, Fernando M. *Politics of Aging among Elder Hispanics*. Washington, D.C.: University Press of America, 1982.

―――, ed. "Public Policy." *Generations*. 12, no. 3 (Summer 1988): entire issue.

Tropman, J. *Public Policy Opinion and the Elderly, 1952–1978: A Kaleidoscope of Culture*. Westport, Conn.: Greenwood Press, 1987.

Van Tassel, David D., and Peter Stearns. *Old Age in a Bureaucratic Society*. Westport, Conn.: Greenwood Press, 1986.

Williamson, J. B., J. A. Shindul, and L. Evans. *Aging and Public Policy: Social Control or Social Justice?* Springfield, Ill.: Charles C. Thomas, 1985.

Williamson, J. B., L. Evans, and L. A. Powell. *The Politics of Aging: Power and Policy*. Springfield, Ill.: Charles C. Thomas, 1982.

Women's Studies Quarterly 17 (Spring–Summer 1989): entire issue.

Yahnke, Robert. *The Great Circle of Life: A Resource Guide to Films and Videos on Aging*. Owings Mills, Md.: National Health Publishing, 1988.

INDEX

/

Page numbers in **bold** indicate main entries

About the Editors

DAVID D. VAN TASSEL is Elbert J. Benton Professor and Chair of the Department of History at Case Western Reserve University. He is the author of *Old Age in a Bureaucratic Society* (Greenwood Press, 1986), among a number of other works.

JIMMY ELAINE WILKINSON MEYER is a former librarian and a doctoral candidate in the Department of History at Case Western Reserve University.